Chuluunbaatar Enkhzaya

Impact of Institutions on Lending

WIRTSCHAFTSWISSENSCHAFT

Chuluunbaatar Enkhzaya

Impact of Institutions on Lending

Informal Constraints and Enforcement of Bank Regulation in Mongolia

With a foreword by Prof. Dr. Alexander Karmann

Deutscher Universitäts-Verlag

Bibliografische Information Der Deutschen Bibliothek
Die Deutsche Bibliothek verzeichnet diese Publikation in der Deutschen Nationalbibliografie; detaillierte bibliografische Daten sind im Internet über <http://dnb.ddb.de> abrufbar.

Dissertation Technische Universität Dresden, 2004

Published with the support of the German Academic Exchange Service (DAAD)

1. Auflage August 2006

Lektorat: Ute Wrasmann / Anita Wilke

Der Deutsche Universitäts-Verlag ist ein Unternehmen von Springer Science+Business Media.
www.duv.de

Umschlaggestaltung: Regine Zimmer, Dipl.-Designerin, Frankfurt/Main
Druck und Buchbinder: Rosch-Buch, Scheßlitz
Gedruckt auf säurefreiem und chlorfrei gebleichtem Papier
Printed in Germany

ISBN-10 3-8350-0024-1
ISBN-13 978-3-8350-0024-7

Dedicated to Emuunee, my Grandma

Foreword

The surprisingly slow process of economic transformation is a well-known but not well-understood phenomenon in economies in transition (EIT). Neither macro-economic arguing nor neoclassic micro approaches turned out to provide helpful tools in explaining the barriers to transform markets and institutions.

Chuluunbaatar Enkhzaya addresses the issue of economic transformation, exemplarily by looking at the Mongolian loan market. Her methodological innovation is not only to employ the New Institutional Economy but also to operationalise the degree of institutional change. This is done by using concept mapping, besides the more standard way of interviewing. It allows to identify „action regulating knowledge" governing the decision behavior of credit officers and leading to an indirect observation of informal rules like attitude to risk, perception of supervision, social and ethic commitments.

Enkhzaya adds to our understanding why the enforcement of banking regulation norms has not led to an efficient allocation of resources in EIT banking systems. Besides she gives an impressive description of the actual state of the Mongolian economy.

Chuluunbaatar Enkhzaya gained a Diploma in International Relations, with a main subject in German Studies and a subsidiary subject in Economics, at the National University of Mongolia, in 1995. She was elected as scholarship holder of the German Academic Exchange Service (DAAD) to start a PhD in Economics at the Dresden University of Technology (TUD) which she completed in 2004, under my supervision. This book is the slightly revised version of her thesis. In 2005, Enkhzaya turned back to Mongolia to engage in building up the domestic market system and its institutional framework.

Alexander Karmann
Chair of Monetary Economics
Dresden University of Technology, Germany

Preface

In the early 1990s an unprecedented "transition" was set in motion, to change the economic co-ordination of economies in transition. As the reforms neither considered the time needed to establish the market, nor dealt with this process itself, microeconomic reforms aimed at establishing the market and at inducing market-oriented behaviour need to be adjusted.

The New Institutional Economics (NIE) legitimises the factors constraining the behaviour of economic agents – institutions or "rules of the game" – as objects of economic analysis by incorporating them into the corpus of Neo-classic theory. Applying the principles of NIE in an analysis of transition problems can support research on the behaviour of economic agents – e.g. bankers – during the transition. NIE argues that it is not only a question of norms and rules (formulated or transferred) but also a question of designing compatible rules which is of crucial importance for economic and institutional change.

The present work seeks to question the "inadequate" behaviour of banks in Mongolia by analysing the institutional framework of the banking system, especially in lending. It focuses on the genesis of informal institutions of lending (as attitude to risk) and their interaction with formal institutions of lending (bank regulation norms). The results, first of all, aimed at contributing to further research on making informal institutions observable and measurable and to suggest some practicable measures to address institutional reforms in the banking system.

Direct observation and gauging of informal institutions is one of the outstanding challenges for present-day economists and psychologists, therefore an approach is evolved to indirectly observe the informal institutions of lending by diagnosing the action-regulating knowledge of Mongolian bankers.

This cognitive approach is based on the principles of NIE – especially the Theory of Economic and Institutional Change by North – and of cognitive psychology by Kahneman and Hacker, thus on the interrelation of institutions, mental models and knowledge. The action-regulating knowledge is diagnosed by means of triangulation of methods with a main method of concept mapping.

The results confirm the inconsistency of formal and informal institutions canalising decisions of bankers which accounts for the "passive" behaviour of banks. Suggestions for as simultaneous as possible a change of formal and informal rules are advanced in order to ensure an effective allocation of the very scarce financial resources of Mongolia. However, the questions addressed by transition go far beyond the transition process itself. Institutional perspectives and the cognitive approach in economics could also support research on the microeconomic foundations of macroeconomic reforms in advanced market economies.

The book presents the PhD thesis completed by the end of 2003. Since that time some positive changes have occurred. Nevertheless, the lack of appropriate (for the chosen economic system) mental models of individuals is observable not only at the economic, but also definitely at the political and social markets – behaviour of politicians during election campaign. Furthermore, the question of whether a pure market-based economy is the optimal one for such countries as Mongolia with only a very low population density, and what might be a more appropriate one, is the subject to a separate study.

The author expresses great gratitude to Prof. Dr. Alexander Karmann who agreed to the research question and supported the interdisciplinary approach as well as to Prof. Dr. Hermann Locarek-Junge and Prof. Dr. Peter Richter for their encouragement. Many thanks go to my friends Dr. Olson Baloi and Ana Dominguez for the constructive discussions and valuable brainstorming, to Ellen Schwarz and Dr. Michael Berlemann for their courteous help. My PhD project could not been finished successfully without every support of my family, especially my beloved parents, who often had to put up with my absence. I am deeply grateful to Dr. Michael Linke – for many Mongolians their first German teacher – for believing and encouraging. And last, but not least, I would like to thank very much the German Academic Exchange Service (DAAD), especially the people working there, not only for the big support during the realisation of my PhD project and of this publication, but also for the opportunity to stay in this country and to learn about it from inside.

Chuluunbaatar Enkhzaya

Overview

Table of Contents

Index of Tables

Index of Figures

Abbreviations

A	Activity
A1, A2...	Suggested approaches (numbered)
BC	Basle Committee on Banking Supervision
BHO	Bank's head office
BIS	Bank for International Settlements
BOM	The Bank of Mongolia, the central bank
C	Condition
CAR	Tier I Capital Adequacy Ratio
CC	Credit Committee
CD	Credit Department
CF1, CF2...	Credit files (numbered)
CIS	Common Wealth of Independent States
CMEA	Council for Mutual Economic Assistance
DM	Decision making action
D	Dependence
DR	Definitional relation
EBRD	European Bank for Reconstruction and Development
EI	Evaluation items
EIT	Economy in transition
EM	Evaluation matrix
ES	Evaluation statements
EXD	Executive director
GDP	Gross domestic product
GKh	The Great Khural of Mongolia, the parliament
HAS	HAS Bank
HC	Head of Credit Committee
HD	Head of Credit Department
IMF	International Monetary Fund
ITI(B)	Bank of Investment and Technological Innovation
LGP	Loan Granting Procedure
LIP	Loan Information Pool in Mongolia
LL	Lawyer responsible for loan affairs
LLR	Lender of last resort

LO	Loan officer
LR	Officer of the Loan Recovery Department
MARA	Mongolian Asset Recovery Agency
MCB	Mongolian Co-operative Bank
MP	Means and Partner
MRPR	Mongolian People's Revolutionary Party
MSE	Mongolian Stock Exchange
N1, N2 ...	Numbered notes of the day
NBFI	Non-bank Financial Institution
NIE	New Institutional Economics
NPL	Non-performing loans
O	Operational action
O(A)	Objection of A (activity)
O(C)	Objection of C (condition)
O(D)	Objection of D (dependence)
O(DR)	Objection of DR (definitional relation)
O(MP)	Objection of MP (means and partner)
O(R)	Objection of R (reason)
O(SC)	Objection of SC (simple characteristic)
O(SR)	Objection of SR (simple relation)
OI	Observation items
OIE	Old Institutional Economics
P(A)	Potentiality of A (activity)
P(C)	Potentiality of C (condition)
P(D)	Potentiality of D (dependence)
P(DR)	Potentiality of DR (definitional relation)
P(MP)	Potentiality of MP (means and partner)
P(R)	Potentiality of R (reason)
P(SC)	Potentiality of SC (simple characteristic)
P(SR)	Potentiality of SR (simple relation)
R	Cause, Reason
RACAR	Total Risk-Assessed Capital Adequacy Ratio
RAROC	Risk-Adjusted Return on Capital
RATCAR	Tier I Risk-Assessed Capital Adequacy Ratio
RI	Response items

SC	Simple characteristic
SCC	Secretary of the Credit Committee
SLO	Senior loan officer
SR	Simple relation
SU	Soviet Union
T	Team decision
TD(B)	Trade and Development Bank
VAR	Value at risk
WR	Work rules of the Credit Committee

Introduction

Motivation

When in the early 1990s the post-communist countries implemented reform programmes to transform their previously centrally-planned economies into market-based economies, an unprecedented "transition" was set in motion and the economies in transition (EIT) emerged. This change of economic co-ordination should lead to a more efficient use of resources with higher economic output.

Closely monitored and financially supported by international organisations, such as the International Monetary Fund (IMF), the process of transition consisted of three main elements: privatisation, liberalisation and stabilisation. It was assumed that liberalisation of prices and the creation of private property would result in the establishment of many enterprises, and competition between these would lead to an efficient allocation of resources and stabilisation. Yet these big bang reforms implying rapid transition process were nevertheless followed by so-called transition crises – especially in south-east European and central Asian EITs – from which many countries are still suffering.

The liberalisation of prices in Mongolia led to immoderately high inflation, peaking at 325 percent in 1992 and remaining in double-digits until the late 1990s. Aggregate output subsequently started to decline, reaching its lowest level in 1995. Stagnation continued long into the late 1990s before picking up to record a growth rate of 3.9 percent in 2002. Whereas the inflation rate has fallen and growth revived in the meantime, the loss of confidence in the national currency, the Tugrug, is proving difficult to restore. Some studies in this context put the Dollarisation ratio in Mongolia at up to 80 percent (Herr, 2003).

The low degree of macroeconomic achievement was put down to the absence of responsive microeconomic reforms. The global big bang strategy based on Neo-classic theory consisted of macroeconomic policies which assume a market mechanism that functions automatically, as if the market suddenly materialises by magic. The strategy neither considered the time needed to establish the market, nor dealt with this process itself. However, if the economic agents in EITs – enterprises, banks, households, the state – do not behave as economic agents do in market economies, the market mechanism cannot operate as it is supposed to. Thus microeconomic reforms aimed at establishing the market and inducing supposed market-oriented behaviour need to be adjusted so that macroeconomic reform policies can realise the initial expectations.

The economic literature on transition processes deals for the most part with the macroeconomics of transition, yet conditions at the microeconomic level are unfortunately almost ignored or taken for granted. The existing models – be these Keynesian, Neo-classic or Monetarist - believe in creating market economies overnight. New Institutional Economics (NIE) includes factors constraining the behaviour of economic agents – institutions – into the corpus of Neo-classic theory and legitimates them as objects of economic analysis. Defined as the "rules of the game" by North (1990: 4), institutions constrain individual behaviour and thus define the outcomes which result from individual action (Schotter, 1986: 117). Both formal institutions – laws and regulations – and informal institutions, such as codes of conduct, canalise individual behaviour. In a world of positive transaction costs - due to market imperfections inter alia – institutions and their design are the root of many problems in the EITs.

Thus applying the principles of NIE in an analysis of transition problems can support research on the behaviour of economic agents during transition. This would deliver insights into the establishment of market-oriented institutions in EITs in general and specific markets in particular – for example, the financial markets of EITs.

The financial system, and particularly the banking system, is of special interest. On the one hand, banking operations had been heavily restricted under central planning, on the other hand, banks now have a crucial role as financial intermediaries in the restructuring of economies and the establishment of effective corporate control.

Despite implementation of the recommended reforms in the Mongolian banking sector, bank restructuring, rehabilitation and privatisation faced strong "resistance" from economic agents, including bankers, politicians and state-owned enterprises. The effective allocation of scarce financial resources expected did not appear because bankers and borrowers did not behave as required (in terms of market orientation). Reckless loan granting policies built up immense inventories of non-performing loans, resulting in two banking crises in 1996 and 1999. Having learned the hard way, amendments to banking law and bank regulation were made.

But the enforcement of bank regulation norms still remains patchy. Despite some progress, the laws and regulations passed – formal institutions - which compel banks to fulfil capital requirements or to build up reserves, have not led to efficient behaviour in the banking system and have not significantly improved the allocation of financial resources. Total loans accounted for about 20 percent of GDP in 2002 (Ariunkhishig, 2003: 3).

This "inadequate" behaviour of banks can be explored within an institutional analysis of a banking system in transition. Hitherto, the institutional analysis of transition processes concentrated mainly on the perspective of rebuilding and modifying institutional configurations (experiences from Poland, the Czech Republic, Hungary). Neither the constitution and genesis of institutions themselves, nor their interaction have been focused (Thomas, 1999: 20). But, NIE argues, that it is not only a question of norms and rules (formulated or transferred), but also the question of designing compatible institutions which is of crucial importance for economic and institutional change.

The present study seeks to question this "inadequate" behaviour of banks in Mongolia by analysing the institutional framework of the banking system, especially in lending. It focuses on the genesis of informal institutions of lending and their interaction with formal institutions of lending. The results first of all aim to contribute to further research on making informal institutions observable and measurable, and to suggest some practicable measures to address institutional reforms in the banking system.

Research Questions

In order to analyse the flaws (deficiencies) in the enforcement of banking regulation reforms, the present work asks the questions of which informal institutions constrain the banks' decision making in lending, and what their impact is on the enforcement of formal institutions of lending in Mongolia. Therefore, the purpose of the study is:

1. to identify specific (informal) attributes of lending practice in Mongolian banks – informal institutions of lending and to ascertain common and specific features of bank regulation, especially bank regulation norms, in Mongolia.
2. to determine the relationship between informal institutional constraints of decision making in lending (the informal institutions of lending) and regulation norms of banks' lending business; to draw conclusions about the impact of this relationship on the enforcement of banking regulation and to suggest measures to address it.

For this purpose, the following research questions are posed:

- What is the content and range of bank regulation in Mongolia? (formal institutions)
- What codes of conduct constrain bankers' decision making on lending? (informal institutions)
- How are the codes of conduct of bankers and the bank regulation norms interrelated? And what significance does this have for the enforcement of bank regulation?
- Which implications could this have for banking reform in general and for the regulation of the lending business in particular?

In order to answer these questions, the present study evolves a cognitive approach to frame methods for indirectly observing informal institutions of lending, which are hypothesised. Hypotheses formulate four kinds of informal rules constraining the behaviour of Mongolian banks: bankers' attitude to risk, bankers' perceptions about the proper functioning of bank supervision, bankers' commitment to an authoritative state and standards of ethic in personal relationships. A triangulation of methods with a main method of concept mapping provides evidence for these hypotheses by diagnosing the action-regulating knowledge of bankers.

Structure

Part 1 below theoretically exemplifies the impact of institutions on lending. It first introduces the theoretical foundations of the New Institutional Economics – chapter 1.1. Basic terms and definitions are introduced there, the crucial importance of institutions to economic performance is highlighted, and the main instruments of institutional analysis are deployed. In chapter 1.2, an institutional analysis is applied to lending processes, thereby showing the set of institutions which channel lending. In order to find answers to the questions posed by the study, a cognitive approach is developed in chapter 1.3 to frame the observation of informal institutions of lending by diagnosing the action-regulating knowledge of bankers (which shape bankers' mental models).

Part 2 applies the theoretical framework to lending processes in Mongolia. It first analyses the overall situation in Mongolia in chapter 2.1, thereby discussing the historical and political background to today's economy and searching for the microeconomic/institutional foundations of macroeconomic achievements. Chapter 2.2 then describes the performance of the financial organisations which have arisen in general – financial intermediation, and of banks in particular – microeconomic behaviour of banks – and examines loan allocation. Chapter 2.3 reviews whether the existing or missing institutions of lending really do account for the described behaviour of banks, thereby analysing the formal institutions – bank regulation norms – and hypothesising informal institutions.

In order to address the hypotheses put forward in Part 2, Part 3 provides a complete description of directions and steps taken to conduct the survey. Chapter 3.1 describes the framework within which the materials (data) are incorporated – the qualitative-quantitative research design. It introduces the main research method within the research design – the method of concept mapping to diagnose the action-regulating knowledge of bankers on lending. Chapter 3.2 details where, how and when data were collected – the participants, instrumentation and procedure. The results of data analysis are presented in chapter 3.3, the survey data are analysed and the findings pointed out which test the hypotheses.

Having formulated findings on informal institutional constraints of lending in Mongolian banks in Part 3, these are then discussed in Part 4. Chapter 4.1 reviews the significant findings and considers the impact of informal, institutional constraints of lending on the enforcement of bank regulation norms on lending. Chapter 4.2 then discusses the implications the study has in practical terms by setting out future challenges and offering suggestions for further reforms.

Part 5 concludes the analysis.

Part 1 The Impact of Institutions on Lending

In order to exemplify the impact that institutions have on lending, this part first looks at the theoretical foundations of the New Institutional Economics – chapter 1.1. Basic terms and definitions are introduced here, the crucial importance of institutions to economic performance is highlighted, and main instruments of institutional analysis are deployed. In chapter 1.2, lending processes are institutionally analysed, thereby showing the set of institutions which influence lending. In order to answer the questions posed by the study, a cognitive approach is developed in chapter 1.3 to observe informal institutions of lending by diagnosing the action-regulating knowledge of bankers (which shape bankers' mental models).

1.1 The New Institutional Economics

1.1.1 Institutions Matter

The question of what institutions are is by no means straightforward. There is no consistent concept of an institution in economic literature. This is not a question of contradictions (and of which definition is wrong and which is right), but rather a matter of broadness in understanding and making sense of this concept. Richter and Furubotn (1999: 513) e.g. characterise an institution as "auf ein Zielgebündel abgestelltes System von Normen einschließlich deren Garantieinstrumente mit dem Zweck, das individuelle Verhalten in eine bestimmte Richtung zu steuern" (in Furubotn and Richter (1991:2) "as a system of norms with respect to a particular set of activities"). Eger and Nutzinger (1999: 24) give a very generalised view of an institution: it is a system of norms which co-ordinates and regulates the interaction of people. More controversially, Veblen (1919: 239) envisages institutions as "settled habits of thought common to the generality of man". Remarkably, many scholars deal with institutional issues without defining or even mentioning the concept institution. This points out that the Institutional Economy is still in its early stages and no comprehensive, self-contained theory exists as particularised below. Nevertheless, the existing approaches are capable of dealing effectively with many current problems of interest to theorists and policy makers.

The relatively broad definition of ***institution*** used here is taken from Schotter (1986: 117) who sees an institution – derived from North - "as a set of rules that constrain individual behaviour and define the social outcomes that result from individual action". An institution is seen here as a system of rules - with their enforcement precautions - through which the actions of individuals are channelled. Different institutions form the framework of individual action, i.e. the incentive structure of society (economy) which determines the choices or decisions made by individuals. Consequently, institutions are "humanly devised constraints that structure political, economic and social interaction" (North, 1991: 97).

For a better understanding of institutional issues, it is useful to differentiate between the terms institution and organisation. ***Organisations*** are the personified or factual dimension of institutions. Using Coase's approach to a firm, the network of contracts (rules) constituting a firm is an institution and the people connected through the firm form an organisation. Similarly, wedlock (with its rules and norms) is an institution and the family (with its members) is a corresponding organisation. Human relationships like friendship or kinship are institutions, friends and kin connected within these relations form the organisations. The attitude to risk (banking norms and rules) is an institution, while loan officers, bankers or banks adopting this attitude make up organisations. The authority of the state is an institution, whereas parliament, government and especially their officials form organisations. North (1994: 361) states that "if institutions are the rules of the games of the society, then the organisations and their entrepreneurs are the players". It is important for institutional analysis to bear in mind that "the purpose of the rule is to define the way the game is played, but the objective of the team [players – Ch.E.] within the set of rules is to win the game" (North, 1990: 4). Thus, the organisations that come into existence will reflect the opportunities provided by the institutions or institutional matrix (North, 1994: 361). Sub-chapter 1.1.3 later details the symbiotic relationship between organisations and institutions and its importance for institutional analysis. It should be noted that the terms institution and organisation are often not differentiated throughout the specialist literature (e.g., Feldman, 1999: 10).

By forming the incentive structure and determining individual choices, institutions have a great impact on the allocation of resources in a world of positive transaction costs, and thus on economic performance (North, 1994: 360). They affect the costs of transacting and hence the costs of producing (finding out relevant information, negotiating and concluding contracts, monitoring and enforcing them) in the following way: individuals base their choices on incomplete information with subjectively derived models, therefore under uncertainty. To reduce this uncertainty in exchange, a system of rules is introduced; thus an institution is devised. That system of rules leads to certain reciprocal expectations about individual behaviour and thereby creates order. It gives a "bargaining power" to individuals channelling their actions. The strength of bargaining affects the efficiency of outcome. Consequently, the systems of rules, or institutions, define the set of choices, which does not necessarily result in the most productive outcome. Only if an institution is able to reduce the costs of transaction and production per exchange so that "potential gains from trade are realisable" (North, 1991: 98), can this be regarded as an appropriate economic environment that induces increasing productivity and economic growth. Thus the main role of institutions is to reduce uncertainty by establishing stable, although not necessarily efficient, structures for human interaction.

The question of how institutions arise, evolve and change is an intriguing one. Different theories exist, ranging from these arising "spontaneously" to being established by a central authority. The most comprehensive description is given by North and this is illustrated in sub-chapter 1.1.3.

Institutions consist of ***formal*** and ***informal rules*** and the precautions to enforce them. There are a multitude of institutions, beginning with a culture of society, its constitution and laws, up to a company's organisational structure and internal regulations. Figure 1.1 categorises institutions into distinct levels. Regarding the interrelation of institutions at different levels, it should be understood that the outer level significantly influences the inner level, but the influence of the inner level on the outer level is not of the same significance. Hence, an interrelation between different institutions is not precluded, but the primary direction of the impact is assumed to be from top to bottom (Erlei et al., 1999: 25).

On the first level, the laws of nature and the non-renewable resources available form the non-influenceable framework of society's economic activities. The second level is culture, which particularly consists of informal ***codes (rules) of conduct*** and habits, but also the language of the considered cultural area, the prevailing religions and the common history. The formal legal framework composes the third level. One conceives it as the fundamental laws of a society, possibly a constitution, which can be altered only by a broad consensus. Variable factors are accumulated within that framework and go to make up the economic variable endowment. The variable endowment factor contains the basic knowledge of the society, its technological and organisational infrastructure and its system of education. These capital goods of the society are decisively "produced" by political decisions – in particular decisions on social and economic policies.

Figure 1.1: Institutions system and institutional framework of lending
Source: adapted from Erlei et al. (1999: 24) and amplified

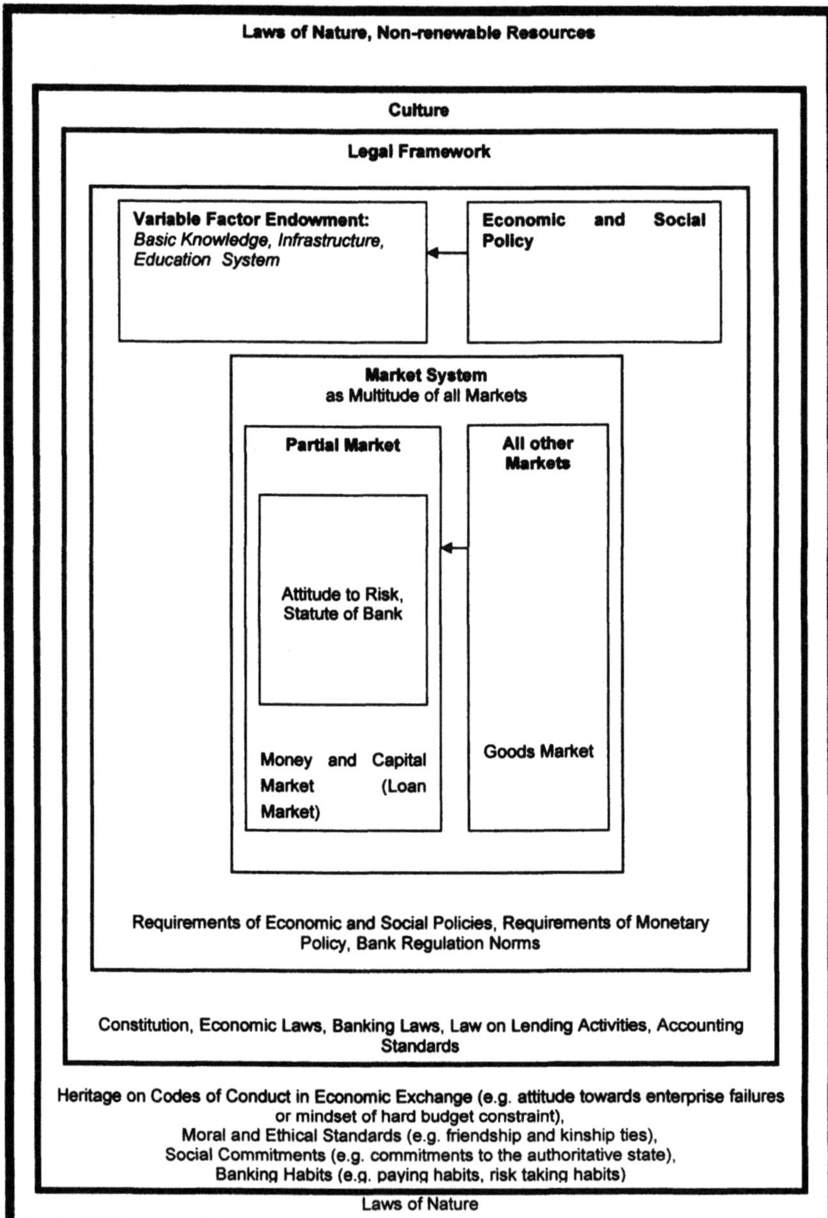

That fourth level, the endowment variable with the corresponding policies, affects the next, fifth, *level of institutions – the market system as the multitude of all markets* in the society. It unveils the conjunction with industrial economics. Although the partial markets – sixth level – are interdependent, they can be analysed separately in terms of causal isolation (Schlicht: 1985, 21), e.g. the impact of variables from other partial markets ought not to be so strong that deviated conclusions have to be annihilated (feedback effects). There are plenty of suppliers on the partial market in question, and some of them decide to organise themselves as firms. The organisational structure of these firms should be reasonably distinct due to institutions and corresponding incentive structures. This scheme of the institutional level can be specified further in this way.

The subject matter of the present work is institutions considered at the second level (informal institutional constraints) down through to the level of one particular partial market (the loan market). This study observes informal institutions which channel the activities of particular individuals – bankers - on the loan market, that are codes of conduct of bankers in the lending process (channelling decision making on lending).

1.1.2 Institutions in Economic Science: the New Institutional Economics

The concept of institutions in economics is not new, its roots can be traced right back to the Classicists: Adam Smith wrote about action restrictions, such as ethics, conventions and traditions. As recently as the method of comparative-static analysis was introduced by David Ricardo, and as the change from Classicist to Neo-classicist began, institutions had taken a back seat until their revival in the 19th century.

Neither Neo-classicists nor Keynesians explicitly analyse institutions or their impact on the actions of economic and political agents. Neo-classic theory is concerned with the operation of markets, not with how these markets evolve or develop (formation of markets). It deals with models of frictionless and static worlds where time and institutions do not matter. Keynesians emphasise the active role of the state in economic processes. But they do not expound on the problem of the behaviour of the state and its decision makers. It is assumed that decisions emanate from a benevolent dictator who is able to diagnose problems correctly and – having the right instruments at his disposal – implement adequate measures. Institutions are taken for granted by both Neo-classic and Keynesian economics; their existence is recognised as far as they play an instrumental role, but they can be ignored in economic analysis because they play no independent role in economic performance.

The Old Institutionalism

Institutions as a subject matter of economic reasoning revived in the 19th century, but only among some selected scholars, a systematic classification of these is rather difficult: the German Historical School (Schmoller, Knapp), Austrian School (Menger, F. von Hayek), American Institutionalist School (Veblen, Commons) and Freiburger Ordoliberal School (Eucken, Böhm).

These schools have one common feature: they all reject Neo-classicism as abstract and static. They all can be characterised as schools of Old Institutionalism or ***Old Institutional Economics*** (OIE), although occasionally, only the American Institutional School is referred to as OIE in the literature, as it is argued that it was largely rooted in North American traditions (Rutherfold, 1994). The Old Institutionalist Economists hope to provide relief by referring to humanities and social sciences and emphasising empirical (historical-descriptive) work. It can be called normative and is characterised by scepticism about theoretical generalisation and the critique of the method of isolation, whereas the ***New Institutional Economics*** (NIE) includes institutional factors in the corpus of Neo-classical theory and legitimates institutions as objects of economic analysis. Despite quite reasonable notions, the schools of OIE never really got beyond their beginnings and did not manage to develop a closed concept as an antithesis to the mainstream.

The New Institutional Economics and their relevance to Neo-classic

Although the writings of NIE theorists are quite diverse in style and content as discussed below, for the most part they accept the tenets of orthodox marginalism. Thus, the analytical framework of NIE can be characterised as a modification of Neo-classic theory externalising the role of institutions. What it retains is the fundamental assumption of scarcity, and hence competition, and the analytical tools of microeconomic theory (North, 1994: 359). What it modifies is the assumption of rationality (bounded rationality), founded in the modification of such assumptions as that of perfect market knowledge (asymmetric information) and of perfect competition etc. What it adds is the dimension of time (North, 1994: 359).

Prior to going into particular theoretical approaches of NIE, firstly its main features, hypothesises and research heuristics. The main features of NIE are methodological individualism within utility maximisation of homo economicus, which is opportunistic in behaviour and is only bounded rationally by transaction costs:

- In Neo-classicism, Methodological Individualism means that "society", "the state", "the people", "the firm", or the "parties" are to be understood as collective entities that behave as though they were individual actors. In NIE, the organisation per se is no longer the main focus. Rather, the theory of such social units must start with and base its explanations on the positions and actions of their individual members.

- Under the utility maximisation principle, individuals are assumed to look after their own interests and to maximise utility, subject to the constraints established by the existing organisational structure. Compared to conventional practice, the dichotomy between the theory of consumer choice and the theory of the firm is ended in NIE by extending the utility-maximisation hypothesis to all individual choices. An individual, whether be a manager of a government bureau or a capitalist entrepreneur, is understood to make his own choices and to pursue his own goals within the limits allowed by the system in which he is operating.
- The term bounded rationality used by Simon (1975) primarily reflects the fact that individuals, assumed in the Neo-classics to be rational beings, evaluate their action contingencies based on utility maximisation, but have only limited ability to acquire and process information. This restriction on rationality means that not all economic exchange can be organised by contract and market and it is impossible to deal with complexity in all contractually relevant respects.

Besides the hypotheses known from Neo-classicism, NIE adds the following hypotheses:

- of not allocative (Pareto principle) but adaptive efficiency; adaptive efficient rules "provide incentives for the acquisition of knowledge and learning, promote innovation, encourage risk taking and creative activity"[1] (North, 1992: 479),
- of institutional design influencing the operation of market mechanism and thus economic growth.

The positive heuristics of NIE instruct (Erlei et al., 1999: 54):

- to consider the institutions as relevant restrictions;
- to analyse, starting from social problems, how institutions influence individual behaviour (their plans, decision making and action), and, problem-oriented, how they evolve;
- to determine institutional erroneous trends, and to show institutional alternatives;
- to develop, starting from the status quo, strategies to implement institutional alternatives in consideration of costs (transaction costs etc.)

1 As in a world of uncertainty no one knows the correct solution to the problems we confront (as Friedrich Hayek has persuasively argued), rules should encourage trials and eliminate errors.

Thus, NIE deals with the systematic analysis of the impact (positive) and design (normative) of institutions through which the actions of individuals are channelled (which channel individual behaviour) (Erlei et al., 1999: 43). It offers new perspectives on both the micro foundations of economics (transaction cost and its significance) and the long-term dynamics of economic development (a theory of development in terms of appropriate institutional change which fosters further economic growth). Hence, it is important as a major development within the dominant paradigm of modern economics. In addition, it is important in the context of economic policy because it has challenged the dominant roles ascribed to the market by the orthodoxies. NIE, moreover, is a body of economic theory which is accessible to other social scientists, seeming to open up the terrain of genuine, interdisciplinary inquiry. In this context, one of the main challenges is to provide them with additional tools to analyse the institutional features of economics which would be an important contribution to the methodology.

Main approaches of New Institutional Economics

In his Nobel-Prize Lecture, Ronald Coase (1992) notes the contribution of many economists, such as Oliver Williamson, Harold Demsetz, Douglas North and others, to the way of thinking, to the transformation of approaches, which aim to increase the understanding of economic issues. They included features of economic systems (institutions and organisations) in economic analysis and that changes the structure of economic theory, especially the theory of microeconomics. The main approaches of NIE to the way of thinking and their application to other areas of social science are followed.

Yet it was Ronald Coase who took the first step towards a modern analysis of institutions. With his statement on the existing "costs of using the price mechanism", Coase (1937: 390) settled the basics of the ***Theory of Transaction Costs***, without using this term. The question of why management was needed, if the pricing system provided all the co-ordination necessary, led him to realise that it is costly to bargain using the price mechanism. It implies that other methods of co-ordination could also exist as alternatives to a free market, which is the only method of co-ordination analysed by economists. Under certain conditions (e.g. lower transaction costs), they may be preferable to the price mechanism. That explained the emergence of the firm, and this was enhanced by Williamson (1967, 1975) and Alchian/Demsetz (1972). The work of Oliver Williamson has contributed to a greater understanding of the factors which govern what a firm does and how it does it. Besides, the Theory of Transaction Costs comprises the significance of long-term relations which build reputation and trust. But above all, the introduction of transaction costs into economic analysis is an important contribution to institutional analysis.

Besides the Theory of Transaction Costs, the ***Property-Rights Theory*** and the ***Theory of Contracts*** expose the way of thinking in NIE, too. The Property Rights Theory (Demsetz (1967), "Coase's Theorem" (1970)) dealing with institutions of law is a significant step towards an analysis of an economy with positive transaction costs. It explains why legal systems differ between economies. The main thrust of the analysis is not the physical exchange of resources, but the exchange of the property rights to these resources. The design and restrictions of particular property rights thereby have an impact on the value of resources and, consequently, the behaviour in trading with them. Property rights consist of the right of usage, the right to derive income from that use, the right to exclude, and the right to exchange. A separate disposition (assignment) of each of the rights to different individuals can have significant impact on individual behaviour and thus on the efficiency of exchange.

The Theory of Contracts deals with the process of contracting. It explains how contracts should be organised to ensure economic efficiency. In a world of asymmetric information, the point of interest is the polymorphism of contracts and contractual relations which affect the exchange. One of the central objects of investigation within the Theory of Contracts is the ***Principal-Agent Theory***. The incongruity of interests of principal and agent can cause agents to act inefficiently (Jensen/Meckling, 1976, and Fama/Jensen, 1983). In order to restrain malpractice on the part of the agent, it is in the interest of the principal to take measures of monitoring and control. Moreover, the principal can only observe the results of agent's activities (and not his activity itself), whereas the results are not solely dependent on the agent's activities (Karmann, 1992: 557 et seq.).

Analysing the institutions not only behind market transactions, but also those in other sectors, such as political sector, is the other achievement of NIE. The economic analyses of institutions applied to political institutions are presented in the ***Theory of Public Choice***, which examines individual behaviour in the political sector (Buchanan, Tullock, Niskanen), and in the ***Theory of Constitutional Economics***, which analyses institutions in respect of their contribution to the efficiency of modern, liberal democracies (Buchanan, Hayek).

The application of the institutional way of thinking to economic history and performance through time, ***The Theory of Economic and Institutional Change***, studies institutions and institutional change and their impact on economic performance. Whereas classical theory seeks to analyse an economy at a particular moment in time, and takes little account of peculiarities of time and space, some institutionalists examine processes and seek to explain why some economies have advanced whilst others have not. The incorporation of political and social matters into analyses of the formation of institutions points to the relevance of NIE for research on economies in transition and developing economies (Harris, Hunter & Lewis: 1995, 5). The following sub-chapter reviews the Theory of Economic and Institutional Change in order to highlight this relevance.

1.1.3 The Theory of Economic and Institutional Change

The basic idea behind the Theory of Economic and Institutional Change was addressed in foregoing sub-chapter (institutions and approaches of NIE). North (1990), in search of a theory of economic dynamics (comparable to general equilibrium) to provide an analytical framework which would enable economic change to be understood, develops the initial framework for an analytical understanding of the way economies evolve through time. The Neo-classical methodology – concerned with the operation of markets but not with their development – is unable to analyse and prescribe policies that are capable of inducing development. When applied to economic development and history, it focused on technological development, and more recently human-capital investment, but ignored the incentive structure embodied in institutions (North, 1994: 359). Namely, that institutions determine the extent of social investment in those factors. By abolishing the two assumptions of Neo-classicism (neither institutions nor time matters), the analytical framework provides – despite crudeness – a necessary guide to policy in the ongoing task of improving the performance of economies. The Theory of Economic and Institutional Change concentrates on the interaction of rules (institutions), the adjustment of rules and economic performance through time.

Institutional framework (matrix) and economic performance

North constructed his Theory of Economic and Institutional Change by combining a theory of human behaviour with a theory of the costs of transacting. In sub-chapter 1.1.1, institutions are characterised as constraints, which structure (channel) human interaction. They are devised by humans to reduce uncertainty and create order (reciprocal expectations on individual behaviour). The uncertainties arise as a consequence of both the complexity of the problem to be solved (incomplete information) and the problem-solving software possessed by the individuals (information processing) (North, 1990: 25). The latter means the computational limitations of individuals, which are determined by a capacity of mankind to process, organise and utilise information. Individuals therefore typically act on incomplete information and with subjectively derived models that are frequently erroneous. Based on this capacity, rules and procedures evolve to simplify the exchange process. Hence together with the traditional constraints of economics, institutions define the choices made by individuals. They determine – with the technology employed – transaction and transformation costs that add up to the costs of production (North, 1994: 360).

The costs of economic exchange are explained by the gains from trade made possible by increasing specialisation and division of labour. Transaction costs, determined by four major variables[2], are the costs of specifying what is being exchanged and of enforcing the consequent agreements (North, 1994: 361). What is being specified in economic markets is the valuable attributes – the physical and property-right dimensions – of goods and services or performance of agents. The level of these attributes varies from one specimen or agent to the next. By ascertaining the level of individual attributes of each unit exchanged, economic agents produce ***costs of measuring*** (first variable). Moreover, measuring can not be performed accurately because information is distributed asymmetrically.

The second variable is market size. This determines whether a personal or an impersonal exchange occurs – the ***cost of impersonal exchange***. Ties of kinship, friendship loyalty etc. in a personal exchange reduce the need for costly specification. Whereas in an impersonal exchange, there is nothing to stop the parties taking advantage of each other. Thus costs rise with the need for more elaborate specification. The larger the market and the number of actors, the greater will be the share of impersonal exchanges (Buch, 1993: 2). Apart from this, transaction costs also consist of the ***cost of enforcement*** (third variable). That means that the problem of monitoring various attributes that constitute the performance of agents raises the costs of monitoring and policing[3]. The enforcement of agreements cannot be taken for granted because of the uncertainty that the agent finds it in his interest to live up to the agreement.

Lastly, ***ideology***[4] is an "individual perception about the fairness and justice of the rules of the games" (North, 1992: 479) – the fourth variable of transaction costs. Individuals use these culturally conditioned ideas to receive and interpret information. The ***cost of ideology*** is important insofar as it is the direct function of the degree to

---

2 See North (1992).
3 More detailed in Jensen et Meckling (1976).
4 Ideology contains all the subjective beliefs, dogmas, sound theories and myths that individuals consult in order to explain the world around them (North, 1992: 485).

which the measurement and enforcement of contracts is costly. The lower the costs of measuring and enforcement, the less important is ideology.

The aforesaid specification made up of institutions is therefore given as a reason for varying economic performances through time and across countries. The comparison of property rights in Mongolia with those of Germany in the beginning of the 1990s ascertains the following difference. In the former, after the abrupt change of the political and economic system, the majority of valuable rights are still unprotected, so that those ready to use violence to be successful can seize them. In the latter, the legal structure defines and enforces the majority of rights. And those which are not protected tend to be allocated by traditional norms of behaviour. The difference between these two countries is the difference between the institutional frameworks in each. An ***institutional framework*** is the set of institutions and their enforcement characteristics in an economy[5]. The economic development of a state depends on whether its population succeed in abating the permanently emerging transaction costs by means of convenient institutional frameworks. There are many economies that have failed to produce a set of institutions (matrix of economic rules of the game) that induce sustained economic growth, as the experiences of developing countries and of some economies in transition (EITs) show.

An important feature of institutional frameworks is consistency of different institutions within a particular economy – one of important questions on the nature of institutional change.

Nature of institutional change

Since institutions define – together with other economic restrictions – the opportunities of a society, organisations are created to take advantage of these opportunities. That means that if the institutional framework rewards crime and ripping off then robbery banks or gambling banks will come into existence, and if it honours productive activities then organisations, e.g. banks, which successfully intermediate funds, will come into existence. Thus, the kind of organisations coming into existence will reflect the institutional framework, and as they evolve they alter the institutions. This interaction between institutions and organisations shapes the institutional evolution of an economy (North, 1990: 7). For a better understanding of it, North (1994: 361) focuses on main elements of institutional change: the source of change, the agent of change, the direction of change and path dependence, the stability characteristics of institutions and of institutional change.

5 It is also referred to as institutional setting, institutional arrangements, institutional structure, institutional environment or institutional matrix throughout literature.

Of major importance is to grasp that the change is an incremental, ongoing process, one that it is a consequence of choices made every day by individual actors within organisations. The daily exchange processes are settled within the existing rules. Yet organisations with sufficient bargaining power will occasionally use policies to maximise their objectives, thereby bending the existing rules. That is the case if the payoff to maximise within the existing structure of property rights and political rules is lower then payoff from maximising within new – modified or eroded – bargaining rules. Thus institutional modifications occur because organisations believe that they could improve by restructuring exchanges. North (1990: 86) describes the process of institutional change as follows:

> A change in relative prices leads one or both parties to an exchange, whether it is political or economic, to perceive that either or both could do better with an altered agreement or contract. An attempt will be made to renegotiate the contract. However, because contracts are nested in a hierarchy of rules, the renegotiation may not be possible without restructuring a higher set of rules (or violating some norm of behaviour). In that case, the party that stands to improve his or her bargaining position may very well attempt to devote resources to restructuring the rules at a higher level. In the case of a norm of behaviour, a change in relative prices or a change in tastes will lead to its gradual erosion and to its replacement by different norm. Over time, the rule may be changed or simply be ignored and not enforced. Similarly, a custom or tradition may be gradually eroded and replaced with another. This very simplified story can be complicated in many ways – by agenda power, by the tenacity of norms of behaviour. But as the skeletal outline of the pattern of institutional change, it provides some basic characteristics.

Hence the source of the changed perception of individuals, i.e. ***source of institutional change***, is the alteration of relative prices or preferences. This is brought about by innovation (such as gunpowder, the deposit activities of goldsmiths in medieval times and clearing activities in the nineteenth century), altered resources (land rate, labour rate, gold rate) or new knowledge (knowledge about the impact of environmental damage increasing ecological awareness, knowledge about the nature of financial products – such as loans – promoting the acceptance and estimation of risk).

An individual entrepreneur (or organisation) who requires new opportunities to make gains from trade is the ***agent of institutional change***. Entrepreneurs perceive and grasp these opportunities depending on their ability (knowledge) to ferret out profitable margins, to estimate the likelihood of success, and to risk resources to make the gains. Amongst other things, this pertains to the foundation of intermediate organisations, such as lobbying groups, associations, action committees etc. Organisations are therefore "purposive entities designed by their creators to maximise wealth, income, or other objectives defined by the opportunities afforded by the institutional structure of the society" (North, 1990: 73). The bargaining power of agents to apply pressure in changing the old rules is of great importance to economic output.

Nevertheless, the change in the relative stock of resources can be initiated externally, such as by war, revolution or by natural disasters. Under such radical, discontinuous changes, formal rules change but not informal ones. This discontinuity of change is characterised by an inconsistency of rules because the persistence of cultural traits causes informal institutions to change at different rate than formal institutions. North (1990: 91) sees the "result over time tends to be a restructuring of the overall constraints – in both directions – to produce a new equilibrium that is far less revolutionary". This interaction of rules is an important factor for the ***stability of change***. Stability means implementing the institutions at the lowest cost. And that is just the case with consistent and complementary formal and informal institutions (***compatibility of institutions***). However, this stability does not mean efficiency in the sense of producing economic growth: "Stability is a necessary condition for complex human interaction, but it is not a sufficient condition of efficiency" (North, 1997: 6).

The direction of institutional change is characterised by a ***path dependence***. This term was originally used by Brian Arthur (1989) and Paul David (1985) to describe the way a particular technological development shaped subsequent downstream technological choices. Applied to an institutional development, it accounts for the characteristic of an institutional framework "that has shaped downstream institutional choices and, in consequence, makes it difficult to alter the direction of an economy once it is on a particular institutional path" (North, 1997: 15)[6]. Once a development path is taken, the particular course is reinforced by the network externalities, the learning process of organisations and the historically derived subjective modelling of the issues. If a path enables a maximum of choices under uncertainty, a pursuit of various trial methods of entrepreneurial activities and an efficient feedback mechanism to identify choices, which are relatively inefficient, and to eliminate them, than it is an adaptive efficient path, that is part of economic growth. Yet an unproductive path can provide disincentives to productive activities. This will create organisations with a stake in the existing constraints. Such institutions give false incentives, encouraging e.g. military domination of politics and economy, religious fanaticism, and simple redistributive organisations. The subjective mental models of

6 For detailed description see North (1990: 92 et seq.).

individuals will evolve an ideology that not only rationalises the society's structure, but also accounts for its poor performance. Consequently, the economy will evolve policies that reinforce the existing disincentives and unproductive organisations (third world economies of Latin America, Asia and Africa).

The foregoing arguments can be concluded with following implications from North's groundbreaking work (1990: 104):

> Long-run economic change is the cumulative consequence of innumerable short-run decisions by political and economic entrepreneurs that both directly and indirectly (via external effects) shape performance. The choices made reflect the entrepreneurs' subjective modelling of the environment. Therefore, the degree to which outcomes are consistent with intentions will reflect the degree to which the entrepreneur's models are true models. Because the models reflect ideas, ideologies, and beliefs that are, at best, only partially refined and improved by information feedback on the actual consequences of the enacted polices, the consequences of specific policies are not only uncertain but to a substantial degree unpredictable. Even the most casual inspection of political and economic choices, both throughout history and today, makes clear the wide gap between intentions and outcomes. However, the increasing-returns characteristics of the institutional matrix and the complementary subjective models of the players suggest that although the specific short-run paths are unforeseeable, the overall direction in the long run is both more predictable and more difficult to reverse.

The dimension of time as it relates to economic and social change is the dimension in which the learning process of human beings shapes the way institutions evolve. In detail, the beliefs that individuals, groups and societies hold and which determine choices are a consequence of long-term learning – not just within the span of an individual's life or of a generation of a society, but the learning embodied in individuals, groups, and societies that is cumulative throughout the times and passed on between generations by the culture of a society (North, 1994: 360).

Human learning as a long-run source of change

According to North[7], the most fundamental ***long-run source of change*** is learning by individuals and entrepreneurs of organisations. Ubiquitous scarcity impels competition among organisations, thereby inducing them and their individuals to engage in learning to survive. The rate of learning will reflect the intensity of competition and there is little incentive to learn in a monopoly (for productive purposes, e.g. to get productive knowledge). The speed of economic change is a function of the rate of learning, but the direction of that change is a function of the expected payoffs to acquiring different kinds of knowledge (North, 1994: 362). Knowledge psychologists (Mandl, Spada: 1988) describe the term ***knowledge***

[7] See hereto North (1990: 80), North (1992: 198) and North (1994: 362).

preferably as the relatively steady mnemonic representations of facts (to know that – factual knowledge) and proceedings (to know how – procedural knowledge) as well as the regulation and planning of actions (meta-knowledge).

During the ***learning*** process, individuals develop a knowledge (structure), by which to interpret the varied signals received by their senses (North, 1994: 362). Although the initial architecture of the structure is genetic, the structure's subsequent scaffolding is a result of the experiences of the individual. Individuals make their experiences from both their physical environment and their social-cultural linguistic environment. The structure is composed of categories or classifications. These gradually evolve from the earliest childhood to organise an individual's perception and pursue his or her memory of analytic results and experiences. These classifications are used by individuals to form ***(subjective) mental models*** in order to explain and interpret their environments – typically in ways relevant to some goals. Using the feedback derived from new experiences, both the categories and the mental models will evolve. This feedback sometimes reinforces an individual's initial categories and models, or may lead to modification – in short, learning. So, with new experiences, the mental models may be continually redefined.

The intimate relationship between mental models and institutions is explained by North (1994: 363):

> Mental models are the internal representations that individuals cognitive systems create to interpret the environment; institutions are the external (to the mind) mechanisms individuals create to structure and order the environment.

That supports analyses into the economic past and current developments in EITs. Human societies which have evolved in differing environments, i.e. with different experiences, evolve different mental models to explain the world around them. These mental models formed informal constraints, which in turn defined the institutional framework and were passed down through generations. This is the key to explaining the powerful influence of the past on the present and future – the path dependence. Institutional prescriptions of a society reflect the learning from past experience.

The understanding of how human learning takes place, and of the kind of learning that individuals in a society acquire through time, are of crucial importance for institutional analysis. Chapter 1.3 will return to this issue at the time it develops a theoretical framework for the succeeding survey.

Understanding of transition problems and weakness of NIE

The failure of communism in 1989 reflected the collapse of the perceived legitimacy of the belief system and a weakening of the supporting organisations. Most formal rules were destroyed as a result, whereas many informal constraints survived. A factor in the varying success of different EITs in reforming their entire societies, and especially their economies, is the heritage of informal norms from the pre-communist era. These enabled a relatively harmonious establishment of new rules in countries such as the Czech Republic, Hungary and Poland. Countries with no tradition of a market economy and democracy – Russia and Mongolia, among others – had no informal constraints or norms to provide fertile ground for the establishment of such economic and political systems. Yet as they have chosen to go with these economic and political systems, the major obstacle is the institutional restructuring that is required. The difficulty in this context is the fact that informal norms have evolved as a result of cumulative past experiences. These do not properly equip the individuals in such societies to confront and solve new problems. For this reason, the analysis of the existing informal constraints of these economies is the key to accurately address economic policies.

However, despite ground-breaking approaches and implications, NIE still does not constitute a comprehensive, new framework with useful instruments of empirical analysis. The approaches of NIE are immensely diverse and separate. This weakness is exacerbated by the lack of effort made so far to measure transaction costs, the failure to "cost out" alternative institutional solutions and the practical difficulty of doing so.

It is the problem of measurement which is a methodological shortcoming for empirical analysis of institutions, institutional features and institutional operations. One of the major tasks for NIE is therefore to provide new tools to analyse institutions and the institutional features of economies (designing and evolution of methods). The present work attempts to address this problem by using a method of concept mapping related to cognitive science to observe and measure – at least indirectly – the informal institutions of lending. The useful tool of concept mapping – based on perceptions of an action-regulating knowledge approach – is applied to diagnose the links and associated ideas of bankers, thus bankers' own interpretations of lending. As the study asks which informal constraints channel decision-making on lending, and what drives decision makers – bankers – during the loan granting process, the action-regulating knowledge of loan officers can be identified using concept maps created by themselves. But before going into details of the relations between institutions, mental models, action-regulating knowledge and concept mapping in chapter 1.3, the lending process should be analysed as seen by NIE.

1.2 Institutional Framework of Lending

1.2.1 Applying NIE to Lending

Applying the approaches (arguments) of NIE to analyse the process of lending in banks offers an opportunity to explain some crucial (fundamental) issues of financial intermediation and imperfections of financial markets that have not yet been justified. Before reviewing the institutions which structure and channel the action of bankers under uncertainty in lending processes, the next step determines transaction costs, which account for uncertainties in lending.

Transaction costs, institutions and organisations in lending

The costliness of exchange is of crucial importance to the existence of institutions. The exchange unit in this case is a service – an intermediation of funds. It entails mediating the excess funds of depositors to borrowers who have a shortage of funds. The service therefore has two sides, receiving deposits and granting loans. The present work accentuates the latter and intends to analyse the institutions channelling behaviour in lending[8]. As argued above in sub-chapter 1.1.3, four types of transaction costs can be identified: cost of measurement, cost of impersonal exchange, cost of enforcement and cost of ideology. The costliness of exchange in lending can be characterised as followed.

The valuable attributes of the service in question – a loan – need to be specified in the financial market. That means that the amount and type of contractual obligations which result from the exchange of this service need to be specified. Ascertaining the level of the physical dimension – size, interest rate, maturity – and the property rights dimension – collateral – produces ***costs of measurement***. In a non-inflationary, stable environment, the value of the money (in the form of the loan) can be easily specified. But where inflation exists, measurements cannot be made accurately, thus impeding long-term lending. Moreover, the market value of the asset used as collateral (to safeguard against unexpected insolvency) also becomes difficult to determine. The property rights dimension of collateral must be exactly specified and well protected (Buch, 1993: 2) through financial laws and other norms or habits, if the cost of measurement is to remain low.

---

[8] Although the impact of institutions is relevant to both – receiving deposits and granting loans – the analysis is restricted to the latter due to the specifics of the research question posed in present work.

As the role of the (financial) market under review here is to receive deposits from a plurality of individuals and allocate them as loans to single investors, this market is large and thus characterised by impersonal exchange. The inherent feature of financial markets – impersonality – makes allowance for a more elaborate, and thus costly, specification of financial services such as loans. This specification is essential to ensure the security of depositors, which depends on the ability and willingness of the intermediary to administer the funds in the depositors' best interests (Buch, 1993: 2). Hence institutional mechanisms, such as rating or bank supervisory requirements, should contain the ***costs of impersonal exchange***. Moreover, the shortage of information in impersonal exchanges can cause extremely high costs and adverse selection, causing an inefficient allocation of resources.

Since economic agents cannot accurately measure and control the performance of borrowers and information is distributed asymmetrically, they have a problem enforcing contractual obligations. The enforcement of financial contracts therefore cannot be taken for granted due to a moral hazard problem. Moreover, the separation in time of a contractual agreement and of its completion emphasises the need of prospective lenders to monitor and to control activities if borrowers have superior information on the project (Buch, 1993: 3). The moral hazard problem is characterised by the possibility that a borrower falsifies the profitability of the project, then disappears with the borrowed money or uses it for projects other than that initially proposed and more risky than lenders prefer. Thus control mechanisms, such as corporate governance, are needed to address the ***cost of enforcement***.

Due to costs of measuring impersonal exchanges, and of enforcement at the financial markets, the initial perception of actors about the fairness of the game played (service with financial funds) also influences costs. Due to the fact that actors do not posses the same information to update their perceptions, they may have different perceptions or interpret information in different ways to other actors – lender or borrower. Hence, there is a ***cost*** and benefit ***of ideology*** in the exchange of financial services. If the ethical and moral standards which served as a reference for a particular law or contract in lending diverge from the subjective beliefs of those actors who are supposed to implement the law or contract, the willingness to apply the law or the contract obligations will be low (Buch, 1993: 3).

In a world of positive transactions in lending, and thus of uncertainty in lending, institutions do matter. They can minimise uncertainty by reducing transaction costs. As already mentioned above, examples of institutions or elements of institutional framework in lending are laws on financial activities, e.g. lending, bank regulation norms, paying habits etc. Figure 1.1 highlights different kinds of institutions and their crude systematisation gives some examples of institutions in lending (lower half of the figure). If the focus lies on a particular market of concern, generally the financial market here and especially the loan market, there are the following institutions to be named[9] in building the institutional framework of decision making around this particular market. They are classified here at two levels: firstly formal and informal levels, and secondly overall economic and branch-specific levels. ***Formal rules of lending*** include overall economic rules, such as a constitution, economic laws, requirements of economic and social policies and accounting standards. Branch-specific formal rules include banking laws, laws on financial activities such as lending, requirements of monetary policy, bank regulation norms and the statutes of banks. The ***informal rules of lending*** can be designated as the inherited code of conduct in economic exchange, ties of family and kinship, commitment to (rejection of) an authoritative state, which are all overall economic rules. Branch-specific informal rules are banking habits, such as paying habits, attitude to risk etc.

As transaction costs can alter throughout time and are also different across countries, the mixture of formal rules (the definition and protection of property rights to collateral or bank regulation norms) and informal rules (paying habits, attitude to risk) varies enormously. Thus different economies can have different institutions and institutional frameworks for lending which shape different opportunities. ***Financial organisations of lending***, such as banks, will arise to exploit the opportunities shaped by existing institutions and reduce transaction costs. Banks, as financial organisations, have a comparative advantage over a multitude of individual lenders. This emanates from the delegated monitoring theory of financial organisation of Diamond (1984), whereupon banks accept a request from many lenders to collect information on borrowers. As Fama (1985) argues, information asymmetries are lower in bank lending agreements than in public bond and equity issues[10]. Yet there are other forms of financial organisations which mediate financial funds. The simplest of them is the market maker – a stock exchange – providing a market place for potential lenders and borrowers but not creating assets. Whereas a dealer – a market specialist on securities exchange – takes a position at his own risk in the asset transacted. Banks and mutual funds are more complex financial organisations, which produce new financial commodities in the course of serving as financial intermediaries.

---

9 Due to the complexity of institutions, the list is far from complete.

10 Since the present work focuses on institutional analysis of lending, especially bank lending in transition, it does not dwell on the issues of why banks exist and if/ why bank lending has a comparative advantage over other forms of financing. See Diamond (1984), Fama (1980, 1985), James (1987).

Thus depending on existing formal and informal institutions in the economy generally and particularly in lending, the financial organisations which arise can have varied forms not only within a single economy, but differ from one economy to the next.

Institutional framework of lending in a market economy

In an environment in which properly defined property rights, regulation requirements and adequate norms of conduct and banking behaviour exist, banks will arise to productively allocate financial resources. They can lower transaction costs by organising money and capital markets: they collect savings and allocate these to the most profitable investments, perhaps loans. In such an institutional environment, thus in a market economy, Buch (1993: 7) argues that banks can achieve the following :

- They are better able to diversify their portfolios and to pool risks. In a market economy, banks are capable of transforming production, liquidity and term-structure risks to suit to the individual preferences of their depositors, these being the basis of banking business.
- In addition to monitoring, controlling, and assessing their borrowers, banks accumulate information on markets and investment projects. With information advantage, banks in a market economy are good at reducing problems arising from moral hazard and from asymmetric information. They provide a solution to the increasingly costly principle-agent-relationships that arise when societies want to utilise gains from specialisation.
- Finally, market-oriented banks are in a position to provide the framework for a functioning payments mechanism.

However, banks set up in an economy with institutions that are still far removed from that of market economy, cannot properly inherit the role of financial intermediary as in case of EITs.

1.2.2 Institutional Framework of Lending in Transition

Some mitigating problems of loan markets in EITs characterise institutional issues of lending there: contract design, efficient use of ever scarcer financial resources, market imperfections.

Transaction costs and institutions of lending in transition

Transaction costs, an inherent feature of all financial markets, are even greater in the money and capital markets of EITs. Besides "typical" transaction costs being higher, the financial markets of EITs have additional transaction costs. These can be explained as having their roots in past economic systems – centrally planned economies. Both of these factors causing high transaction costs come into play when banks lend to enterprises in transition.

An EIT represents an environment with hardly any financial information and extreme uncertainty – privatisation issues, especially in banking, remain unresolved - so that measuring becomes extremely costly. Due to uncertainty concerning property rights and the market values of assets, it is difficult for banks to evaluate the value of a borrower. The lack of appropriate collateral is also due to the lack of adequate accounting standards. Whereas the general lack of financial information enhances the role of collateral in lending, and bank lending focuses on secured loans (Ickes and Ryterman 1994: 67). Especially in the early stages of transition, even secured loans become difficult because firms do not own the land the factory is built on, and therefore cannot use it to secure loans. Loans are therefore very often only secured by written pledges to repay, or are mostly collateralised by inventories and sometimes also by machinery. Furthermore, most EITs have had no experience in enforcing property rights though the legal system, nor in the treatment of seniority issues (Buch, 1993: 4). These problems drive up the cost of measurement.

Impersonal exchanges in transition are more costly compared to those of advanced economies because information mechanisms, such as rating and supervisory systems, are non-existent or extremely underdeveloped. Specialisation of financial services (or financial commodities) is hardly possible under these circumstances. Many banks in the loan markets in EITs therefore tend to stick to old, well-established business relations and activities. These activities and relations, however, often hamper a proper allocation of resources.

Deficiencies in the legal infrastructure make it costly to enforce contracts. Poorly developed commercial laws make it hard – if not impossible – for banks to demand repayment and reclaim assets. Banks therefore look to find administrative solutions (instead of solutions via courts of arbitration): as soon as a firm received funds on its bank account, the account was immediately debited in favour of priority creditors (Perotti, 1994: 73). Even filing bankruptcy cases is extremely difficult, despite the bankruptcy laws passed. Bankruptcy proceedings were initiated against very few enterprises because judges were reluctant to tackle politically precarious cases and lawyers lacked experience. Moreover, bankruptcy proceedings and failures of enterprises were perceived to be socially undesirable and morally reprehensible (Buch, 1993: 4). Thus banks continued to extend loans to ailing firms, expecting to be bailed out by the Government if the worst came to the worst. This also points to the lack of commitment to hard budget constraints and the different attitude towards enterprise failures (compared to advanced economies). The aforesaid costs of enforcement can also serve as factors for high costs of ideology. Hence the fundamental distinction between transaction costs in transition and in developed market economies can be seen in the costs of ideology. A high level of public ignorance, based on the perception of the fairness of the game played, can make financial services extremely costly, if not impracticable.

A common denominator for all four kinds of transaction costs is the lack of information on the outcome of the transition process. Sudden shifts in policy, actual or potential, or even a change of regime or government, increase the uncertainty of the economic environment. The future viability of borrowers is thus more difficult to asses, and credit history (indicator for future solvency) unimportant. Bank lending under these conditions is associated with exorbitantly high transaction costs.

The magnitude of transaction costs in lending, especially during transition, means that economic exchanges are heavily reliant on institutions. Yet in the financial systems of EITs, many basic rules of money and capital markets are unknown and economic agents have no experience of market-based financial transactions. The regulatory and legislative framework - the formal institutions – is riddled with loopholes (Buch, 1993: 5). Thus the rules of the game in lending (institutions), such as well-defined commercial and banking laws, regulatory norms and accounting standards and sustainable, assignable economic, social and monetary policies, are part of the process of building a framework to confine uncertainties. Well-established rules of conduct in economic exchange, existing ethical standards and social commitments (informal institutions) are also of similar weight in EITs. Some formal and informal rules in lending practices in EITs are best described by showing their roots in the planned economy.

The institutions in a planned economy and the incentives shaped by them gave economic actors little or no discretion over their financial transactions. According to the former ***laws and regulations on lending activities*** (production and investment targets of central plan), banks were dependent upon central directives and could not allocate savings individually. They did not have to conduct financial analysis: there was no need to assess the solvency and credibility of borrowers, not to mention assessing the value of collateral. The absence of risk considerations in the lending decisions and weighting the risk involved in a particular project underpin the lack of experience in the ***attitude to risk***. The accounting systems in planned economies were set up as accounting mechanisms rather than full-blown information systems (Buch, 1993: 5). Banks monitored whether the planned amount of goods was produced and sold. As long as costs equalled sales, i.e. as long as the firm's account of transactions was balanced, the firm would receive credit. Thus, banks analysed the current financial position and there was no ***banking habit of forward-looking evaluation*** of a borrower or a project.

Under the former monetary policy (as far as it can be called such), interest rates were kept artificially low, so banks had no experience in pursuing their own pricing policies. The ***moral and ethical standards*** did not involve activities such as refusing applications for financial funds or forcing enterprises into bankruptcy. In case of difficulties, ***social commitments***, such as the authority of the state – e.g. being bailed out by the state – took over. They gave important incentives for the activities of actors and should not be underestimated in transition analysis. The authority of the state also allowed banks to allocate part of their budgetary outlays for subsidy payments. Owing to the lack of proper institutions, bank lending, and thus credit allocation, was not efficient until long into transition.

Transforming the financial system therefore means changing the institutional framework (creating new institutions and rebuilding existing ones) in order to provide an impetus to form proper financial organisations, such as banks. The role of banks has to shift from being passive agents of fiscal policy to becoming active participants in a market system.

Banks (financial organisations of lending) and their behaviour during transition

Against this background, different kinds of - banks shaped partly by prompt, partly by fragmentarily changed institutions - came into existence at the beginning of transition. They can be classified, according to their behaviour and role for credit allocation, into four categories based on Johnson et al. (1993: 183).

The former state bank branches, which were transformed into legally and financial independent state banks, are in the first category. In most EITs, they have independently started to sell shares to large enterprises. Despite this spontaneous action to raise capital and to reduce the proportion of state shares in the banks, the state still claims responsibility for these banks. Due to the dominant role of political decision makers (no rules to prevent it), the lending decisions made by state banks were subject to intense negotiations and lobbying. They thus continued to act purely as agents implementing state-directed loans aimed at sustaining the operations of whole industries. As long as such directed loans were warranted by Ministries of Finance and yielded very high returns, banks had no incentives to refuse the state credit programmes or change their lending behaviour. The high profits come from the interest rate spread (e.g. banks received the credits at an interest rate of 3% and lent the money on at 10%) and from foreign exchange activities (banks delayed passing on the credits, bought foreign exchange and profited from depreciation in the meantime). Moreover, the general public held the state responsible for the way these banks functioned (social commitment). This amounted to an implicit assurance that the state stood warranty for their deposits, allowing these banks to collect the majority of savings – especially in the early stages of transition.

After markets had been opened up, there was rapid increase of consumption curiosity in the early years of transition[11]. A number of traders accumulated considerable capital during this time and some of these private persons founded the so-called "zero" banks – second category – with their earnings. In order to expand into other profitable fields of business, they created banks and were able to protect themselves from high inflation by reinvesting their trading profits in stocks of goods, which preserved their real value. Being mostly controlled by their owner-managers, zero banks are usually not involved in political processes and have a relatively good level of corporate control. Exploiting opportunities presented by the low level of commercial information, large returns can be made on intermediate trade. Due to the "unworkability" of bankruptcy laws, trust in the form of ties of friendship and kinship plays an important role in their lending and "serves" as collateral. Under these conditions, such banks predominantly engage in trade finance, which yields high profits, and do not grant any long-term loans.

The third category, the so-called "pocket" banks, were usually founded by a single state-controlled enterprise or co-operative. In fact these banks played the role of the financial departments of the founding enterprises. Due to the lack of formal rules, they offered easy access to the central bank's refinancing facility and provided an opportunity to hedge against inflation (operations on foreign exchange markets) and engage in speculation. These banks were usually founded in a hurry and also facilitated self-privatisation (buying up shares in voucher auctions), thereby allowing the firm's managers to remain in control of their firm.

The fourth category of "spin-off" banks comprise former state organisations, like the former directorates of industry ministries or regional branches of former state banks, which have been spun off from the state organs to which they originally belonged.

[11] The adjustment of relative price after price liberalisation, the confusion concerning internal trade networks and the new external trade opportunities created a large scope for traders to reap windfall profits (Freinkman 1995: 54). Regulations and controls on some goods' prices and the requirement that goods had to be sold for non-cash money led to a large spread between wholesale and retail prices for traders so that very high profits could be yielded.

These financial industrial conglomerates were formed by state organisations as a means of survival after central planning had been dismantled. Their good relations with the remaining state organs were important in lobbying, e.g. for subsidies. These banks are mutually intertwined with the enterprises they once attended to as a ministry or state bank through cross-ownership of shares. The lack of rules governing relationships between ownership and bank management means that the cancerous relationship between enterprises and banks – pocket as well as spin-off banks – prevails (Ickes, 1994: 10). As enterprise surveys indicate, the largest shareholder enterprises control half of the banks' capital (ownership concentration), implying cross-subsidisation within the group of banks owners (Ickes and Ryterman, 1994: 347).

Johnson et al. (1993: 195) reported in detail on the ways used by banks to reduce transition costs and to make lending profitable. Large enterprises, and even ministries, co-signed debt contracts that should reduce the adverse selection problem. The short time horizon of loans and credit extension solely for trade finance show how banks try to address moral hazard. Transaction costs could be held relatively low by lending only to state organisations or to affiliated enterprises within a network of enterprises.

Playing to win the game, these banks took advantage of all opportunities given by existing or failing institutions. As a result, enterprises that could not obtain credit on the "tighter" official credit markets started to build up an inefficient network of inter-enterprise credit. As repressed inflation turned into open inflation, inflation-hedges and foreign exchange holdings were accumulated; bribery and lobbying became a successful way to obtain credit. As this kind of financial organisation takes root, it enforces new rules of interest, making it ever more tricky to leave this path. And changing the inefficient allocation of financial funds gets more difficult as the nature of institutional change reveals.

Consistency of formal institutions with informal institutions in lending

Thus extreme friction characterises the transition process from one economic system to another. This friction needs to be taken into account in estimating the impact of policies. The switch from the centralisation to the decentralisation of banking services, such as lending, does not lead per se to greater efficiency. Supporting reforms need to be enacted by addressing the institutional framework and its change in order to encompass the new system. The banking system, thereunder its lending activity, has to be transformed from passive to active.

The main implications for improving the institutional framework of lending in EITs can be formulated as followed:

- Formally changed laws, even legal allowance for private ownership of banks, liberalised interest rates and precisely devised or copied bank regulation norms are insufficient if people's subjective mental models of behaviour do not shift (Buch, 1993: 6). Informal constraints, such as paying habits or bankers attitude to risk, shape economic behaviour, they cannot be changed overnight, they need much more time to develop than formal rules.
- Informal rules cannot adjust if formal changes are inconsistent in themselves (Buch, 1993: 6). That means that changes to banking laws and bank regulation norms must be implemented by adequate (aright) economic and social policies. Privatising enterprises without credibly protecting the property rights of the new owners would not give the hoped-for incentives.
- Making information on the new situation (new socio-economic coherences) available as well as giving incentives to learn are essential for the consistent change of formal and informal rules. Recognising new opportunities presented by by changed formal rules of the environment, bankers would start to adjust their behaviour accordingly and change/ create banking habits (informal rules). Moreover, they would then further evolve the formal rules by pushing through rule changes in order to maximise their gains. So path dependence also characterises institutional changes in lending (once set onto the proper path). Incentive structures to build up information capital (e.g. technical or expert knowledge) are of great importance.

Thus not only the existence of proper institutions is important, but also their compatibility with each other, especially the ***compatibility of formal and informal rules***. That means that the amendment of both formal and informal institutions has to be addressed simultaneously. And this consistency of formal rules with informal rules is subject to gradual reform. The consistency of banking regulation norms (which aim to rein in the risky behaviour of banks with legal rules) with the banking habits (which control bankers' actions), such as the attitude to risk, should therefore be the focus of further research and policy targets. Precise observation and diagnosis of these norms is required for this purpose. However, as already stated, observing and measuring informal institutions is one of the outstanding challenges for NIE. In this work, a method to indirectly diagnose the informal institutions of a particular sector of the economy – lending – is evolved based on the cognitive science approach. The next chapter therefore introduces the cognitive science approach to decision-making (in lending).

1.3 Cognitive Approach to Analysing Institutions of Lending

As already argued in sub-chapter 1.1.3, human learning is a long-term driver of institutional change. During the learning process, the mind appears to order and reorder the mental models reflecting the feedback derived from new experiences. On this basis, the following sub-chapter evolves a cognitive framework (Figure 1.2) to analyse institutions by addressing the interrelationship between mental models, institutions and knowledge (1.3.1). Following on from this, models of knowledge organisation used by cognitive psychologists are introduced (1.3.2) in order to frame the diagnosis of action-regulating knowledge of bankers during decision making in lending (1.3.3).

1.3.1 Cognitive Approach to Institutional Analysis: Institutions, Mental Models and Knowledge

The analysis of institutions is a growing field within the discipline of economics. Although the theory to analyse informal institutions is nothing like complete, cognitive science has made immense strides in recent years – enough progress to suggest a tentative approach that can help understand decision-making under uncertainty (North, 1994: 362).

Half a century ago, decision-making was introduced by Edwards (1954) as a research topic for psychologists. Allais (1953) outlined a psychology-based positive theory of choice under uncertainty, while Simon (1956, 1957) proposed an approach to information processing and decision making based on bounded rationality. However, research in cognitive psychology finally came into its own only recently after Daniel Kahneman and Amos Tversky (1976 or 1979) published their findings on judgement and decision-making. Although Kahneman[12] adhered to the tradition of cognitive psychology, his research has equally well been directed towards economists. Given the barriers to communicating across traditional disciplines, considerable efforts have gone into building a bridge between research in economics and psychology[13]. The interrelationship of cognition and institutions is now determined by introducing the conception of decision making in cognitive psychology.

---

12 Many of his articles have been published in economics journals one of which, Kahneman and Tversky (1979), even has the highest citation count of all articles published in *Econometrica* up to 2002.

13 An insightful comment on it is made by Kahneman (2003). The current wave of work in behavioural economics (or economic psychology) is based on bridges: experimental methods and theoretical modelling.

Figure 1.2: Conceptualising the cognitive approach

Source: own illustration, ——— interrelations in the literature

.... interrelations implicated within this work

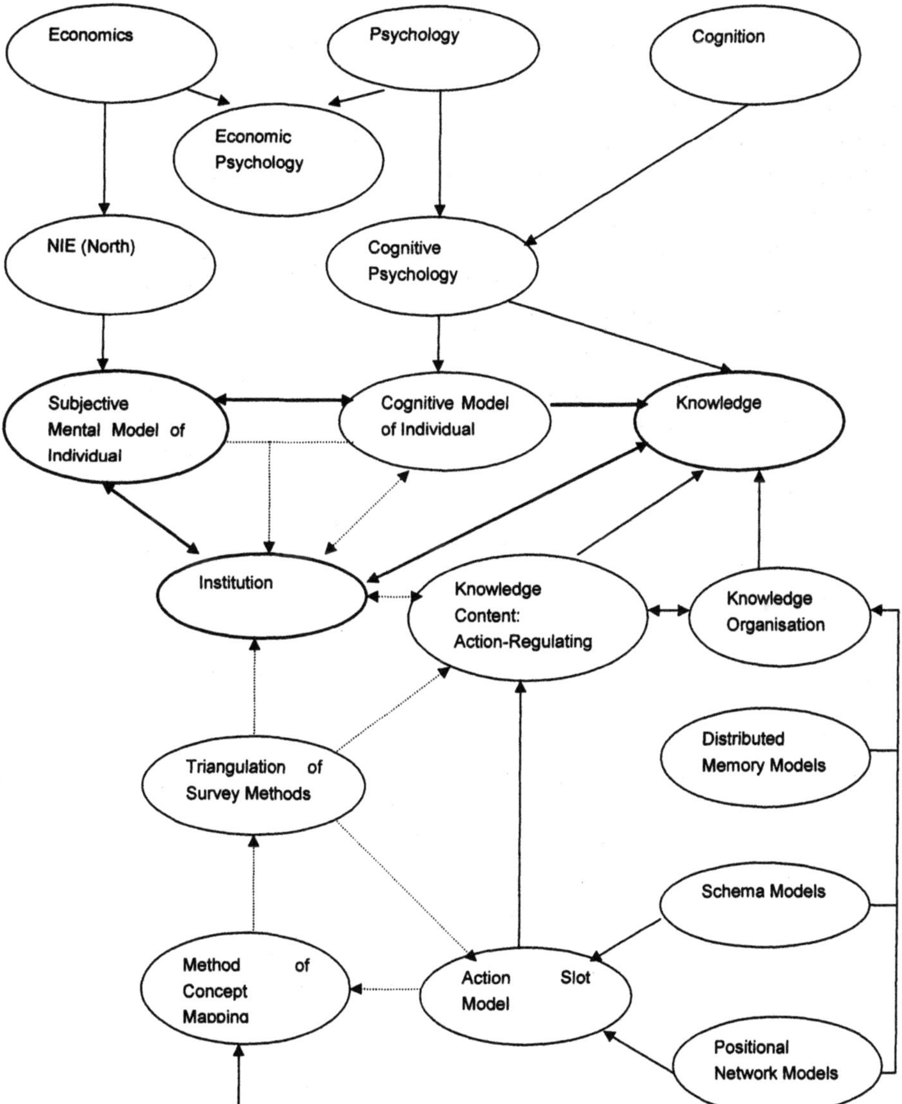

Decision-making within cognitive psychology

Herbert Simon (1986: 210-11) observed succinctly:

> If... we accept the proposition that both the knowledge and the computational power of the decision-maker are severely limited, then we must distinguish between the real world and the actor's perception of it and reasoning about it. That is to say we must construct a theory (and test it empirically) of the process of decision. Our theory must include not only the reasoning processes but also the processes that generated the actor's subjective representation of the decision problem, his or her frame.

On its way to becoming major field of research in psychology, ***cognition*** refers to the process of how human beings perceive and process information. ***Cognitive psychology*** is concerned with "how human beings analyse information obtained from the environment, how it is stored in memory, and how the stored information can be used to acquire and interpret new information and direct behaviour towards the attainment of goals" (Grunert, 1994: 92). Cognitive psychology regards the human being as a system, one which codes and interprets available information in a conscious and rational way. But other, less conscious or unconscious, factors are also assumed to govern human behaviour. Unconscious cognitive processes determine what people perceive, determine their reaction, determine what they remember and how they solve problems. It is this complex view – where intrinsic incentives help shape human behaviour – that has come to penetrate recent developments in economic theory, as in NIE – the Theory of Economic and Institutional Change.

The Neo-classicists reduce the cognitive process to a problem of forming and maximising expectations. It assumes that decision-makers behave as if they correctly assigned probabilities to relevant events and chose an action that maximised the expected value of their resulting utility.

Cognitive psychologists, however, consider an interactive process where several factors may influence a decision in a non-trivial way (Grunert, 1994: 98). These components include perception, which follows its own laws, as well as beliefs. Intrinsic motives, such as emotion – the state of mind of decision-maker – and ***attitudes*** – stable psychological tendencies to relate to a given phenomenon in one's environment – may influence decision making. Additionally, the memory of previous decisions and their consequences serves a critical cognitive function that also has a strong influence on current decision-making (Kahneman, 2003: 165). Given this complex view, human behaviour is regarded as logically conditioned to a given situation. Typically, behaviour is adaptive; it is dependent on the context and transitory perceptual conditions (Simon, 1986: 30).

In order to enhance the understanding of how people make economic decisions[14], Kahneman has used insights from cognitive psychology regarding the mental processes of answering questions, forming judgements and making choices. In a series of studies, Kahneman – in collaboration with the late Amos Tversky (1992) – has shown that, under the circumstances of uncertain future consequences, people are incapable of fully analysing complex situations in which a decision is required. These and other results contradict predictions from the traditional theory of expected-utility maximisation, thereby showing that human beings can systematically deviate from Bayesian logic. Thus modern research at the border line between economics and psychology has shown that concepts, such as bounded rationality, restricted self-interest and limited self-control, are important factors behind a range of economic phenomena. Yet in the context of the present study, much more interesting is the fact that it is essential to explicitly consider the phenomenon of cognition and its characteristics.

Under conditions of uncertainty, individuals' interpretation of their environment will reflect their learning and thus the impact of cognitive processes. Economic behaviour of individuals is guided by ***(subjective) cognitive models*** of the environment: it is assumed that these are created by the human mind. In his Theory of Economic and Institutional Change (1.1.3), North refers to them as subjective mental models. Individuals with common cultural backgrounds and experiences will share reasonably convergent mental models; individuals with different learning experiences (both cultural and environmental) will deploy different theories (models) to make sense out of the world around them (North and Denzau, 1994: 3).

Cognitive psychology differentiates between two conceptually distinct levels at which learning occurs. The first of these – learning, which changes the categories of mental models – has been described in 1.1.3. The second level of learning keeps the categories and concepts intact, but provides changed ideas about the details and applicability of existing knowledge. And together, "learning within a given set of concepts and learning which changes the structure of concepts and mental models suggest a widely known approach to the dynamics of learning" (North and Denzau, 1994: 13). Relating to the context of this work, no difference between the two has been made. Much more important to bear in mind is that individuals build cognitive/mental models on the basis of the knowledge (structures) they gain during their (individual) learning experiences. Thus mental models are shaped by knowledge.

---

14 And has been honoured with the Nobel Prize in Economics in 2002.

Institutions, cognitive/mental models and knowledge

Based on this close relationship between knowledge and cognitive/mental models, the present study intends to frame a cognitive approach to analyse informal institutions. Figure 1.2 illustrates this approach.

As the Theory of Economic and Institutional Change have shown, there is an intimate relationship between the mental models of individuals and the institutions created by individuals to order interpersonal relationships. Thus the "external to the mind mechanisms individuals create to structure and order the environment" - institutions – can be observed through the internal representations that individual cognitive systems create to interpret the environment – mental models. North and Denzau put it differently in 1994 and view institutions as classes of so-called shared mental models. If different individuals have similar models, they are able to better communicate and share their learning (North and Denzau, 1994: 4). So some types of mental models can be shared inter-subjectively, building institutions for the interpersonal relationship within a certain group of individuals in a certain domain (banking/lending) and thereby reducing uncertainty[15].

The kinds of knowledge, skills and learning that the members of an organisation (bankers) acquire reflect the payoff – the incentives – imbedded in the institutional constraints (in banking system). Another constellation of institutions will produce different incentives for knowledge[16] (North, 1990:81). In other words, the particular institutions will not only determinate the types of economic activity that will be profitable and viable, but also shape the adaptive efficiency of the internal structure of firms and other organisations (banks) by, for example, regulating governance structures, and the flexibility of organisations. North (1990: 82) argues that the rules that encourage the development and utilisation of knowledge, and therefore creative entrepreneurial talent, are important for efficient organisation.

The relationship between institutions and knowledge, however, is reciprocal, i.e. the way knowledge develops shapes individuals' perceptions of the world around them and in turn those perceptions shape the individuals' search for knowledge. North (1990: 76) cites intellectual life during late Middle Ages in the West as an example. This was dominated in matters of learning by the church, and even today ideologies in many parts of the world are intolerant, to one degree or another, of the

15 Cognitive/mental models are assumed to be influenced by the process of socialisation (Hayek, 1952, North 1990). During the process of socialisation institutions are internalised, i.e., external enforcement mechanisms are increasingly supplemented by internal ones. In this way, an institutional environment shapes the mental models of human actors.

16 Tacit knowledge.

development of pure knowledge. The way in which knowledge develops influences the perceptions people have about the world around them (mental models of bankers or institutions of lending), and hence the way in which they rationalise, explain and justify that world (lending practices), which in turn influences the costs of contracting.

The understanding of how human learning takes place and of the kind of learning that individuals in a society acquire through time are, therefore, of crucial importance to institutional analysis. This approach can support the study in observing informal institutions. In consideration of the relationship between institutions and cognition, the process of institutional change can be exemplified as followed. According to North (1994: 363), "the languages and mental models formed the informal constraints that defined the institutional framework of the tribe and were passed down intergenerationally as customs, taboos and myths that provided cultural continuity". In the course of time, due to growing specialisation and division of labour, the tribes evolved politics and economies. The more diverse their experiences and learning were, the more different the societies and civilisations that arose were with respect to the degrees of success in solving the fundamental economic problems of scarcity. Evolution requires that a society develops institutions that will permit anonymous, impersonal exchange across time and space (North, 1994: 363). The telling point in the foregoing narrative is the kind of learning that individuals in a society acquire through time. Yet the literature barely mentions the links between institutional structure (e.g. belief systems), knowledge and the incentives and disincentives to acquire knowledge.

Ultimately, the literature is not able to describe in depth the dynamics of the interplays between mental models, institutions and knowledge. The questions on how and to what extent knowledge forms mental models, how the mental models evolve and within which mechanisms they co-act (concur) with institutions and how this influences the development of institutions, are the challenges facing ongoing and future research. If these were properly understood, social science would make a quantum leap towards improving the black box recording the assumption of rationality. With some wringing of hands, North and Denzau (1994: 5) proclaim "we need to develop a framework that will enable us to understand and model the shared mental constructs [institutions – Ch.E.] that guide choices and shape the evolution of political-economic systems and societies".

Thus although the systematic interplays between institutions and cognitive/mental models are nowhere near fully explored, they must suffice for the purpose of this study. As this work intends to identify informal institutions as such, the insights into the interrelationship which exists between institutions, mental models and knowledge enables informal institutions of a process (lending) to be examined via cognitive/mental models by diagnosing the status quo of learning – knowledge – of those individuals taking decisions within this process (bankers).

A growing number of approaches to the question of how information is perceived and processed by the human mind have been developed by cognitive psychology (e.g. Gigerenzer 1993, 1994; Holland et al., 1986). Yet in the context of economic reasoning, the question is how, and to what extent, can these approaches be applied to develop a model of man that allows economic behaviour to be better explained and predicted. The next sub-chapter looks at the methods of cognitive psychology to analyse cognitive/mental models by diagnosing knowledge.

1.3.2 Models of Knowledge Organisation and Elicitation of Action-Regulating Knowledge

There are many basic aspects of a cognitive process: information selection (awareness), information categorisation and integration, storage, retrieval etc. A distinction should be made here between information and knowledge. Knowledge[17] is a fraction of information flood mnemonic-saved in a recallable form. Moreover, only a part of the knowledge in memory regulates the actions of individuals. The actual knowledge which regulates actions, such as decisions made by bankers, is discussed below. As previously mentioned, detailed insights into cognitive aspects related to economic events is a major issue for ongoing and future research. The present study focuses on the models of knowledge organisation (storage) and knowledge content in order to use these to diagnose knowledge. Whereas a knowledge psychologist places more emphasis on the form that expert knowledge is organised, an industrial psychologist is interested in the content of the knowledge, thereby adopting the term "action-regulating knowledge" (Hacker et al., 1993: 64), Figure 1.2.

Knowledge organisation

The discourse which takes place between individuals and their environment give these individuals their identities through a series of (intentional) decisions, actions and perceptions. This identify is based on a pattern of sense-making, a meaningful integration of experiences into an existing structure of one's self (Weick, 1995: 18). In order to explain processes such as perception, sense-making and modification of

[17] A definition of the term knowledge is given in 1.1.3, page 21.

behaviour, cognitive psychologists (Neisser, 1976) have introduced the concept of a ***cognitive map***. These maps can be described as a relational set of cognitive representations (Weick and Burgon, 1986: 106). The cycle of cognition in Figure 1.3 shows that the cognitive map represents a scheme of the individual's current environment. According to this cycle of cognition, cognitive maps conduct the behaviour of the individual, provoking reactions from the environment. The experiences accumulated by individuals during interaction with their environment in turn modify their cognitive maps and alter their knowledge. Cognitive maps represent a mentally-created painting of the world, built up through the range of human experiences (Handlbauer, 2000: 163), which are based on each individual's biography or on their observation of others. Handlbauer (2000: 164) emphases that a cognitive representation is a construction based on the existing representations accumulated in the cognitive map.

The major competing models of cognitive structure - knowledge organisation in memory - are positional networks, distributed memory and schema models (Figure 1.2). In his work on cognition and economic psychology, Grunert (1994) gives an overview of them and characterises their areas of application. ***Positional network models*** assume that "the organisation of knowledge can be modelled as a set of nodes and links: the nodes represent cognitive categories and the links associations between these categories" (Grunert, 1994: 98). The links can vary in strength, and in some models, also in type. Anderson (1976a, 1983a), Norman and Rumelhart (1975), and Quillian (1968) have developed major models of this kind. Grunert (1982a, 1990, 1992), Lunt (1989; Lunt and Livingstone, 1991) applied them to the economic behaviour of consumers and voters. Figure 1.4 shows an example of a positional network concerning economically relevant knowledge. It illustrates the cognitive map of a Conservative voter[18], which was build during an empirical study by Lunt (1989). He had measured the perceptions of the causal determinants of unemployment for people with different political affiliations. These kinds of model are called positional network models because a piece of knowledge has a specific position in the network (Grunert, 1994: 100).

Although ***distributed memory*** models are also networks, the difference is that they are not positional. That means that a node does not correspond to a single piece of knowledge (e.g., Kohonen et al., 1981; McClelland and Rumelhart, 1985): the entire wealth of knowledge is distributed across the whole network. Newly acquired information provides a pattern of activation which spreads throughout the network

[18] For other maps, e.g. the map of Labour voter, see Lunt (1989).

Figure 1.3: Cycle of cognition
Source: adapted from Neisser (1976: 112)

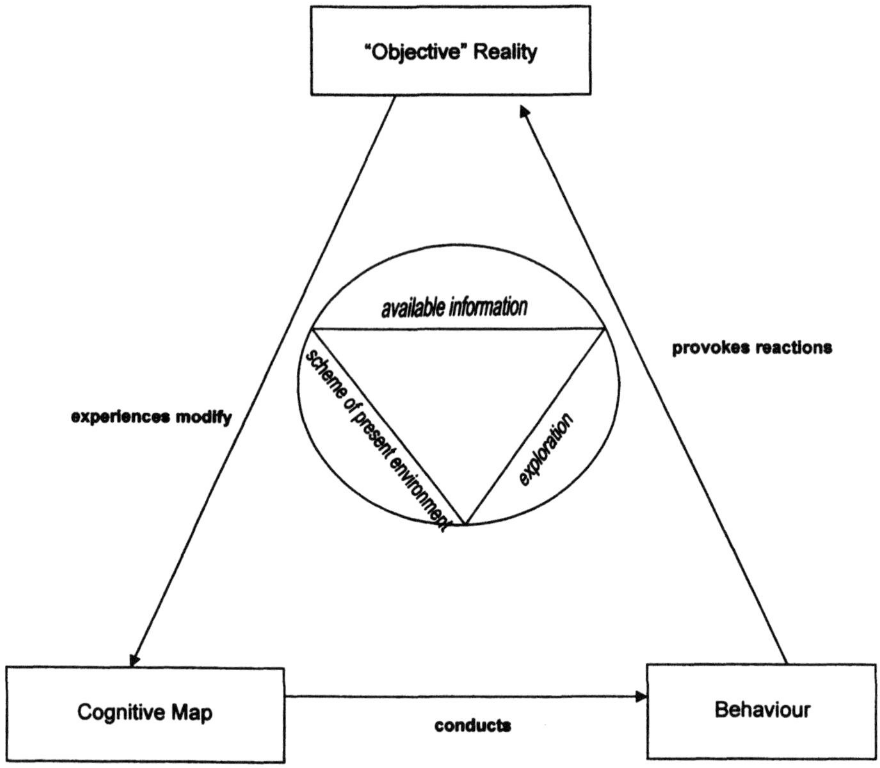

and changes the strengths of the links in the network (Grunert, 1994: 100). Learning thus occurs by consecutive changes in the strengths of links. The application of part of the original activation pattern retrieves knowledge. After this has spread throughout the network, the resulting response activation pattern resembles the one originally caused. Distributed memory models can impressively explain recognition and recall phenomena, but they have still not been applied to economic behaviour.

As the ***schema models*** are not only models of knowledge representation, but also models of cognitive processing, in a certain respect they are a richer concept than networks. A schema not only stores information, but, when incoming information substantiates the schema, it also leads to the formulation of expectations, poses relevant questions to the environment and suggests defaults for missing information (Grunert, 1994: 100). Grunert (1993), Peter and Olson (1990), Sujan and Bettman (1989) have used the schema concepts in connection with the economic behaviour of managers. Schema models are also alternatively called scripts or frames (Minsky, 1975; Rumelhart and Ortony, 1997; Schank and Abelson, 1997).

The question which of the models are the best cannot be answered definitely. As the three approaches obviously complement each another, it depends on the initial purpose. Distributed memory models are probably much closer to the neuro-physiological functioning of memory than the other models, but their explanatory power is restricted to very basic phenomena of storage and retrieval (Grunert, 1994: 100). Positional network models can more easily be adapted for modelling knowledge structures in an applied area, such as the behaviour of bankers. Schema models go further than positional networks in that they represent not only factual knowledge (to know what), but also procedural knowledge (to know how). They combine a cognitive structure and cognitive processes in a dynamic element.

In order to serve the specific emphasis of this study, a combination of the positional network model and schema model would appear appropriate. The positional network and the schema model are incorporated into a more complete model – action-slot model[19] – systematising the knowledge of bankers and explaining the way bankers behave in the lending process. Whereas the interplay of institutions and knowledge is founded on the conception of knowledge organisation in memory, the conception and approaches of knowledge content should allow informal institutions to be observed indirectly by diagnosing the content of this knowledge in memory, which regulates the actions of individuals (Figure 1.2).

---

19 More hereto in 3.1.1.

Figure 1.4: Example of a network representation of the causal structure of unemployment, a Conservative voter
Source: adapted from Lunt (1989)

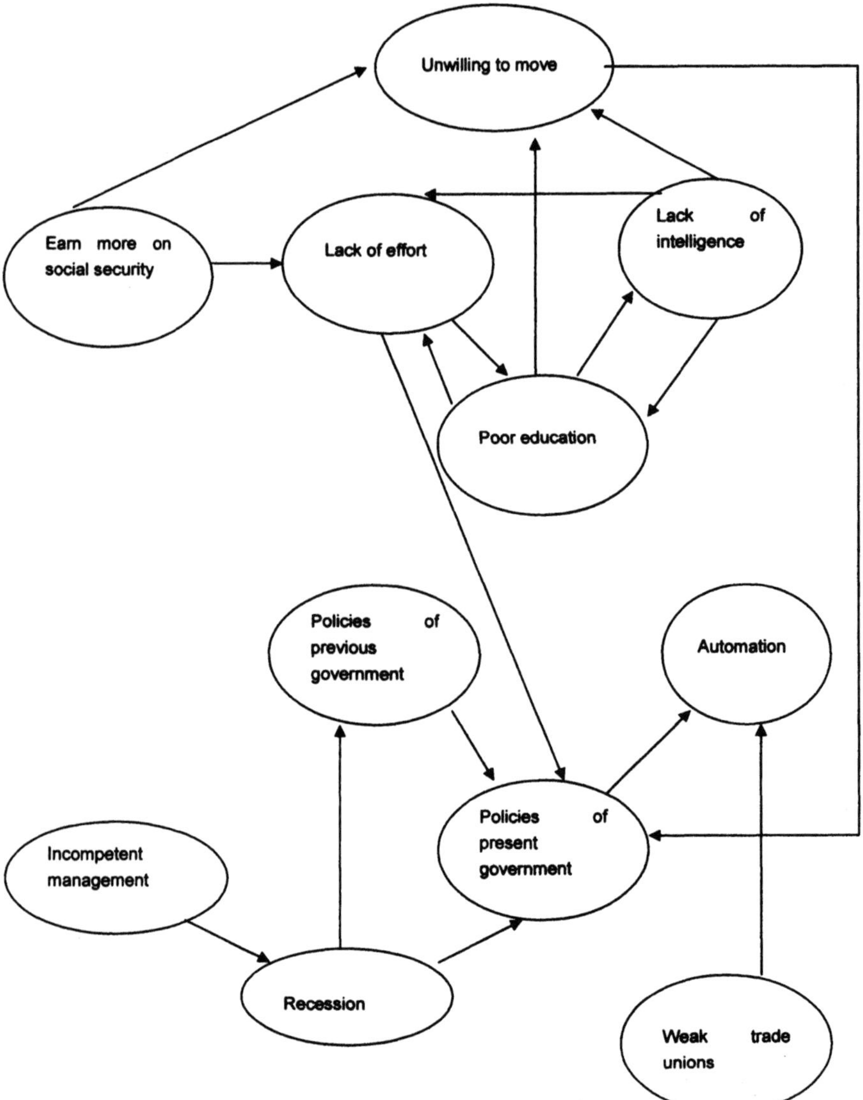

Action-regulating knowledge

An example of such a combination of two knowledge organisation models are models which underpin the approach to diagnose expert knowledge – knowledge content of particular people – and analyse problem solving. Part 3 explores one type of such models – action-slot model[20] – in greater detail, which underlies the assessment of action-regulating knowledge[21] of bankers in this study.

As to Hacker's Action-Regulation Theory (1999, 2003), only a particular part of an individual's knowledge truly regulates his or her actions. It means that ***action-regulating knowledge*** consists of intention-cue-measurement-patterns: individuals cannot succeed unless they have a clearly defined goal, identify the cues of the conditions of goal accomplishment and command suitable measures (Hacker, 1999: 2). Thus the action-regulation process firstly involves preparation for action and redefinition of the order (Hackman, 1969: 438) into self-set goals, secondly the orientation on the conditions of goal accomplishment, the design or reproduction of methods with decision making, and the co-ordination of own actions with those of co-workers (Hacker, 2003: 4). And the final phase of implementation and evaluation is accompanied by continuous feedback on goal accomplishment.

It is essential to keep in mind that the characteristic of action-regulation is that "actions are controlled by goals which work cognitively as anticipations of the intended results and motivationally as intentions" (Hacker, 2003:4) – a goal-oriented activity. This definition is a fundamental psychological approach in the mental regulation of work. The inner specific regularities of human beings, such as knowledge, experience or values, determine their activity in an indirect, mediated way. It is a (mediated) mental regulation of activity. Different people perceive and interpret – redefine – identical work orders differently due to their differing experiences, levels of aspiration or values (Hackman, 1969: 441). In addition, knowledge is content-specific. This means that there are content-related pieces of knowledge on cognitive categories such as goals, situational cues, reasons, causes, means and partners – ***knowledge fields*** (Figure 1.5).

On the basis of the characteristics of Action-Regulation Theory introduced above, the concept of action-regulating knowledge can be applied to diagnose the content of knowledge which regulates the actions of bankers in lending under the circumstances prevailing in the Mongolian economy.

---

20 Hacker (1996) gives a review and comparison of analogue models.

21 For the same meaning action-guiding knowledge, action regulation knowledge (Hacker et al: 1993, Hacker: 2003).

Figure 1.5: Fields of action-regulating knowledge
Source: Hacker (2003: 11)

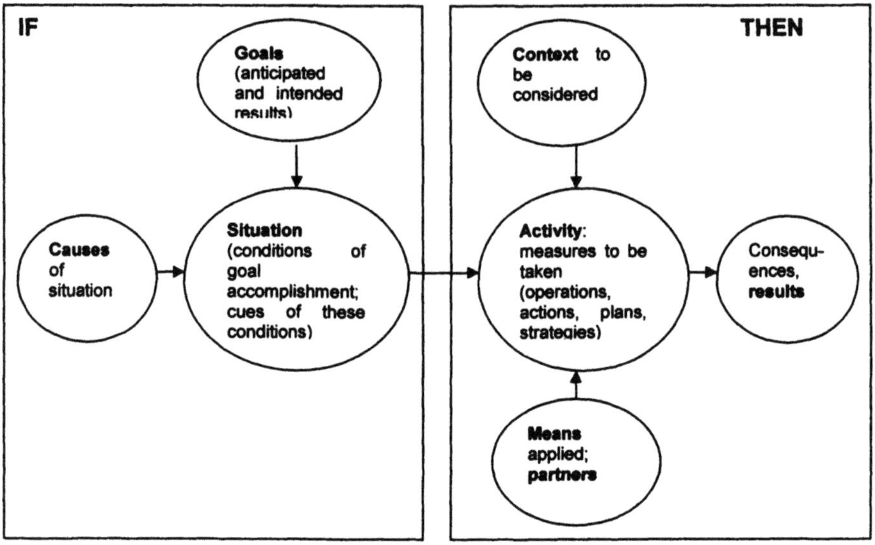

From the point of view of cognitive psychology, actions of experts guided by their knowledge and reflected in mental models can have both conscious and unconscious forms. The knowledge of bankers could have been acquired unconsciously during lending actions through psychological automation, or was gained unconsciously from the start as an experience integrating feedback during the lending activity.

NIE, especially North (1990, 1994) says very much the same about knowledge. Expert knowledge cannot be verbalised completely. Hacker et al. (1991: 861) reasons that knowledge application in action-regulation is not a mere reproduction, but a reconstruction procedure. Consequently, they suggest the application of intervention techniques for activating reconstruction in order to elicit action-regulating knowledge. Such techniques should also enable unarticulated pieces of knowledge to be diagnosed which cannot be elicited by questioning alone. There are several models that help to elicit the content and structure of the action-regulating knowledge. But as Hacker et al. (1991: 863) acknowledges, there is no "one-shoot" method of knowledge elicitation. A carefully combined package of methods is required to capture the multi-faceted, action-regulating knowledge of experts. In many studies, Hacker (1991, 1993, 1996) has compared different elicitation models and examined the variety of their combination. Chapter 3.1 of Part 3 introduces the methods and the methodological triangulation that have been chosen in this study. Before that, the next subchapter briefly addresses the sub-domains of action-regulating knowledge of bankers within the domain lending.

1.3.3 Bankers' Action-Regulating Knowledge in Lending

Bearing in mind the purpose of this work, the cognitive maps of bankers ought to consist of three sub-domains: action-regulating knowledge on risk, on credit risk management and credit investigation, and on bank regulation and supervision.

Bankers' own perception of the economic interrelation involved in "Risk and Risk Taking" should help to identify the meaning given to risk by bankers, and to show bankers' understanding of risk as subject to bank regulation. In detail, this involves:

- revealing whether and what kind of risk exists for bankers;
- demonstrating the influence of information on risk and risk taking;
- proclaiming the role of bankruptcy probability in risk;
- examining whether risk is seen as subject to bank regulation norms by bankers;
- indicating if and which tasks of bank supervision are recognised by bankers in respect to risk.

Bankers' own conception of the economic interplay between "Credit Risk Management and Credit Approval" aims to show how bankers understand credit risk management and to identify the ideas held by bankers on which factors influence the decision making process in lending, how and to what extent:

- proclaiming the role of credit risk management on lending;
- revealing which kind of collateral and guarantee instruments exist for bankers;
- showing whether and to which extent personal relations influence credit approval;
- showing the scope of influence that state authorities have on credit approval;
- proclaiming the single aspects of the credit investigation process in their lending practice;
- showing what the authority line of decision making in lending is in banks.

And finally, bankers' own perception of the interrelation between "Banking and Bank Supervision" intends to show how bankers understand the aim of bank supervision and how bank supervision may influence their decision making:

- indicating how bankers consider the general role of bank supervision;
- revealing how bankers see the tasks of bank supervision in respect to banking activities in general and to lending in particular;

- detailing which instruments of bank supervision are known by bankers;
- showing which bank regulation norms are taken into account by bankers during lending;
- finding out whether bankers are familiar with internationally known bank regulation concepts and authorities;

In each sub-domain, action-regulating knowledge is used to look for critical fields of knowledge in cognitive maps. In lending, the knowledge fields can be outlined as follows: causes of lending activity, situation signals for lending activity, goals of lending, process or condition of lending, measures (and sites) of lending activities, means of lending, and results of lending activity. These knowledge fields are elaborated in a composition of key concepts for decision-making in lending in sub-chapter 3.2.2.

Part 3 introduces the method of concept mapping in detail and use it to implicitly diagnose both the current informal institutions and the informal constraints of lending process in Mongolia. But before doing so, Part 2 below reviews the overall economic and banking situation in Mongolia.

Part 2 The Economic and Banking Situation in Mongolia

After having theoretically exemplified the impact of institutions on lending in Part 1, Part 2 intends to apply that theoretical framework to lending process in Mongolia. It first analyses the overall situation in Mongolia in chapter 2.1, thereby questioning the historical and political past of today's economy and searching for microeconomic/ institutional foundations of the macroeconomic accomplishments. Chapter 2.2 then describes the performance of arisen financial organisations in general – financial intermediation, and of banks in particular – microeconomic behaviour of banks – and examines the loan allocation. Chapter 2.3 enquiries about whether the existing or missing institutions of lending do account for the described behaviour of banks, and thereby analyses the formal institutions – bank regulation norms – and makes hypotheses on informal institutions.

2.1 The State of Economic Transition in Mongolia

Sandwiched between Russia and China, Mongolia is a large, land-locked country with a population density of 1.6 people per square kilometre. Mongolia is well endowed with natural resources – sizeable reserves of copper, gold, coal, oil and other minerals. These, however, are difficult to exploit due to the extreme weather conditions and a lack of infrastructure. Traditional nomadic herding – with 23.6 million head of livestock in 2002 – employs nearly half the population. The other half lives in urban areas, which consist of the capital, Ulaanbaatar, and a few very small towns and villages. Major industries are cashmere processing, copper and gold mining, construction materials and food processing – a narrowly based, vulnerable economy. Due to geo-historical developments, **Mongolia has had no experience of a market economy, such as that now being "installed"**. Table 2.1 gives the main characteristics of the political, economic and cultural systems in Mongolia today.

2.1.1 The Historical and Political Background of the Mongolian Economy

Three socio-political systems within one Century

Locked between two neighbours, Mongolia's independence - apart from its self-supremacy under Genghis Khan - has always been limited by the need to balance external relations with its neighbours. After coming under Manchurian domination in 1691 and a long enduring feudal system, Mongols proclaimed their own independent state on 1st of December 1911. Before this theocratic-feudalistic state with a lamaistic "God-king" (hutugtu) as a head of state could become stable – the erstwhile bounded political directions and social levels were now looking in different directions - the so-called revolutionary leaders brought about the People's Revolution in 1921 with Russian support.

Table 2.1: Main characteristics of the political, economic and social systems in Mongolia today.

Source: The Ministry of Economy and Finance (2003)

Issues	Characteristics (2002)
Form of Government	Republic, parliamentary democracy
Land area	1,566,5 million sq. km
Population	2,459 million
Official language	Mongolian
Religions	Mainly Buddhists, minority of Muslims and Christians
Main cities	Ulaanbaatar (807,200), Darkhan (69,600), Erdenet (72,300)
Labour force	0,857 million
Unemployment rate	3.4 percent
Inflation rate	1.6 percent
Exchange rate	1125 Tugrugs = 1 US$
GDP growth	3.9 percent
GDP per capita	500.7 thousand Tugrugs (453 US$)
GDP composition by sector	Industrial sector 26.3 percent, agriculture 23.6, construction 1.5, transport and communication 11.9, trade and storage 25.2, services 11.5
GDP use	Private consumption 67.8 percent, state expenditure 15.8, investment 23.0
Main products	Cashmere, wool, leather; copper and gold, construction materials and food
General government debt	93 percent of GDP
Domestic credit to private sector and non financial public enterprises	19.1 percent of GDP

At that time, the economy was based in principle on pastoral nomadism[22] within a subsistence economy. The industry consisted of gold mining factories, power stations and a few, mostly foreign-owned leather and wool processing industries. Apart from direct bartering, a convenient way for nomad families, bullion fulfilled the function of

[22] Concerning nomadism as a way of life, Braun (1997: 515) comments : „ Das Nomadentum als bewußte Negierung einer Bindung an Grund und Boden darf keineswegs als ‚primitiv' angesehen werden: Sozusagen im Innenverhältnis einer Gruppe von Nomaden herrschte eine straffe Organisation mit engen Verantwortungs- und Autoritätsabstufungen; dieses war auch notwendig, um innerhalb der in der Regel aus zwei bis drei Jurten (gers) bestehenden kleinen Lager die breiten Aufgabenbereiche arbeitsteilig bewältigen zu können. Auch zwischen den Gruppen beziehungsweise ihren Stämmen mußte rechtlich geklärt sein, welches Gebiet von wem und wann genutzt werden könnte."

money. Other commodities, such as sheep or pressed tea in the form of bricks, were also used as units of account and units of value. Moreover, Russian Roubles and Mexican Dollars served as measures of payment.

Hence, no "industrial capitalism" in terms of Marx's theory existed, so that there was no workers proletariat to carry the revolution. Marx's socio-economic "Stufenlehre" was modified and a special way "by-passing capitalism" (Sanders, 1978: 159) was defined. The Mongolian People's Revolutionary Party (MRPR) was created in 1921 and the Mongolian People's Republic was proclaimed in 1924.

The first Constitution (26th of November 1924) formulated as its ultimate ambition the socialist modernisation of Mongolia with the aim of overcoming the stagnation of centuries ascribed to old structures of feudalism and colonial domination. According to new constitution, transcending the agrarian-nomadic subsistence economy was to be shaped consistently with the traditional way of living. Murzaev (1954:33) construes this as animal husbandry based on nomadism, and private "ger" as a domicile will remain untouched.

But the realisation of this high aim of immediate socialist modernisation had to wait until the end of 1940s. In the first instance, the Mongolian Trade and Industry Bank was established as a central bank and the Tugrug was introduced as a national currency. The central plan was introduced and the collectivisation of agriculture took place as recently as 1948. Industrialisation began after the World War II and its primary object was to access the Council for Mutual Economic Assistance (CMEA), which succeeded in 1962. The main industries included mining, especially copper mining, (40 percent of exports) and processing of agriculture-related raw materials. In addition, some import substituting industries emerged, such as building materials, wood processing, light food products, textiles and clothing. The contribution made by Mongolia's manufacturing sector had increased from 14.6 percent in 1960 to 36 percent of national income by 1990. Agricultural production was arranged in a system of state-owned farms and co-operatives that produced grain, but were dominated by approximately 25 million head of livestock by 1990.

The majority of industrialisation projects were financed by the CMEA, especially by USSR credits, which averaged 35 percent of GDP annually. Apart from this, Mongolia received 40 percent of its consumer goods and 90 percent of technical equipment from these countries. This became ever more habit-forming, and Mongolia's economic and political system became inextricably linked with that of

Russia and the countries of CMEA. The ability to fund self-supporting economic growth was non-existent.

These links suddenly broke on January 1st 1991. Soviet credits to Mongolia were abruptly stopped, and trade volumes with the CMEA countries dropped sharply. The economic collapse that ensued was possibly the greatest in any of the peacefully transformed, formerly socialist countries with the exception of the countries of former SU. The decline in domestic consumption was approximately 62 percent of GNP, much more than the decline experienced in Eastern European countries or during wartime destruction. Mongolia's political leaders responded to civil protests by calling elections in early 1990, and Mongolia's first elected Parliament thus met in October 1990. Mongolia has since **struck out on a new path of democracy and market economy, the third socio-economic system within a century after the feudal and socialist ones.**

Table 2.2: Selected economic data
Source: BOM, IMF

	1996	1997	1998	1999	2000	2001	2002
GDP nominal, milliard Tugrug	646.6	832.6	817.4	925.3	1,045	1,131	1,245
GDP growth, %	2.4	4.0	3.5	3.2	1.1	1.0	3.9
Inflation rate, %	44.6	17.5	6.0	10.0	11.6	8.0	1.6
M2/GDP, %	19.9	20.4	20.5	23.8	24.8	29.3	34.6
Total loans/GDP, %	10.0	6.1	10.5	8.4	6.4	11.9	19.1
Exchange rate, Tugrug/USD	697	813	902	1,001	1,082	1,099	1,116

Present socio-economic system

The first democratic election created a coalition government that was dominated by the MPRP, but also included several prominent members of the new opposition. There was a clear cleavage in policy making during 1991, not to mention the absence of any consistent concept for the intended socio-economic system. As with the majority of EITs, Mongolia strived for a democratic society with a market economy in early 1990s, but without any convincing strategy for comprehensive transition. Some officials wanted to delay the implementation of policy until the political outcome in Russia became clear, whilst others called for immediate radical reform to a market system similar to that of Poland. The outcome was a mixture of both approaches (Boote et al., 1997: 103) dominated by the "big bang liberalisation" programme of multilateral donors. Some prices were freed; some trade was liberalised; the banking system was deregulated; and, most surprisingly, the world's first voucher privatisation program was launched.

During the early years, when it was still unclear what would happen in the Soviet Union (SU), the government received vigorous support from Western governments. The United States and Japan provided emergency credits, and in July 1991 the Government signed its first standby agreement with the International Monetary Fund. In 1991, aid from the West amounted to 8 percent of GNP, partially making up for the loss of Soviet financing. At present, it accounts for about 27 percent of GDP (2002). The agreement with the IMF led to further price liberalisation in 1991, but exchange controls and state intervention persisted.

The major political reform of October 1991 brought about a new constitution and a parliamentary system was created. The constitution created a strong parliamentary democracy with a relatively weak president as the head of state. New elections were called for June 1992[23]. While the competition for votes had at times slowed reform during this period, the development of a democratic process may in time prove to be Mongolia's greatest strength. The last few years have allowed the political system to develop a process for co-ordination of powers amongst the various actors, and have ingrained the right of political competition and free speech in political parties, particularly in urban areas. It appears that a relatively stable political process arose in the 1990s. Although at first glance democratic institutions might seem new for Mongols, certain fundamental elements of Mongolian culture – including egalitarian values, such as social consensus of the population and a widely held vision of what constitutes fairness and justice - underpin a democratic, political culture.

2.1.2 The Stylised Facts of Transformation

When the transformation began, a package of measures aimed at macroeconomic stabilisation was implemented as agreed with the IMF. Privatisation succeeded in the retail sector, herding and, recently, in banking, whereas that of processing industries - such as cashmere processing and copper mining - is still on the agenda. Prices and tariffs were liberalised, a free exchange rate system adopted, and tight monetary and fiscal policies were introduced. Within the framework of legal reform, new legislation on economic relations was passed, such as budget taxes, foreign investment, statistics, social insurance and the regulation of unfair competition.

Macroeconomic accomplishments: Output and inflation

Output started to decline in the wake of the transition reforms. This fall in output is comparable to those experienced by western economies during the Great

---

23 Since then, each election (three parliamentary and three presidential elections) resulted in a change of majority in parliament or the appointment of a new president.

Depression. However, this considerably understates the severity of the fall in effective income in Mongolia. Prior to the transition, consumption was approximately 30 percent higher than income. This reflected the transfers from the former SU. After the collapse of the SU and the dissolution of the CMEA with its subsidiaries system, most of the larger industries went bankrupt without markets and new investments. At the same time, the prices of Mongolia's basic exports fell, such as copper, which reduced consumption even further. The cumulative affects of these shocks and the prolonged fall in output which they induced are, on several measures, larger than any comparable episode during the twentieth Century (Chimeddagva et al., 2000: 44).

Mongolia underwent a severe economic crisis. Declining from 1990 to 1993 (annual rates of growth -2.5, -9.2, -3.0 percent), output began to recover slightly in 1994 (2.3 percent) and growth has now been experienced in recent years. The output components of GDP indicate the way in which the shocks impacted on the different sectors (Table 2.1). The picture in terms of real output is far less dramatic in terms of sector restructuring. The decomposition highlights the impact of transition on construction and transport. The relative experience of sectors is shown more clearly by their growth rates in real terms. It is evident that the shocks to output were especially sever in the construction and transport sectors where imports of basic inputs, including fuel, virtually ceased during the early part of transition. Manufacturing was also severely curtailed but succeeded in achieving robust growth. As noted earlier, it is clear that agriculture, although subject to a decline in real output, did not experience the cataclysmic falls suffered by the other sectors and quickly returned to positive growth.

While output declined, price levels increased extraordinarily. The percentage change in the consumer price index, shown in Table 2.2, indicates the extent of inflation in the wake of the crisis. In the immediate aftermath of transition, the inflation rate rose dramatically reaching 325.5 percent in 1992 and then gradually fell each year until it reached a respectable 17.5 percent in 1997, before dropping to just 6 percent in 1998 and 1.6 percent in 2002.

In the early period of transition, the government attempted to maintain a fixed exchange rate against the Dollar and instituted a two-tier system. This, however, quickly broke down and the decision to float was taken on May 28th 1993. The Tugrug immediately depreciated, reflecting the cumulative inflation over the previous three years. It continued to depreciate steadily in subsequent years, stabilising with inflation during 1997. Its course through time is show in Table 2.1. Although officially a free-floating system, it can actually be characterised as a managed float due to interventions by the BOM to iron out excessive exchange rate fluctuations. With regard to foreign debt (80 percent of GDP in 2002), the current account deficit (15 percent of GDP in 2002) and the highly Dollarised state (foreign currency deposits at 40% of total deposits) of the Mongolian economy, one can imagine the consequences of a potential depreciation of the Tugrug.

Macroeconomic policies and the lack of microeconomic adjustments

The IMF, which monitored and supported the process of transition in almost all EITs, mentioned five points on the reform programme of transformation in Mongolia (IMF, 1994): the liberalisation of prices and quantities on all markets, macroeconomic stabilisation by constraining central bank lending to the Government and to the banking system, privatisation, opening up the economy for foreign trade and creating a social safety net.

Despite some economic achievements as shown in the Tables 2.2, the difference between initial expectations about the outcomes of reforms and the eventual realities gave reasons for research. Although reforms followed the suggested approach with large-scale liberalisation at the beginning and a subsequent rapid implementation of privatisation measures, the adjustment response at the microeconomic level remained disappointing over the years. It was expected that price liberalisation and privatisation by selling shares to the public would be sufficient to create a market, but that did not occur. The transformation programme placed a greater emphasis on macroeconomic policy (Portes, 1994: 1181), whilst not paying adequate attention to microeconomic issues. These were only integrated on an ad-hoc basis.

Hence, distortions at the microeconomic level make it difficult to implement restrictive macroeconomic policies. The reason is that the implemented programmes and the models they are based on mostly **failed to take into account the behaviour of economic agents in transitional Mongolia** (enterprises, bankers etc.), which differs from the behaviour of that in market economies (Ernst et al., 1996: 211). Economic agents do not operate under perfect competition in markets with developed infrastructure, they do not have clearly defined property rights and cannot count on rapid legal enforcement.

The legacy of the past, the incompleteness of reforms and the reactions of economic agents to the latter make macroeconomic processes and systematic change complicated in Mongolia. Reviewing the microeconomic conditions and considering the existing incentives for economic agents should thus bring greater insight for the purpose of shaping future economic policies aimed at stabilisation and growth.

2.1.3 Institutions in Transition

As mentioned above, IMF measures of the economic performance of EITs show that Mongolia has not fared that badly. Real GDP, which in 1998 had reached 93 percent of the level of 1989 (100 percent) in Mongolia, is compared to that of 27 other countries. Only Poland, Slovakia and Slovenia have done significantly better. CIS countries only reach 54 percent whilst the average amongst eastern European countries is 94 percent. This simple measure has limitations, and does not reveal much about the development of institutions.

Some studies on Mongolian transition[24] argue that the IMF-supported global strategy, with its standardised package of reform steps, simply ignored the historical experience of economic agents and the resulting economic style and ethos of Mongols. Some useful examples help clarify the institutional framework of the Mongolian economy at the time of reform began. Chapters 2.2 and 2.3 then go into details of the institutional framework, specifically in lending.

At the time reforms were started, the institutional framework of the Mongolian economy consisted of "traditional" institutions with their roots in pre-revolution time on the one hand, and institutions derived from socialist central planning on the other.

The so-called traditional institutions channelled the behaviour of nomads using common grazing land. These, as previously mentioned, are egalitarian values, such as social consensus among the population and joint decision making, for instance, on the use of recourses without formalised authorities. These customary defined property rights (of common property) represent an institutional framework that reduces uncertainty in exchanging and enforcing rights to gain access to and control the resource – land (Mearns, 1995: 22). These informal institutions are regarded to be operating at minimised transaction costs.

As soon as the livelihood of nomadic herders came into consideration, they were able to organise themselves and defend themselves by acting collectively – almost without state administration or legislation. They were able to succeed - even against the state or state involvement in their matters - as is shown by their effective opposition to state intervention in 1930s (collectivisation) and in 1993 (livestock taxation). Moreover, the wilful refusal to bind oneself to property (real-estate, land) is the crucial point of nomadic life. Hence, accumulating wealth has a totally different

24 As for example Schmidt (1995) and Braun (1997).

dimension and scale for nomads then for settled persons. That attitude is found among informal institutions (often unconsciously), which channel individual decision-making.

Whilst the principle of "community-based management of common grazing land" was predominantly retained in the herding sector during the socialist period, other institutions evolved to channel behaviour of economic agents within the planned economy. Under the planned socialist economy, institutions evolved and incentives were derived to channel economic behaviour at administered markets[25] steering individual activities. After the introduction of a central plan in early 1950s, economic decisions within administered markets were taken as follows. The requests of enterprises for resources were accumulated as they moved up the administrative ladder until they reached an agency authorised to assign production tasks to producers – the State Planning Committee. The State Planning Committee distributed the production tasks among manufacturing enterprises, which responded with new requests for the necessary supplies. The planning cycle then repeated itself over and over again[26]. The upward movement of each request for materials and the downward movement of each production order was accompanied by furious bargaining between superiors and subordinates trying to achieve maximum resource allocation and minimal production tasks (Naishul, 1992: 490). This bargaining proceeded among a few "top managers" with bureaucratic leverage and power – heads of enterprises, department heads of ministries, party officials etc. However, institutions in the middle and lower management provided incentives for waiting and obeying – passively following directions (some of them outstanding employees).

Another example of a planned economy institution is the institution of money. Due to the fact that money was limited in its functions as an universal tool of exchange, there were special types of pseudo-money. Cash could only be used by the general public for purchasing certain consumer goods. Banks (the state bank and its branches) issued it to enterprises for salary payments and the shops handed it over to banks. The industrial sector used non-cash payments. Non-cash payments primarily had an accounting function, being essentially the same nature as transfer pricing accounts between companies of large western corporations. It is important to realise that the types of non-cash money vary greatly, since accounts of different types were not mutually convertible. Finally, lack of money in an enterprise's account did not mean that it could not access goods easily, whilst possession of money –

[25] James Buchanan's termed it as a bureaucratic market.

[26] Naishul (1992: 490) refers to this from-the-bottom-up economic planning as Brezhnev-era economic planning compared to from-the-top-down under Stalin; its nature was not directive but iterative and cyclical.

cash or non-cash – in no way entitled an enterprise to acquire the necessary consumer or industrial goods (Naishul, 1992: 492).

The transition from planned economy with administered markets to a free market economy is a systemic transformation in Mongolia constituting an institutional revolution: the old high-cost institutional framework is vanishing to make way for an ultimately superior low-cost setting. However, **the emergence, establishment and consolidation of new institutions and institutional arrangements channelling individual behaviour can not be accomplished overnight** as have seen in many cases. After the liberalisation and privatisation reforms had began, co-ordination of the actions of economic agents was channelled by self-contradictory, chaotically adopted, and partly unrealistic laws (formal institution). It resulted in a legal indeterminacy and in such a constellation of institutions that organisations (and individuals) sprung up to literally exercise "economic freedom".

The actual consequences of privatisation and liberalisation in Mongolia are not comparable to those of deregulation in established market economies. The "fate" of one of many medium-sized enterprises privatised in early 1990s serves to illustrate this. A leather processing enterprise with 250 employees was privatised in 1993 just after the prices had been decontrolled. In order words, the firm was turned into a stock corporation and the shares were "sold" to the employees. In fact, the asset value of the firm was handed over in a form of so-called pink vouchers, non-cash. The new shareholders were not aware of their ownership and the non-existent equity culture resulted in them selling their stocks for peanuts – preferably to managers. The management retained the same and as the accustomed ways of co-ordinating the complex division of labour no longer existed - erstwhile (socialist) institutions for intermediation were no longer in place – managers once used to directing production systems now had to perform other functions, such as acquisition, sales etc.. In the old system, a firm's management often did not know the outlets for their products or the sources of their supplies. Seeing no chance (having no incentive) to keep production going, the management sold the machinery and rented out the space. Many processing enterprises met the same fate and most of them were unable to bounce back. The institutional framework at the beginning of transition (in this case) had provided disincentives for processing industries in Mongolia.

The next chapters address a similar problem faced by Mongolia during transition in one particular branch of economic activity – lending.

2.2 Performance of Lending Organisations in Mongolia

2.2.1 Financial Intermediation and the Role of Lending

As pointed out in 1.2, the key element of transition from a centrally planned to a market economy is the establishment of financial markets and organisations that can support an economy by mobilising savings and efficiently deploying resources among various competing demands through the process of financial intermediation. Since the role of the financial sector in a centrally planned economy was completely different, the transition to a market economy required the transformation of the financial sector as a whole. In order to build up the financial sector, special emphasis needs to be given to the development of financial organisations – banks – which are required to perform this role.

Types of financial organisations

After the fragmentation of the monobank into a central bank, the Bank of Mongolia (BOM), the bank has been vested with relative powers of autonomy to conduct monetary policy and supervise banks. The Central Bank Act gives the BOM responsibility for ensuring financial stability and protecting depositor's funds. It licenses, regulates and supervises banks and non-banks. However, as it is accountable to Parliament, there have been numerous cases of intervention in monetary policy, exchange rate policy and in aspects of banking supervision in the past.

The second tier of the financial sector consists of financial organisations, such as commercial banks on the one hand, and non-bank financial institutions, such as insurance companies, micro finance institutions, credits unions and securities unions on the other. Banks dominate the financial system, whereas no data is available as yet on the size and operations of non-bank financial institutions. Despite recent dynamism in the non-bank financial sector, total assets of non-banks represent only 1 percent of the total assets of the banking system, and consequently the scope of financial intermediation performed by them is very limited.

Little information is available regarding informal money lending (e.g. private lending or pawn brokering) which caters mainly for the short-term retail and personal credit needs of borrowers and which accepts any items of value as collateral. There is some evidence of traders making advances to herders against the future supply of cashmere or other animal products. These advances are usually calculated using a relatively low value for the product.

Table 2.3: Main indicators of financial intermediation in Mongolia, 1991-2001
Source: BOM 2001

Values, milliard Tugrugs	1991	1992	1993	1994	1995	1996	1997	1998	1999	2000	2001
Nominal GDP	18.9	47.3	194.8	324.4	550.3	646.6	832.6	817.4	925.3	1,045	1,131
Money supply or M2	9.9	13.1	42.8	76.8	102.0	128.4	170.1	167.2	220.2	258.8	331.1
Cash outside banks	1.7	1.8	8.8	18.8	25.6	41.7	49.8	56.4	87.3	100.9	109.2
Total loans	12.9	19.1	31.6	52.8	63.4	64.8	50.4	85.6	77.5	66.8	135.1
Total time deposits	2.6	4.5	12.5	32.4	47.1	45.9	58.5	59.3	70.0	92.7	134.6
NPL	n/a	1.1	4.1	7.3	13.5	33.0	14.5	32.6	42.1	15.9	10.9

Ratios, in %	1991	1992	1993	1994	1995	1996	1997	1998	1999	2000	2001
M2 / GDP,	52.4	27.6	21.9	23.7	18.5	19.9	20.4	20.5	23.8	24.8	29.3
Cash outside banks / M2	17.1	14.1	20.5	24.4	25.1	32.5	29.3	33.7	39.6	39.0	33.0
Total loans / GDP	68.0	40.4	16.2	16.3	11.5	10.0	6.1	10.5	8.4	6.4	11.9
Total time deposits/ GDP	13.8	9.6	6.4	10.0	8.6	7.1	7.0	7.3	7.6	8.9	11.9
NPL / total loans	-	5.8	13.0	13.0	21.3	50.9	28.8	38.1	54.3	23.8	8.1

Financial intermediation and lending

The four indicators of financial intermediation shown in Table 2.3 – the financial deepening or the ratio of money supply M2 to GDP, the ratio of total loans to GDP, the ratio of total time deposits to GDP and the ratio of non-performing loans (NPL) to total loans – give a rough idea of the extent to which the Mongolian financial system is fulfilling its role. The first three indicators show its success, whereas the latter provides evidence of its efficiency. Additionally, Enkhhuyag (2002: 1) uses an extra indicator, the ratio of cash outside banks to M2, which measures the level of confidence amongst the general public.

With GDP[27], the almost constant base of indicators (except ratio of cash outside banks to GDP), all indicators worsened from 1993-1995, bottoming out during 1995-1999, and start to show signs of improvement from 1999. The years of worst performance clearly coincided with first wave of banking crises in 1996, culminating in the closures of Ardyn Bank and Insurance Bank, and with second wave in 1998-1999 when the Bank of Investment and Technological Innovation (ITIB), the Reconstruction Bank and the Agricultural Bank either went bankrupt or were close to bankruptcy. For example, substantial increase in the ratio of non-performing loans of 50.9 percent in 1996 and 54.3 percent in 1999 is explained by these bankruptcies. In exact parallel to worsening ratios of financial intermediation, the indicator for the level of confidence amongst the general public has been steadily indicating a widespread erosion of trust in the banking system and growing reliance on cash instead of using banks. Thus, the demand for loan and savings products has not been adequately met through official financial intermediation.

This state of financial dis-intermediation can be compared with the situation in other EITs. Table 2.4 shows ratios of money supply to the GDP of some EITs. The level of Mongolia's M2/GDP ratio is lower than those in advanced transition economies such as Czech Republic, Hungary, Poland and Estonia, otherwise Mongolia's ratio is at the same level or slightly higher than those in other EITs. However, the levels of financial intermediation in EITs are still much lower compared to the levels in developed countries.

On the basis of the aforesaid indicators, Enkhhuyag (2002: 4) distinguishes three different phases of banking system development since 1991:

- The first phase, 1991-1993, is characterised by the establishment of the basic infrastructure of a two-tier banking system parallel to the first commercial banks starting up in business (the number of banks had risen from one in 1991 to 13 by 1993): setting up formal institutions, such as Banking Law, defining the new role of the central bank and its monetary policy instruments, introducing the first bank regulation norms, such as reserve requirements, prudential ratios and loan classification regulations etc. The first steps to implement the new means were subsequently taken. During this time, the M2 aggregate was boosted by 77 percent in 1991, 32 percent in 1992, 227 percent in 1993 and inflation climbed to 325 in 1992[28].
- The second phase, 1994-1999, was afflicted with banking crises, beginning with a deterioration in financial positions in 1994 as a result of poor decisions on lending

27 In this context, see the growth rates of GDP in Mongolia during 1996-2002 in the Table 2.2.
28 See hereto inflation rates in the Table 2.2.

made during the initial phase. Loans not been paid on time soured into bad loans. Those bad assets eventually caused several banks to go bankrupt (Enkhuyag et al., 2002: 2). Two waves of banking crises can be identified: in 1996 with great concern for Ardyn Bank (57.7 percent NPL ratio[29]) and Insurance Bank (82.4 percent), and in 1998-1999 where ITIB (96.4 percent), Reconstruction Bank (100 percent) and Agricultural Bank were involved. The loss inflicted on such a weak economy as that of Mongolia was immense, as demonstrated by the ratio of bank restructuring bonds to GDP (Table 2.5) and other payments such as US$ 2 million[30] payment made by the BOM to German banks on behalf of ITI bank, 80 million Tugrugs paid by the BOM to depositors of the Central Asia Bank, 131 million Tugrugs to write-off the BOM's claims against Mercury Bank, 6.4 milliard Tugrugs to write-off the BOM's claims against Ardyn Bank and Insurance Bank.

- In the third phase, from 1999 to date, relative stabilisation sets in. After learning from experiences of the past, the first strategies (long-term by the Government and medium-term by the BOM) for developing the financial system were approved in early 2000 and important amendments concerning legal provisions on lending and loan collateral were authorised by Parliament in early 2001. Some improvements in the BOM's supervision of banks can be observed, although they are more on the level of bank regulation norms and area-wide enforcement of them leaves much to be desired. In addition, the stable Tugrug exchange rate enabled predictable levels of inflation, and competition was boosted within the financial sector by the newly established banks and NBFIs (2 domestic private banks, a branch of a foreign bank, a bank with fixed domestic and foreign funding and an NBFI with foreign investment) with total capital injection of 22.7 milliard Tugrug. Distribution of rural finance has improved with the presence of Agricultural and HAS banks and rural NBFIs. The accumulation of capital since 1991 has slowly been building a steady inflow cash, which has provided funding and some pledgeable collateral.

On the question of if, how and where funds come from, Itgel et al. (2001) reveal in their survey with 2000[31] households throughout Mongolia the size and presence of savings in the country. Despite a very low level of savings (only 54.8 percent of all households), households with excess money prefer to hold it in cash (31.3 percent) due to low confidence in the banking system and poor but expensive banking services (e.g. fees for cash withdrawal or minimum balance requirements for opening a current account). Just 3.4 percent of households hold their savings in bank

29 NPL ratios are taken from Enkhhuyag (2002: 6).
30 Plus pending US$ 4 million (state of end 2002).
31 At that time there were 554 thousand households in Mongolia (Itgel et al, 2002: 3).

Table 2.4: Ratios of money supply to GDP (M2/GDP) of some selected EITs, in percent

Source: BOM, 2001

	1991	1992	1993	1994	1995	1996	1997	1998	1999	2000	2001
Albania	69	57	40	38	47	55	58	52	58	61	61
Armenia	n/a	n/a	n/a	n/a	n/a	6	6	6	6	7	7
Bosnia	n/a	n/a	n/a	18	15	19	19	21	26	27	0
Bulgaria	n/a	n/a	n/a	n/a	n/a	n/a	n/a	n/a	n/a	35	39
Czech Republic	n/a	70	71	74	75	71	73	70	73	76	74
Estonia	n/a	n/a	33	34	33	35	41	35	42	48	53
Yugoslavia	n/a	n/a	n/a	n/a	n/a	n/a	n/a	n/a	21	18	15
Macedonia	n/a	n/a	n/a	n/a	11	11	13	14	17	19	21
Georgia	n/a	n/a	n/a	n/a	n/a	n/a	6	5	5	6	n/a
Hungary	47	51	50	46	42	48	47	46	47	46	47
Kazakhstan	n/a	n/a	n/a	13	11	10	9	7	10	9	8
Latvia	n/a	n/a	31	33	22	22	27	26	26	29	32
Lithuania	1	1	23	26	23	17	19	19	21	23	27
Moldavia	69	43	19	14	15	15	17	13	13	14	17
Poland	32	36	36	37	36	37	40	40	43	43	43
Romania	47	31	22	21	25	28	25	25	25	23	24
Slovakia	n/a	64	64	64	65	69	66	62	65	69	68
Tajikistan	n/a	n/a	85	84	20	8	9	8	7	9	10
Ukraine	67	50	33	27	13	11	13	15	17	18	22
Mongolia	52.1	27.6	21.9	23.7	18.5	19.9	20.4	20.5	23.8	24.8	29.3

accounts. Admittedly, 6.2 percent of them claimed to be in favour of making payments through their current account and 10.1 percent consider the appropriateness of using payment cards. That can be explained by recently introduced payment card services (Golomt Bank, Anod Bank), which allow card holders to purchase goods and services on credit and at a discount, thus improving their income level.

Deficient financial intermediation in rural areas is characterised by the limited supply of basic financial services, such as credit, savings and payment systems. Credit in the rural sector is provided through Government programmes and donor credit lines. These programmes have a limited reach as regards servicing the entire demand for credit in rural areas. There is some evidence that the demand for credit is met through inter-family borrowings, barter and short term lending from pawnbrokers. Savings mobilisation in rural areas is also low. Some business operators have expressed their willingness to save if offered an alternative they believe to be safe.

Table 2.5: Ratio of bank restructuring bonds to the GDP (in milliards of Tugrugs)

Source: BOM, 2001

	31.12.1999	31.12.2000	31.12.2001	30.04.2002
Savings	25.0	25.0	25.0	25.0
Bank of Mongolia	19.6	19.6	9.4	12.4
Reconstruction Bank	3.3	3.3		
Agricultural		4.2	4.2	
Total Bonds	47.9	52.1	38.6	37.4
GDP	925.3	1,044.5	1,130.5	
Bonds / GDP, %	**5.2**	**4.9**	**3.4**	

When considering financial intermediation in Mongolia, the second important channel of financial intermediation cannot be ignored. Although the Mongolian Stock Exchange (MSE) made a quite vigorous start in 1991 on sales of privatisation vouchers – primary market, it became dysfunctional towards the end of the 1990s (Enkhuyag, 2002:11). At present, there is in principle no corporate financing via capital markets – neither via primary nor via secondary markets. The general public has 1 milliard Tugrug worth of outstanding claims deposited at the MSE, which needs to be addressed first of all. Reviving the capital market would deepen financial intermediation, help break the monopoly of banks and bring down the level of interest rates.

Hence, bank lending remains the most important form of financial intermediation in Mongolia on the allocation side. Despite the low ratio of total loans to GDP (11.9 percent in 2001), bank loans in Mongolia are the predominant source of external funding. Businesses primarily address capital shortages through bank loans, lending between individuals is the second biggest source after bank loans (Enkhhuyag, 2002:

20 et sqq.). As demonstrated above, despite the economic contributions of Mongolian banks during last decade, **the banking sector has not been able to satisfy the needs of financial intermediation**. Thus investment in the real economy, especially the absence of medium and long term loans, is still insufficient. Moreover, borrowing tends to involve only certain groups of people and larger business entities, and there is evidence that other social groups and rural people cannot get access to financial and loan services (Enkhhuyag et al., 2002: 2).

The other question of if, how and where financial funds are allocated – where they go during lending – is tackled in next sub-chapter.

2.2.2 Bank Behaviour: Loan Allocation and Lending Uncertainties

The first financial organisations – commercial banks – were founded in Mongolia at the very beginning of transition. It started with the launch of the first truly private commercial bank – Mongolian Co-operative Bank (MCB), and by separating the books of the Trade and Development Bank (TDB) and ITIB from the balance sheet of the State Bank[32] in early 1991.

Bank behaviour and loan allocation

Since then, a total of 22 banks have been created, six of these have either merged with larger banks or been wound up. The banking system is small and – with 16 banks currently operating – over-banked. Most banks concentrate their activities in the capital and provincial centres. Under the Banking Act, banks have to apply to the BOM for a banking license. The various types of banking business are defined in Article 4 of this Act. An initial banking license allows banks to lend, take deposits and operate money transfer services. After six months, the bank can apply for an expansion of the initial license to allow additional transactions, such as foreign exchange or securities.

Real interest rates remain among the highest in Asia despite a significant reduction of central bank interest rates, and this is jeopardising economic development. The weighted average of interest rates on bank loans in 2002 was 33.4 percent p.a. for Tugrug and 19.8 percent p.a. for US-Dollar loans (Ministry of Finance and Economy, 2003: 51). Short term bank loans are made at 35 percent p.a., whereas banks pay 18 percent p.a. for domestic currency time deposits, so a spread of 17 percent is usual. Branch density is clearly better in urban areas and worse in rural ones. This,

---

[32] The main bank in the previous mono-bank system, its successor is The Bank of Mongolia.

however, has remained relatively stable despite the closure of some banks – and is better than the comparative figure for East Asia[33]. Banks intend to open more branches in areas with well-developed infrastructure, agriculture and industry, thereby following developing markets.

There is only a narrow range of financial instruments available to the public. The majority of bank assets and liabilities have a short-term maturity profile, bank liabilities are limited to demand, saving and time deposits and foreign currency deposits, while government bonds, treasury and central bank bills dominate the assets side. Empirical evidence of the survey of bank profitability in Mongolia (Davaajargal et al., 2001:5) confirms this, showing that banks prefer to keep a large share of their assets in more liquid forms, such as central bank bills. As mentioned above, access to term credit at present is mainly limited to the largest companies with links to foreign banks and markets. The main borrowers are the Government and big state-owned enterprises.

State loan provision has been very common, especially until recently with the Agricultural and Reconstruction banks. Subsequently, the Reconstruction Bank, which was set up by state with a clean start-up balance sheet in December of 1996, disgracefully fell only two years after its establishment and the Agricultural bank underwent a deep crisis. The outright asset-stripping or shameless fraud of mostly privately owned banks, such as ITIB, Mongol Business, Central Asia, Mercury and Exim banks, brought about their failure. Cases of non-performing bank loans made by their executives to themselves, their relatives or other cronies have become "best performing assets" in a form of real estate, hotels, bars or restaurants, or in some cases even new banks. This illustrates how initial capital accumulation took place by all possible legal and illegal means in start-up societies like Mongolia in the early 1990s.

Abuse of "free borrowing of loan resources" had thus became a wide-spread practice among banks, with the MCB and ITIB in particular providing risky lending accompanied by cases of criminal misuse of bank loans in early 1990s. Competition amongst banks has received a substantial boost with the relative stabilisation since 1999. In 2001 alone, 2 banks with domestic capital (Inter bank and Kapitron bank), a branch of a foreign bank (Menatep SP) and a bank with mixed domestic and foreign

---

33 In Mongolia, bank density is one branch/sub-branch per 5,300 inhabitants. In East Asia(South Korea, Malaysia, the Philippines, Thailand) around 8,950 people are serviced by one branch, in Latin America (Brazil, Chile, Colombia, Mexico, Per) the figure is around 15,000, while the comparative figure for developed countries (Australia, Euro zone, Hong Kong, Japan, Singapore, Switzerland, United Kingdom, United States) is 2,770 (all figures from 1999, own calculation based on BOM).

funding (HAS) came into existence. Agricultural and HAS banks are compounding their engagement in rural areas, thereby bringing competition to rural areas and covering different regions with financial services.

Although co-financing provides an opportunity for banks to pool their limited resources, and consequently diversify risks in financing projects which require substantial funding, such as in manufacturing or infrastructure, co-financing has never materialised for Mongolian banks.

The behaviour not only of commercial banks, but also that of the newly restructured central bank, the Bank of Mongolia, is telling. In the early 1990s, some top management officials at the Bank of Mongolia were implicated in speculative foreign trading which ended in substantial losses. This further hindered both the prestige of the new central bank and its operational stability.

What, then, is the state of loan allocation in Mongolia? The lender's survey prepared by Enkhhuyag et al. (2002) in which 1,600 borrowers participated, gives some quantitative evidence on this question. Most borrowers are currently engaged in trade (45.9 percent) and services (17.7 percent) according to Enkhhuyag et al. (2002: 19), which might be related to current loan availability, maturity and terms. Only trading businesses with fast turnovers are able to repay the loans in today's situation with high interest rates, short maturity and inflexible loan terms. Borrowers in industry, manufacturing and mining currently come in a poor second. Borrowers defined interest rates and maturity as being the major difficulties and insufficiencies that they face in taking out and repaying loans. Credit extension is an inherent feature of lending in Mongolia, whereas small lenders had largely been ignored by bigger banks.

Uncertainties and transaction costs in lending

From a professional point of view on banking behaviour, one would argue hitherto that the structures of corporate governance in banks led to the dominance of lobbing or relational lending in the mechanism of loan allocation. However, even if the mechanisms of corporate control were quite elaborate, the NIE provided other arguments on why loan allocation could still be subject to extreme inefficiencies.

Firstly, the high transaction costs that banks incur when they lend to enterprises in transition. Johnson et al. (1993, 194) see the newly established bank structure as a sensible way to reduce these transactions costs. High costs result from the extreme case of asymmetric information prevailing in transitional Mongolia. Its economy represents an environment with fairly incomplete financial information and extreme uncertainty, so that **measuring becomes extremely costly**. Due to uncertainty concerning property rights and the market values of assets, it is difficult for banks to evaluate the value of a borrower. The absence of capital markets and the lack of adequate accounting standards makes it hard for banks to evaluate the borrower's worth. So, in an environment with little financial information and extreme uncertainty, screening and monitoring is extremely costly in Mongolia.

Kletzer and Roldos (1996) see a fundamental distinction between problems of information in economies in transition and those in developed markets: a high level of public ignorance representing the costs of ideology. In the early stage of Mongolian transition, the outcome of transition processes was unknown and compounded by the lack of information. Changes in the environment induced by the change of regime made it difficult to assess the future viability of potential partners. The changes in relative prices rendered the credit history of a borrower, which is usually taken as an indicator for future solvency, unimportant (Johnson et al., 1993: 186). The increase in non-performing loans and inter-enterprise arrears reduced the information base further and led to a complete lack of knowledge about a partners' solvency (Ickes and Ryterman 1992: 336). Further uncertainty derived from sudden actual and potential shifts in policy. Such shifts, or even regime or government changes, increase the uncertainty of economic environment, as the developments between 1996-2000 show (crises within governing Democratic Union). Under these conditions, bank lending is associated with **exorbitantly high costs of ideology**.

Once a debtor had defaulted, the costs of collecting payments were also incredibly high because of deficiencies in the legal infrastructure and enforcement of legal regulations. Filing a bankruptcy case had been rendered impossible by the underdevelopment of bankruptcy laws until the amendment to Civil Law in 2001. Even then, the reluctance of judges to engage in the politically delicate cases and the inexperience of lawyers meant that bankruptcy procedures were either not enforced at all, or only very slowly. Economic agents in Mongolia have had no experience in enforcing property rights, never needed to think about the legal system, nor had any experience or practicable routines for the treatment of seniority issues. That **increases the costs of enforcement**.

Moreover, the costs of payment collection are increased by the lack of appropriate collateral. The general lack of financial information enhances the role of collateral in lending in transition. It makes banks reliant on secured loans (Ickes and Ryterman 1994: 67). A firm does not own the land its factory is built on, and therefore cannot use it to secure loans. Therefore, loans are frequently only secured by written pledges of redemption (Johnson et al. 1993:187). However, virtually every loan is collateralised by inventories and sometimes also by machinery.

The behaviour of Mongolian banks can thus be explained by their efforts to address these considerable transaction costs of specialisation: to reduce the named transaction costs and to make lending profitable. Yet since specialisation in financial services (or financial commodities) is hardly possible under described circumstances of high transaction costs, many banks in the Mongolian loan market stick to old, well-established business relations and activities. Banks mostly started to explicitly extend credits for trade finance and lent only to state organisations or to affiliated enterprises with a network of enterprises in order to reduce collection costs. These activities and relations, however, often impede a proper allocation of resources.

Missing incentives[34] or lenders passivity

As the transaction costs prevailing in the Mongolian transition are considerably higher than those in developed market economies, the role of institutions which form the incentives becomes more relevant than ever. This adds increased significance to inertial behaviour and the slow process of the establishment of economic institutions, and thus of false incentives.

Banks were entangled in the tradition of the planned economy, under which they monitored the financial behaviour of state-owned enterprises for tax and non-waste purposes. They had to conduct neither financial analysis nor any assessments of creditworthiness whatsoever (Bigman and Leite 1993: 3). The difference between monitoring under central planning and assessing creditworthiness in a market economy is the forward-looking nature of the latter. Instead of evaluating the future prospects of a firm, banks analysed its current financial position. And instead of considering the current liquidity position of a firm and the competitiveness of its products, the banks monitored whether the planned amount of goods was produced and sold, regardless of mounting arrears. As long as costs equalled sales, i.e. as long as the firm's account of transactions was balanced, the firm would receive credit, since it could point to its viability (Ickes and Ryterman, 1992: 346). The allocation of loans will therefore not be efficient until long into transition owing to the lack of know-how and a tradition of due diligence.

---

[34] Incentives are insofar missing here as they are incentives for a market-based financial system and lending.

In order **to abolish this passivity of banks and to activate them, a strategic approach has to be taken which aims to improve the institutional framework of bank lending**. If the banking system is to be the centre of economic development, institution building in banking is the main focus in supporting reforms to build up a sound system. Among other things, the next chapter reviews bank regulation norms in Mongolia and identifies potential inconsistencies.

2.3 Institutions of Lending in Mongolia: Some Hypotheses

Playing to win the game, the players – the financial organisations created, such as banks – took advantage of all opportunities given by existing or failing institutions in transitional Mongolia. Thus, **the existing or missing institutions of lending account for the behaviour of Mongolian banks described above and their contribution to overall economic development.**

There is an empirically founded argument in economic literature that the success or failure of financial systems, in respect of financial sector reforms, depends on country-specific institutional factors (Arestis and Demetriades,1997; Demetriades and Hussein, 1996). As Arestis and Demetriades (1997: 791) demonstrate, the success of financial sector reforms in Latin America depends heavily on country-specific factors, such as the reliability of the financial information systems, the situation of real sector, the legal framework and the regulatory system. It has been argued in many studies that these factors have heavily retarded the nature of financial intermediation in developing countries and in EITs. However, the factors for comparison in these studies are formal institutions with their enforcement characteristics, such as laws, regulatory norms and issues which can be more or less quantitatively determined. As argued in Part 1, the role of informal institutions is of no little importance and the interrelation of formal and informal institutions is of the utmost significance. Thus, there is a need to analyse the overall institutional framework and assess the informal institutions in detail.

2.3.1 Incentives Shaped by Existing or Missing Institutions of Lending

Many basic rules of money and capital markets are unknown in Mongolia's financial system, and economic agents have little experience of market-based, financial transactions. The regulatory and legislative framework - formal institutions - has many loopholes. The rules of the game (institutions) which should confine uncertainties in lending, such as well-defined commercial and banking laws, regulatory norms and accounting standards as well as sustainable, assignable economic, social and monetary policies, are still being set up. Of equal weight in transitional Mongolia are also the rules of conduct in economic exchange, existing moral standards and social commitments – informal institutions. A short description is given below on how some formal and informal rules in lending practices in Mongolia have come into being by showing their roots in previous economic systems, especially in the planned economy, before going into details in the following sub-chapters.

In the years of planned economy, **the incentives shaped by the institutions at that time gave economic actors in Mongolia little or no discretion over their financial transactions**, because the leeway for autonomous individual actions was drastically curtailed. Just as the monetary side of transactions hardly influenced the behaviour of firms, banks were not organisations for voluntary financial intermediation between savers and investors. Due to the laws and regulations which existed for lending activities - production and investment targets of the central plan – banks in socialist Mongolia were dependent upon central directives and could not allocate savings individually. They were simply passive instruments for central financial control over the productive sphere. Hence, they did not have to conduct financial analysis, there was no need to assess the solvency and credibility of borrowers, not to mention valuing collateral.

Thus, just after the introduction of a market economy, the lack of internal control procedures, the failure to see loan making as competition and the total absence of loan appraisal influenced the widespread practice of "free borrowing of loan resources" as seen at ITIB and MCB. The vagueness of existing legal stipulations on loan relations and unsatisfactory observance of the few legal regulations that existed were both at fault in this.

The failure to consider risk in lending decisions and to assess the risk attached to projects underlies the lack of experience in the attitude to risk. The previously mentioned case of speculative foreign exchange trading at BOM makes this abundantly clear. As there were **no accounting systems in the Mongolian planned economy to function as a comprehensive information system**, the lack of information and accounting systems and pervasive uncertainty about the value of things were characteristic of the early years of transition in Mongolia. This helps to explain why client firms were favoured whose top managers had been known to the banker for a long time. Whilst this may be rational enough, such systematic favouritism in the abnormal situation of transition, however, also reflects a perverse system of mutual insurance. Trusting each other and trying to keep their cushy old jobs for as long as possible, bankers and firm managers tried to bail each other out in order to avoid bankruptcy proceedings and other kinds of outside scrutiny; they collaborated to cook the books and to channel financial flows in ways that made both the bank and the firms look sufficiently healthy for the time being, as the insolvency experiences of Ardyn Bank and ITI Bank show.

Moreover, the banks monitored whether the planned amount of goods was produced and sold during plan economy. Credit was granted as long as costs equalled sales, i.e. as long as the firm's account of transactions was balanced. Thus, banks analysed the current financial position and there was **no banking custom of forward-looking evaluation of a borrower or a project**. This is one of the reasons why virtually all loans were short term until quite recently. And initial attempts made by some private banks, such as Golomt Bank and Anod Bank, to extend loans for more than 12 months, face many operational problems (Onoodor, 2001: 5)

Due to plan-based monetary policy – as far as it may be called such – interest rates were kept artificially low, so that banks had no experience of pursuing their own pricing policies. That explains the inability of Mongolian banks to respond to the monetary instruments deployed long into transition.

The moral and ethic standards of lending did not include action such as refusing applications for financial funds or forcing enterprises into bankruptcy. Banks continue to act as if they cannot go bankrupt. The expectation that the government will bail out banks is so deeply entrenched due to the existing institution of social commitments, such as the authority of the state. In addition, the government has little political alternative but to stand good for existing deposits, as few depositors even had a choice of banks when they opened their accounts in socialist times.

Moreover, in the first and second phases of financial transition, early steps of BOM's monetary policy, such as automatic clearing loans from BOM to banks, have given misplaced incentives: management of banks ignored a fundamental concept of cash flow, giving rise to extreme NPL ratios. They also exploited the lack of banking expertise among authorities and shareholders in putting money aside, as in the case of banking crises in the second phase. The absence of functional political markets and institutions – no explanation of privatisation decisions and lack of transparency – led to strong public resistance, despite the right approaches, as in the case of the de-merger of Reconstruction Bank from Golomt Bank.

Some substantial changes to institutions have occurred since the beginning of third phase of financial transition. Firstly, long and medium term strategies on financial system development have evolved, which is contributing to the credibility of sustainable economic and monetary policies. Principal amendments concerning legal provisions on lending and loan collateral have been approved, thereby enhancing the property rights of banks to pledged assets. Bank's Management Information Systems are improving slowly due to assistance from international projects and the activities of independent, internal audit units have been expanded.

Nevertheless, there are many gaps to be bridged in the institutional frameworks of lending in Mongolia. There is obvious state intervention in loan matters, lending is not impersonalised, nor does lending properly understand the concept of risk – risk perception, risk management and co-operation between banks in pursuing their professional interests etc. - to name but a few.

In summary, transforming the financial system in Mongolia means changing the institutional framework – **creating new institutions and rebuilding the existing ones – in order to give incentives to form proper financial organisations, such as banks**, so that scarce investible funds are not wasted, but rather targeted to productive investments. The role of banks must shift from being passive agents of fiscal policy to becoming active participants in a market system. With this goal in mind, many formal institutions of lending have been set up, among them bank regulation norms.

2.3.2 Formal Institutions of Lending: Bank Regulation Norms on Lending Activity

Most countries have established supervisory agencies to enforce regulations and, more generally, to promote a prudent attitude to risk. Banking supervision in Mongolia is undertaken by the Bank of Mongolia with "the aim to promote sound banking practices" (Central Bank Act, 1996).

Institutionalisation of bank regulation

In the early stages of transition long into late 1994, lending activities of the banks created were channelled within very lax formal institutions – broadly defined, basic economic laws such as banking law – due to the absence of a law regulating lending activities. Though the BOM tried to establish such criteria for financial solvency for banks on its own, such as reserve requirements and directives to determine and pursue a particular credit policy, to classify loans etc, it has failed to enforce them because the supervision duties of BOM were not properly defined and legally obligated.

Bank regulation has now been institutionalised by a number of separate laws (the Central Bank Act and the Banking Act of Mongolia in 1996, the special Law on Deposit Taking, Payment Services and Lending Activities in 1995, and many legal regulations, such as Prudential Ratios Regulation, Regulation for Calculating and Controlling Reserve Requirements, Regulation on Asset Classification and Provisioning etc. in the late of 1990s). These acts introduced the conception of bank supervision as an inherent function of the Bank of Mongolia in order to ensure the stability and safety of the banking system. The bank regulation authority, regulation procedures and bank regulation norms were thus set up.

The Supervision Department functioning within the structure of the Bank of Mongolia is the authority which regulates banking activities. It consists of three divisions: Policy Regulation Division, Banking Division and Supervision Division. The Policy Regulation Division works out the concept and principles of banking supervision policy with respect to the purposeful development of the banking sector and the financial soundness of banks. It develops prudent regulation norms, co-operates with other institutions in that respect and studies experiences made abroad. The Banking Division elaborates regular bank economic analyses with respect to their financial situation, prudent behaviour and effectiveness, on the basis of which it specifies the banking sectors' basic problems and defines areas for executing banking supervision. It generalises experiences acquired during bank inspections, submits proposals for methodological control of risky areas in banks and outlines further procedures to prevent dangerous banking situations. It also puts forward proposals for the financial recovery of banks in jeopardy and the methodology for bank examination. The Supervision Division makes inspections. Ensuring contacts with banks, it carries out on-site and off-site supervision and makes sure that banks comply with prudential norms. The Supervision Division takes action to correct shortcomings in banks and their activities and monitors its fulfilment. It submits proposals for the imposition of conservatorship, including proposals for conservator appointments. The supervision is carried out by the supervisor, who has the power of state inspector and is appointed by the Governor of the BOM.

The overall structure, procedure and norms of bank regulation in Mongolia are modelled on that of advanced market economies. Credit risk classification was tackled for the first time in 1994, whereby the term risk as such had not been properly defined at that time. The bank regulation norms in lending "are directed at assessing and limiting credit risk at banks" (Onoodor, 2001: 4). The prudential ratios regulation for evaluating the compliance of banks came into force in 1995 and internationally used bank accounting standards were introduced in 1996. The Core Principles for Effective Banking Supervision of the Basel Committee (Basel I) were accepted as guidelines for bank regulation norms in 1997. Auditing the financial statements of banks was introduced in 1998 in order to enforce bank regulation norms more effectively.

Setting up regulation norms

After the banking crises of 1998-99, several measures were taken to strengthen the banking sector and boost confidence by improving bank supervision and regulation. Since then, 20 regulations and numerous amendments to banking laws have been drafted and put into force. The main contents of two important regulations, the Regulation for Calculating and Controlling Reserve Requirements and the Prudential Ratios Regulation are attached in Annexes 1 and 2. The main steps are outlined below:

- An increase in the minimum capital requirement from Tugrug[35] 400 million to Tugrug 2 milliard, which banks were required to meet before June 2001. Due to a follow-up, mandatory increase requirement to 4 milliard by end March of 2004 (with the option of further increase), consolidation of some banks may take place. Moreover, the BOM's Supervision Department plans a further increase to 6 milliard within the next few years to improve the equity ratios of banks.
- The BOM has been empowered to ensure better governance within the sector. Individuals of doubtful character can be prohibited from holding managerial and executive board positions.
- Banks audit standards have been established. Auditors are required to report directly to the BOM.
- Banks whose total assets represent more than 10 percent of the total banking system assets are required to submit accounts audited by internationally recognised auditing companies. Domestic auditing firms audit the financial statements of other banks.
- The BOM has issued guidelines for licensing the auditing firms allowed to perform bank audits.
- Automatic loan rescheduling for defaulting borrowers has been prohibited.
- Banks are now required to report to the BOM monthly rather than quarterly and to disclose their financial statements quarterly to the general public. They should

35 The exchange rate of Tugrug on 1st of June 2003 was 1 EUR = 925 Tugrug and on 1st of June 2003 1 EUR = 1319 Tugrug, The Bank of Mongolia.

submit the following reports to the Bank of Mongolia within the 10th day of every month:

1) capital adequacy report,
2) liquidity ratio report,
3) report on loans, guarantees, letters of credit granted or issued to 20 large borrowers,
4) report on loans, guarantees, letters of credit granted or issued to shareholders, Board of Directors, senior management, employees and their related parties,
5) report on the sufficiency of loan loss provision,
6) report on outstanding guarantees and letters of credit,
7) foreign exchange risk report.

The bank and the officer of the bank responsible for any violation of this regulation should be prosecuted in accordance with the relevant legislation.

In early 2001 Parliament approved further amendments to the framework for banking supervision. Other areas of attention were the further mitigation of credit risk and the disposal of collateral. To improve financial supervision, on-site and off-site guidelines have been drafted. These papers contain paradigms for financial analyses, risk assessment, evaluation of the probability of insolvency and corrective action.

The BOM is currently endeavouring to implement prudential supervision in accordance with the (Basel I) Core Principles for Effective Banking Supervision. It has established a 10 percent minimum requirement of the risk weighted capital adequacy ratio, with the banking system, at the end of 2000, averaging above 20 percent. Banks increased their profitability and concentrated their activities on a few reliable clients. During 2001, the liquidity ratio of the banking system stabilised at 55 percent, proof that banks have allocated their resources in high liquidity and lower risk assets.

The Loan Information Pool (LIP) was introduced at the BOM to attempt to mitigate credit risk and limit lending to borrowers with NPLs. The LIP collects information about borrowers from banks and NBFIs and now holds data on almost 12,000 borrowers with outstanding credit amounting to US$ 116 million. Information is also available on over 4,000 borrowers of insolvent banks, with total outstanding loans of US$ 24 million, which has been transferred to the Mongolian Asset Recovery Agency (MARA). Banks interested in information on borrowers can make telephone enquires, so that not only "official" information, but also "unofficial", private opinion can be exchanged within this LIP.

As the experience of institutionalisation of bank regulation and setting up bank regulation norms in Mongolia shows, establishing and maintaining a strong financial sector requires consequent enforcement of bank regulation norms. For this purpose, skilled bankers and supervisors will be needed, who are able to understand the implications of risk for financial activities and establish an adequate framework for prudent regulation. This depends largely on the knowledge and experience they provide. This cannot be acquired overnight and must be accumulated in the medium and long term by giving the correct incentives within the institutions in turn, especially informal ones.

2.3.3 The Inconsistency of Informal Institutional Constraints with Formal Norms

As seen in sub-chapter above, the formal institution of lending in Mongolia – bank regulation norms – is based in principle upon the bank regulation norms of advanced economies. It resembles the latter in both conception and normative content. Thus, the aim is to channel the behaviour of "advanced" banks in their decision-making on lending. It calls for corresponding informal institutions to guide the decision-making of these banks. As the New Institution Economics stated in Part 1, not only the existence of proper institutions is important, but also their compatibility with each other. The underlying hypotheses of NIE is that the key of efficient enforcement of formal rules – banking regulation norms on lending – is the compatibility of formal rules with informal constraints – informal rules. That means that the alteration of both formal and informal institutions has to be addressed simultaneously.

Formally amended laws, even legal allowance for private ownership of banks, liberalised interest rates and precisely devised or copied bank regulation norms are insufficient if people's subjective mental models of behaviour remain unchanged. Informal constraints, such as payment habits or banker's attitude to risk shape economic behaviour, but they can not be changed overnight, they need much more time to develop than formal rules do.

Consequently, the question is what are the informal institutions of lending in Mongolia and are they consistent with the formal institutions of lending. Banking regulation norms, which aim to confine the risky behaviour of banks with legal rules, must be consistent with banking habits, which also guide the bankers' action. In order to answer this question, informal institutions are diagnosed by hypothesising them as follows.

Hypothesis 1 on the attitude to risk: risk perception and management

The discrepancy between the actual behaviour of bankers and the existing regulations is due to the following attitudes to risk and acts of bankers (risk behaviour):

Hypothesis 1.1

Despite the perception of risk as an important factor, it is not operationalised (risk management) in the day-to-day business of banks.

Hypothesis 1.2

Risk taking and reserves are not recognised as being related to one another in terms of bank supervision.

Hypothesis 1.3

The process of credit risk management is not perceived as a matter subject to bank supervision.

The way that bankers see the role of bank supervision, thus bank regulation norms, should also help to observe informal institutions channelling bankers' behaviour during lending.

Hypothesis 2 on bankers' perception concerning bank supervision

Bankers' perception concerning the functions of bank supervision is to guarantee loan repayment and to provide information.

The informal institutions channelling the behaviour of Mongolian banks differentiate from that of banks in "advanced" economies. Not only the concept risk and risk management, but also ethic standards and social commitments still strongly influence decisions in lending.

Hypothesis 3 on social commitments: commitment to the authoritative state

Decisions on lending are distinctly affected by official representatives (of the Government and Parliament).

Hypothesis 4 on ethic standard: family ties

Decisions on lending are strongly influenced by personal relationships.

As mentioned above, observing and measuring informal institutions is one of the outstanding challenges for the NIE. In the present work, an approach to observe the informal institutions of lending indirectly is evolved on the basis of cognitive science. It examines the foregoing hypotheses on informal institutions of lending with Mongolian bankers. Part 3 which follows goes into the details of the method used in the survey on bankers' action-regulating knowledge of lending.

Part 3 Discrepancy between Bank Regulation Norms and Lending Practice in Mongolia

In order to address the hypotheses listed in Part 2, Part 3 now provides a complete description of directions and steps to be taken to conduct the survey. Chapter 3.1 describes the framework within which the materials (data) are incorporated – the qualitative research design. The main research method within the research design – the method of concept mapping to diagnose the action-regulating knowledge of bankers on lending – is introduced there. Chapter 3.2 goes into details of where, how and when data were collected – participants, instrumentation and procedure. The results of data analysis are presented in chapter 3.3 and the findings are then tested against the hypotheses (in form of evaluation statements).

3.1 Diagnosing Action-Regulating Knowledge (Method)

Based on the cognitive approach developed in Part 1 (chapter 1.3), this chapter frames the observation of informal institutions channelling the actions of Mongolian bankers by diagnosing their action-regulating knowledge. There are about a dozen method groups to diagnose action-regulating knowledge (Hacker, 1992, 1996). The diagnostic methodology used in this study centres on operations and persons. In other words, an operation-centred approach observes the operational aspects of the activity and analyses its condition and results. A person-centred approach evokes thinking out loud, interviews with structural assistant techniques, claims non-verbal descriptions etc. Thus the qualitative research design utilised can be characterised as follows.

3.1.1 Research Design and Methods

The purpose of the study is to give empirical evidence for the subjective mental models of bankers in lending, thus for the informal institutional constraints which exist in practical lending processes in Mongolia. It focuses on bankers' knowledge of goals, of situational cues or conditions, of reasons, causes, measures, means and partners and of consequences (see Figure 1.5) in lending activities. The findings should provide a reliable base, firstly, for describing who is doing what in the lending process, and, secondly, for judging this process on the basis of whether and how the aspects of activity are valuable in themselves. The intended results of the survey were formulated in detail in sub-chapter 1.3.3: these are to identify how Mongolian bankers understand the factors which influence decision making during lending, especially those concerning risk and risk management, and about the relevance of risk to bank supervision. Insights should also be generated on whether lending can be implemented as designed de jure (as pretended by formal institutions) and funded, this being the central policy issue for a bank's management as well as for economic policies and development projects.

An inductive approach is chosen to describe and understand the lending process and the particular aspects which constrain it. The emphasis of this crossing design (qualitative-quantitative) is on describing in depth and on better understanding the meaning and nature of operations of lending practice and effects at some particular banks in Mongolia.

The qualitative-quantitative approach

Research strategies or approaches differ in terms of the problems they address and the outcomes they produce. According to Polkinghorne (1991: 112), methods of qualitative design are especially useful in the "generation of categories for understanding human phenomena and the investigation of the interpretation and meaning that people give to events they experience". Whereas the quantitative strategy is suited to recording a smaller set of previously identified variables, the qualitative approach seeks a psychologically rich, in-depth understanding of the individual.

Despite the great heterogeneity within the literature on qualitative methodologies, Patton's (1980) three assumptions of qualitative research are generally recognised:

- A holistic perspective of the analysis, one which stresses that the whole is greater than the sum of its parts. Thus qualitative methods seek to understand phenomena in their entirety in order to completely understand a person, situation, or process.
- A naturalistic inquiry: by capturing whatever happens to occur, a qualitative method is open and sensitive to deviations from plans, unanticipated variations and important idiosyncrasies of process experience (phenomena in their naturally occurring states).
- An inductive approach: qualitative research begins with specific observations and moves toward the development of general patterns that emerge from the cases under study. The deductive approach of experimental designs prescribe specification of variables prior to data collection, while the qualitative approach does not necessarily have to make assumptions about the interrelationships among the data prior to making observations.

Whereas quantitative data are generally evaluated using descriptive and inferential statistics, qualitative data are usually reduced to themes or categories and evaluated subjectively. In research practice, there is very often a crossing or collaboration of qualitative and quantitative approaches with different emphases. On this basis, this study utilises a crossing design (qualitative-quantitative) with a greater emphasis on qualitative data and in-depth analysis. Findings are pre-estimated by hypothesising the informal institutional constraints of lending on Mongolian banks (hypothetico-quantitative part). The detailed description and an in-depth understanding of decision making on lending and its informal aspects are carried out as a whole on the basis of the qualitative data. The aim is to try to understand the meaning and nature of operations of the lending process as it emerges from direct contact and experience with naturally occurring activities. The lending process of a particular bank should be observed with formulated questions to subsequently draw general conclusions on the basis of findings.

Weaknesses in such a qualitative approach could be the subjectivity of the researcher and the problem of correctly interpreting the findings. The researcher's subjectivity can be reduced by using multiple sources of data and by deploying a variety of instruments and data handling procedures. Pilot studies or pre-tests are also made to demonstrate the suitability of procedures. Proper traceability can be achieved by a proper coding of the raw data and findings to ensure that different observers reach similar conclusions. This should be followed by a detailed description of the methods and instruments used and the data collection procedure.

Methodological triangulation

In view of the characteristics of action-regulating knowledge described, (1.3.2) a ***methodological triangulation*** – the use of multiple methods to study a single problem – is adopted. A triangle is the strongest of geometric shapes, and triangulated research is aimed at increasing its strength and rigor. This study uses a triangulation of the method of concept mapping, the method of individual interviews of bankers, and the method of (credit) document observation. Before describing each method separately in order to answer why and how they served as an effective device to focus discussion on the research questions of the study (sub-chapter 3.2.2), the synergy effects of triangulation of the three methods is presented.

Building checks and balances into an approach by using multiple methods, such as credit documents records and in-depth interviews, deals with the problem of relying too much on any single data source or method. It undermines the validity and credibility of findings because of the weaknesses of any single (main) method.

Denzin (1978: 28) introduced the concept of triangulation into the debate on qualitative research, he explains that the logic of triangulation is based on the premise that: "no single method ever adequately solves the problem of rival causal factors. [...] because each method reveals different aspects of empirical reality, multiple methods of observation must be employed". This is termed triangulation. According to Hacker's investigation results (1996: 17), no single method could identify the entire action-regulating knowledge of experts: a single, "best" method does not exist. This statement shows that different methods diagnose different parts of knowledge and, when combined, they can complement one another.

By deploying a number of complementary methods and data collections to produce relevant and useful insights on subjective mental models of lending in Mongolian banks, the methodological triangulation in this work ought to gain positive effects in the way of:

- inquiries of conscious and unconscious knowledge of the bankers regulating their actions (with concept mappings), which is
- supported with an evaluation of self-reported personal experiences of the bankers about their day-to-day work (by open-ended individual interviews) confronting it with
- observation of some records and documents concerning the loan granting process in one particular bank.

The action-regulating knowledge elicitated with these three methods then needs to be structured or arranged for further analysis. The action-slot model is chosen for this purpose, this being the basic evaluation method for all assessments made. A memory schema represents typical relations of reality which are generalised on the basis of the experiences. It integrates and organises the information. The ***action-slot-model*** tries to expel the blurs of the schema-concept using research findings concerning the inner and inter relations between concepts. The generalised, typical relations of reality, regulating action by knowledge, is specified by concept interrelations which are well-known (among others actor, object, finality, instrument relations) and concept inner relations (among others character, superordinate, subordinate concept relations). The relations hereby refer to a consolidated "semantic core", the action. The relations are called action-slots, which should be "filled" if the action is to be accomplished successfully and efficiently.

The first part of the Figure 3.1 demonstrates the typical semantic relations – or knowledge fields - in an activity. There are, for example, finality relations (goals of the measures, results of the measures), instrumental relations (means, partners) and causal relations (reasons for the situation, which call for measures). The second part shows the W-questions which should help to fill the slots. The third part contains the knowledge fields which could be ascertained by means of W-questions and which help to perform the particular activity.

Figure 3.2 shows a hypothetical knowledge model (knowledge parts and relations) for a particular activity – credit investigation. This knowledge model is built as a hypothetical model based on banking theory in market-based economy (Hartmann-Wendels et al., 1998; Mishkin and Eakins, 1998; Neuberger, 1994) and complemented with results of pre-tests among German bankers. It can be used as a reference for knowledge elicitation and as a common instrument for evaluating the data collected by different methods: bankers' concept maps, open-end interviews with them and observation of credit documents.

3.1.2 Concept Mapping as a Tool Based on Cognitive Science

A ***concept map*** is a structural representation consisting of nodes and labelled lines (Novak, 1998: 22). The ***nodes*** correspond to important terms (standing for concepts) in the domain, whereas the ***lines*** denote a relation between a pair of concepts – nodes, and the label on the line tells how the two concepts are related (Ruiz-Primo and Shavelson, 1996: 570). The combination of two nodes and a labelled line is called a ***proposition***. A proposition is the basic unit of meaning in a concept map and the smallest unit that can be used to judge the validity of the relation (line) drawn between two concepts (Dochy, 1994: 25).

A ***concept map*** thus aims to demonstrate interrelations between concepts by means of propositions (Novak and Gowin, 1984: 15) in order to reflect some important aspect of individual's knowledge – cognitive framework – in a particular content domain (e.g. banking or lending). It is a "network" of concepts showing the links between them, thus illustrating how a person sees the relations between things, ideas, or people (White, Gunstone, 1992:15). Figures 3.3 and 3.4 show examples of concept maps for the domains "Living things" and "Money".

Figure 3.1: Aspects of action-slot model
Source: Hacker (1996:31)

Semantic relations:

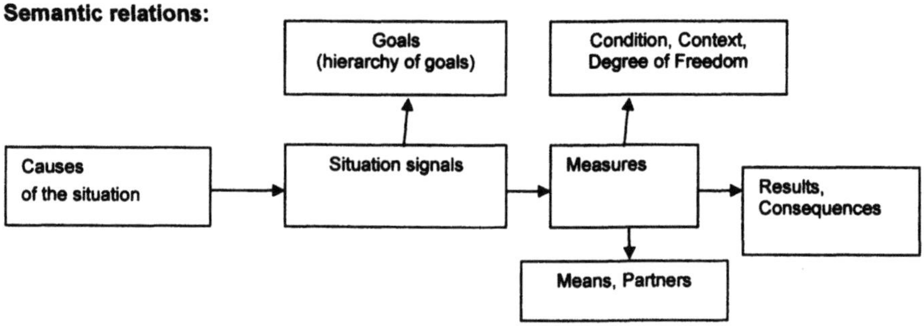

W-questions of industrial psychology:

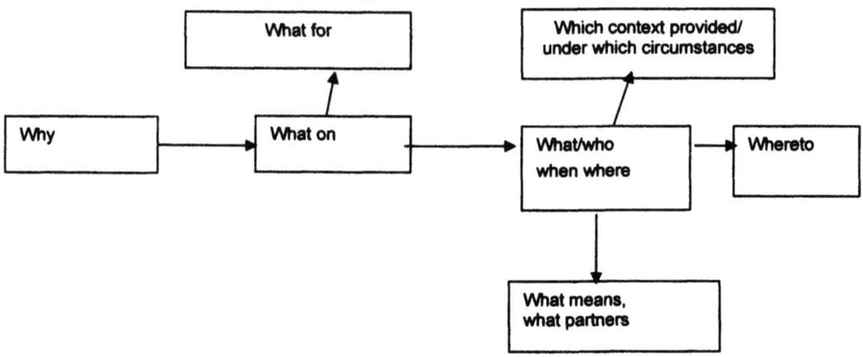

Knowledge fields:

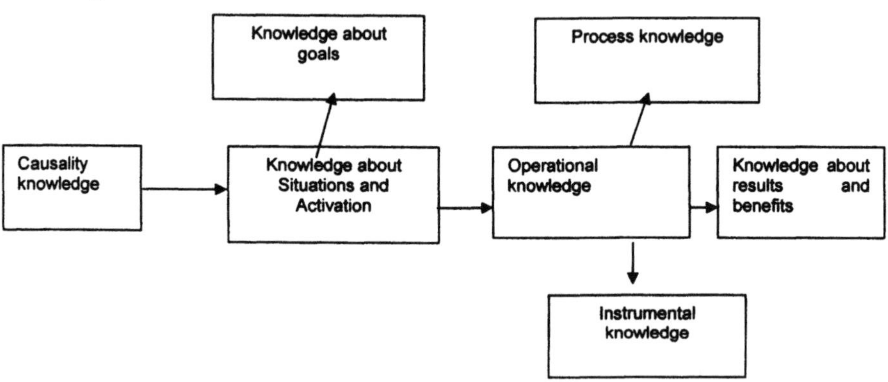

Figure 3.2: Reference map for action-regulating knowledge on semantic core "Credit Investigation" within action-slot model

Source: own illustration

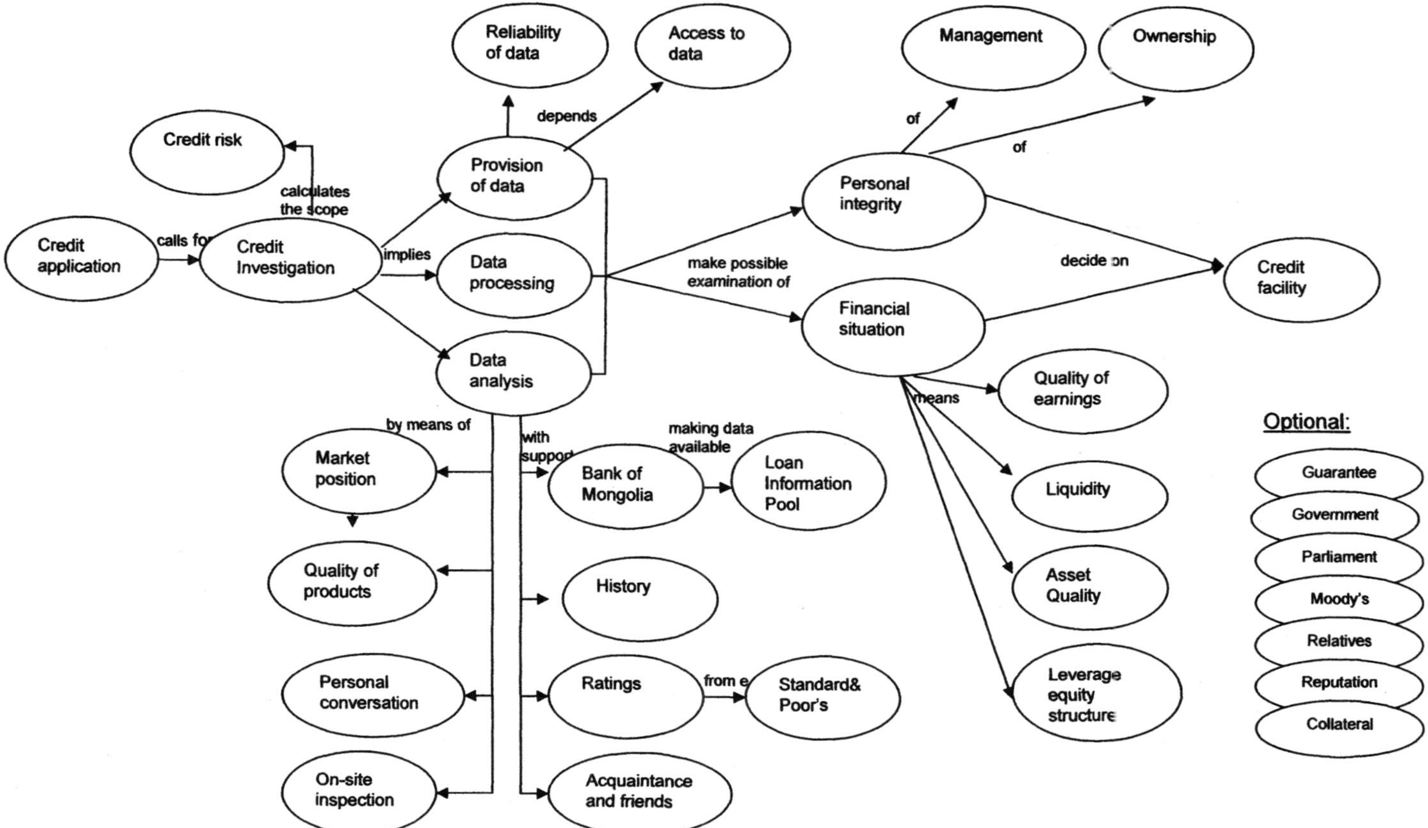

Figure 3.3: Concept maps on domain "Living Things"

Source: reconstruction of concept mappings of survey's pre-test persons; concepts adopted by White and Gunstone (1992: 17) and modified

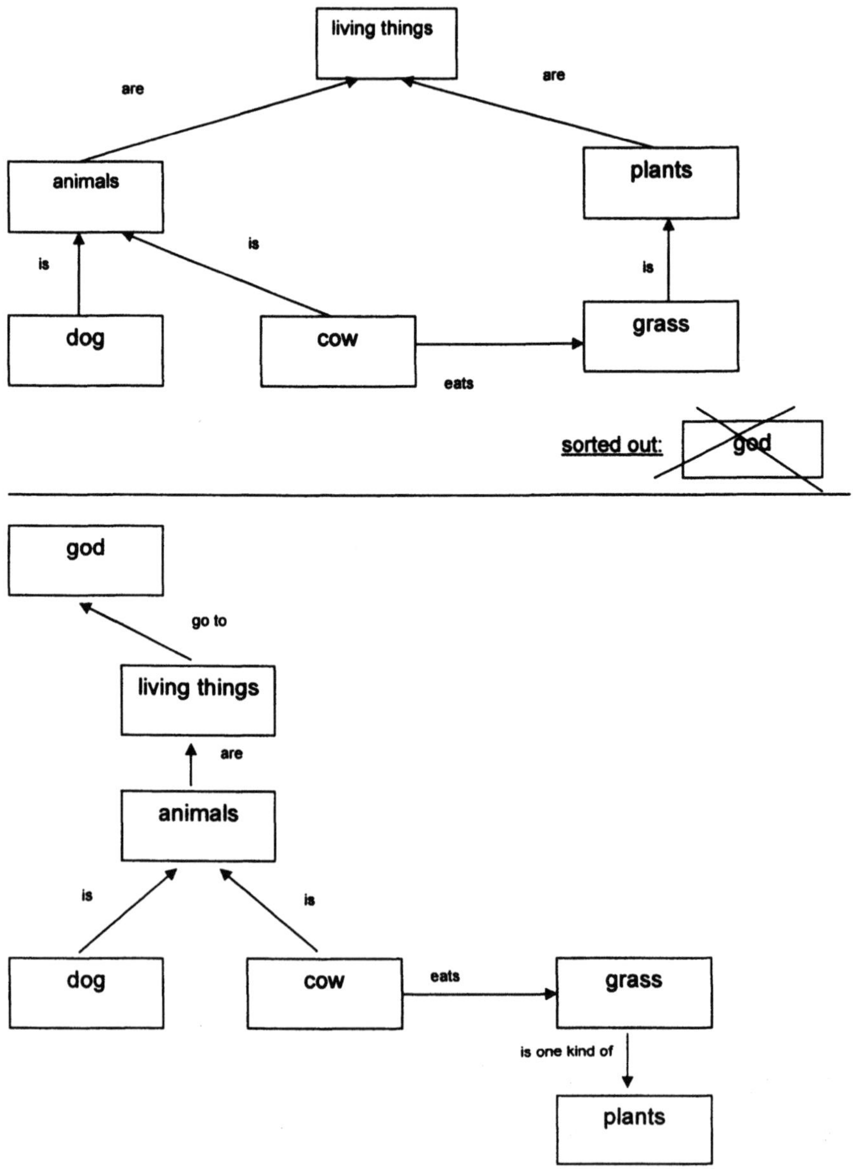

Concept mapping – the process of producing a concept map – has been used as a research and evaluation tool in science education for nearly 30 years. The technique grew out of the work of Novak (1972) and his graduate students at Cornell University (Rowell, 1978). It was originally intended as a vehicle for exploring meaningful learning acquired through audio-tutorial instruction in elementary school science – the students' understanding of science concepts. Since then, many teachers have adopted concept mapping and have employed it all levels of diagnosis and testing, instructional design and curriculum development, and later on as a meta-cognitive aid to help students "learn how to learn" (Novak and Gowin, 1984; Novak, 1990). According to Novak (1998: 113), "meaningful learning must underlie the constructive integration of thinking, feeling and acting if learners are to be successful and achieve a sense of empowerment – and also a sense of commitment and responsibility".

That concepts are interrelated is assumed in most cognitive theories as an essential property of knowledge (Ruis-Primo and Shavelson, 1996: 570). Indeed, the definition of competence in any domain is based on the premise that knowledge is well structured (Glaser and Bassok, 1989: 22). As individuals acquire expertise in any domain through learning, training and experience, the elements of their knowledge become increasingly interconnected. This knowledge increasingly resembles the tightly integrated structures that characterise a subject-matter expert's representation of knowledge (Royer et al., 1993).

Based on the assumption that knowledge within a content domain is organised around central concepts, to be knowledgeable in the domain thus implies a highly integrated structure among these concepts. This organisational property of knowledge can be captured with structural representations (White and Gunstone, 1992) – the concept mapping technique.

Concept mapping in science relies on cognitive theory, which has its roots in related traditions: the hierarchical memory theory of Ausubel (1968) and the associations memory theory of Deese (1965). Ausubel's theory posited a hierarchical memory structure, whereas Deese posited a network of concepts that did not assume but could accommodate a hierarchy. Both theories eventually arrived at the same place – a concept or cognitive map. Each of them is sketched briefly below.

Figure 3.4: Concept maps on domain "Money"

Source: reproduction of concept mappings of survey's pre-test persons

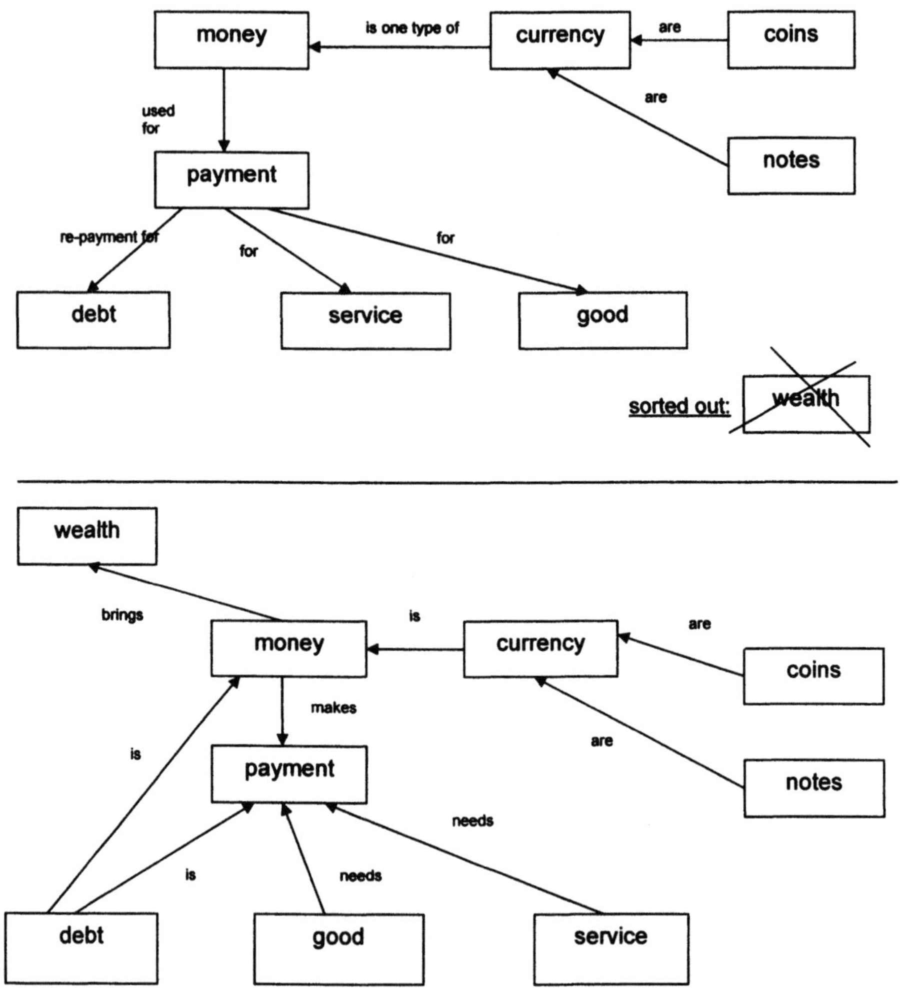

Concept mapping in Ausubel's hierarchical memory theory involves the process of organising concepts and the relationships between these concepts in a hierarchical manner. It has been used successfully both as a learning tool (Fraser and Edwards, 1985; Pankratus: 1990) and as a cognitive research tool (Novak and Musonda, 1991; Winitzky et al., 1994). Concept maps serve to externalise concepts and propositions that a person holds. Malone and Dekkers (1984: 231) described concept maps as "windows to the mind" of students, "for seeing in (by the teacher and other students), for seeing out (by the student) and for reflecting on one's own perceptions (by everybody)." It has been used as a suitable tool for gaining insights into students' cognitive framework for the material learned and for evaluating the extent to which that topic has been understood.

Deese's associationist network theory places requirements on concept mapping similar to those of Ausubel's theory, but with the important exception that maps do not have to be hierarchical. Based on this theoretical approach, then, (a) concept maps are networks with concept nodes linked directionally by labelled lines (arrows) to produce propositions, (b) the lines between the nodes represent various relations, (c) any number of lines may connect two nodes, and (d) the network may divide nodes into subsets and indicate the link (crosslink) between these subsets (Ruiz-Primo and Shavelson, 1996: 572).

The more researchers began to employ the tool of concept mapping to study cognitive structures and conceptual change, the greater their attention has concentrated on the reliability and validity of this technique (Novak and Gowin, 1984; Novak and Musonda, 1991; Ahlberg, 1993; Wandersee et al., 1995). Novak and Gowin (1984) believe that concept maps have construct validity in terms of evaluation theory. There is a correspondence between the assessment of cognitive performance and what Ausubelian learning theory predicts should be the cognitive organisation resulting from meaningful learning.

Concerning scoring in order to evaluate concept maps, Novak and Gowin (1984) noted that any scoring key for concept maps has a certain degree of subjectivity inherent in it, but this, is the case with all evaluation instruments. Although objective, multiple choice tests may score "objectively", the choice of topics and the wording of questions are subjective. Moreover, reporting and short-answer questions will naturally involve subjectivity in both the design of questions and the scoring of answers. According to Novak, Musonda (1991: 134), "concept maps are not only reliable and valid but also measure aptitudes not commonly assessed by typical objective tests. On both theoretical and empirical grounds, concept maps are useful for the assessment of cognitive structure and changes in cognitive structure."

These theoretical conceptualisations implicated a framework for designing concept maps as a potential assessment tool in science and management (Ruiz-Primo and Shavelson, 1996: 573). Based on this framework, a concept map is used as an assessment tool and can be characterised as: (i) a task that invites experts to provide evidence bearing on their knowledge content and structure in a particular domain, (ii) a format for one's response, and (iii) a scoring system, by which one's concept map can be evaluated consistently. Ruiz-Primo and Shavelson (1996) argue that without these three components, a concept map cannot be considered an assessment and give a register of various forms of concept maps.

Concept mapping is thus widely used as an evaluation and learning tool in science education – in lessons, in tests at schools and universities – and very recently but increasingly in the management of companies for decision making, tests and evaluations of expert's knowledge (Novak, 1998). In academic research, however, concept mapping has been used as a cognitive research tool in education and psychology.

The study applies this tool to diagnose the links and associated ideas, thus bankers' own interpretations of key concepts in the "lending" domain. The instrument of concept mapping reflects, in terms of validity, the conceptualisation of the phenomenon in manner that is consistent with the research approach of this study.

3.1.3 Diagnosing the Action-Regulating Knowledge of Bankers with Concept Mapping

Because the method of concept mapping was developed specifically to "tap into a learner's cognitive structure and to externalise what the learner already knows" (Novak and Gowin, 1984: 40), it can be used to understand the semantic sense of the "lending" issue by illustrating their understanding with maps of concepts and the interrelationships between them (within the "lending" domain).

The authors of this tool say they "do not claim that a concept map is a complete representation of the relevant concepts and propositions the learner knows" (Novak, 1990; White, Gunstone, 1992), but they do claim that it is a workable approximation, from which learners (bankers) as well as others (teachers, researcher, managers etc.) can expand and move forward. Concept maps are very helpful insofar as they can identify whether a banker has comprehensive ideas on the topic of "lending" (and what there are). Concept maps should help to observe the conscious and unconscious action-regulating knowledge of bankers which cannot be identified by means of other tests, oral or written.

The mental model of bankers is reviewed in this work for three sub-domains: the action-regulating knowledge of bankers on risk, the action-regulating knowledge of bankers on credit risk management and credit approval, and the action-regulating knowledge of bankers in issues of banking and bank supervision. That means that bankers are asked to build concept maps on these three sub-domains.

As argued in sub-chapter 1.3.3, bankers' own perception of economic interrelation, thus a concept map concerning "Risk and Risk Taking", should identify what bankers think about risk and show how they understand risk as subject to bank regulation. The nodes (concepts) they choose correspond to important terms in the sub-domain "Risk and Risk Taking". The combination of nodes and the lines labelled (by bankers), i.e. concept maps, aims to diagnose the action-regulating knowledge of bankers and to illustrate:

- whether and what kind of risk exists for Mongolian bankers;
- the influence of information on risk and risk taking for Mongolian bankers;
- the bankers' understanding of bankruptcy probability on risk;
- whether risk is seen as subject to bank regulation norms by Mongolian bankers;
- if and which tasks of bank supervision are recognised by Mongolian bankers in respect to risk.

The concept maps on "Credit Risk Management and Credit Approval" aim to show how bankers understand credit risk management and to identify the ideas given by Mongolian bankers about which factors influence the decision making process in lending, how and to what extent. The maps should show :

- the role of credit risk management in lending in Mongolia;
- which kind of collateral and guarantee instruments exist for Mongolian bankers;
- whether and to which extent personal relations influence credit approval in Mongolia;
- the scope of influence of state authorities on credit approval in Mongolia;
- how the authority line of decision making in lending is in Mongolian banks.

Concept mapping on "Banking and Bank Supervision" illustrates bankers' own perception of the interrelation between banking and bank supervision and shows how bankers understand the aim of bank supervision and how bank supervision may influence their decision making. It should provide evidence of:

- how Mongolian bankers consider the general role of bank supervision;
- how Mongolian bankers see the tasks of today's bank supervision in respect to banking activities in general and to lending in particular;
- which existing instruments of bank supervision are known by bankers in Mongolia;
- which bank regulation norms are taken into account by bankers during lending in Mongolia;
- whether Mongolian bankers are familiar with internationally known bank regulation concepts and authorities;

The characteristics of an action-regulating knowledge were used to compose the nodes (concepts) in each sub-domain. In other words, concepts were chosen in a way that the critical fields of knowledge (Figure 1.5) in sub-domains were shown: cause, situation signals, goals, process or condition, measures (and sites), means and results of lending activities. These knowledge fields are elaborated in composition of key concepts for decision-making in lending in sub-chapter 3.2.2 on instrumentation.

Complementary methods are used to support concept mapping in pinning down this multifaceted knowledge of bankers – conscious and unconscious - so as to improve validity. Methods are required whose elements and sequence are carefully attuned to the main method. The arrangement of such packages has been researched by Eberleh et al. (1989), Hacker (1992, 1996), Kluwe (1988) etc. Since a discussion on the combination of different methods is beyond the terms of reference of this work, an approved approach to combination is chosen in which illustrative interviews with bankers serve as a main method – concept mapping – supported by open-ended interview of bankers and partial documentation observation – case study of credit files.

3.2 Bankers' Mental Model on Lending (Survey)

Qualitative research requires methods that are based on a philosophical orientation different to that utilised by rationalistic inquiry (quantitative research). It adopts sampling, instrumentation and data analysis, the components of which may not be possible to predict with the same degree of precision as in a quantitative study. In a qualitative study, the detailed descriptions of events, people, interactions and observed behaviour, including direct quotations, and case documentation are collected as an open-ended narrative without attempting to fit activities or peoples' experiences into pre-determined, standardised options, such as the response choices that constitute typical questionnaires or tests. Thus the special features of survey sampling (what are the units of analysis, where are they located and how are they selected?), instrumentation (which methods used to collect the data?) and procedure (when, where and how were the data collected?) in qualitative analysis is briefly discussed at the beginning of each sub-chapter.

3.2.1 Sampling

The appropriate units of analysis are, on the one hand, individual people – bankers, and on the other hand, granted or withdrawn loans. That means that the primary focus of data collection is on how decisions are made and what drives bankers during the lending process (action-guiding knowledge).

The logic of so called purposeful sampling in qualitative methods is quite different from the logic of probabilistic sampling in statistics. The power of statistical sampling depends on selecting a truly random and representative sample, which will permit confident generalisation from the sample to a larger population. The power of ***purposeful sampling*** lies in selecting cases rich in information for study in depth. Information-rich cases are those from which a great deal can be learned about issues of central importance to the purpose of the study, thus the term "purposeful" sampling. If, for example, the purpose is to increase the effectiveness of an aid program in reaching the lower socio-economic group, a great deal more would probably be learned by focusing in depth on understanding the needs, interests and incentives of a small number of carefully selected poor families, rather than gathering a little information from a large, statistically significant sample.

The purpose of this study is to gain insights for the enhancement of lending effectiveness in Mongolia by improving the decision making process for granting loans. Hence by focusing in depth on understanding the content and structure of action-regulating knowledge of bankers from different banks, supplemented by comprehending the content, the organisation and standardisation of a small number of carefully selected credit files (documentation on everything concerning the application and granting of a loan), more can be learned than by gathering a little information from a large, statistically significant sample covering all banks.

Thus decisions about sampling cannot be made by using statistical tests, such as the t-test, as is the case of power analysis in quantitative research. There are several strategies to purposefully select cases rich in information: extreme case sampling, maximum variation sampling, homogeneous sampling, critical case sampling or snowball sampling etc. As far as the size of the sample is concerned, it should be large enough to be credible given the purpose of the evaluation, but small enough to permit adequate depth and detail for each case or unit in the sample. Literature on qualitative research shows that samples of from 5-8 up to 20-30 are common practice, depending on the purpose and depth requirements of each study (Novak, 1990, 1998; Patton, 1987; Dochy, 1994). Lastly, it is difficult to generate a great deal of really useful information with scarce resources. The extent to which data collection is broad or narrow thus depends on the resources available.

In this study, a combination of critical case sampling and maximum variation sampling (Patton: 1987, 51ff.) is used. Cases that make a point quite dramatically or, for some reason, are particularly important in the scheme of things are called critical, thus ***critical sampling***. A clue to the existence of a critical case is a key informant observation to the effect that "if that group is having problems, then we can be sure that all groups are having problems." (Patton: 1987, 55). Choosing critical case sampling is particularly important where resources may limit the evaluation to studying just a single site. It therefore makes strategic sense to pick the site that seems likely to yield the most information and have the greatest impact for drawing conclusions. The key dimension that turns chosen banks and chosen loans into critical cases is, on the one hand, the market share of these banks – more than 70% of loan markets – and on the other hand, the existence of various loan types - long term loans even though more formally - as well as loan term training of bankers during international development projects.

Moreover, as a further step, critical case sampling is combined with ***maximum variation sampling***, which involves capturing and describing the central themes or principal outcomes that cut across a great deal of participants or events. As individual cases are so different from each other, a great deal of heterogeneity can be a problem for small samples. The maximum variation sampling strategy turns that apparent weakness into a strength by applying the logic that "any common patterns that emerge from great variation are of particular interest and value in capturing the core experiences and central, shared aspects or impacts of a program" (Patton: 1987, 53). The research lacks sufficient resources to randomly select a sufficient sample of projects to generalise to the whole process. Yet by covering the most important economic branches – variation of loans for enterprises from different branches – it is at least sure that the branch variation among loans is represented in the study. So after choosing the maturity for building the sample first, the diverse characteristic for constructing the sample at the next stage is the branches variation.

The survey with concept mapping and open-ended interviews was conducted extensively during a six-week visit to three Mongolian banks in Ulaanbaatar in January and April 2002. The author had the opportunity to study appropriate materials concerning the lending process of one particular bank, as well as to have deeper discussions with the staff. Due to organisational difficulties – getting a meaningful insight into the credit documents of other two banks was really difficult and very time consuming – this additional survey is limited to just one bank. As obtaining permission turned out to be troublesome as expected, the chance to observe credit files and other credit documents for two weeks at that bank was of great importance to the author and the study. Due to banking secrecy agreements, the study does not name any institution.

A total of 15 bankers – 10 loan officers and 5 heads of lending departments – participated in the survey. In their day-to-day work, the loan officers receive loan applications, screen these, investigate creditworthiness, pass their opinions on to the credit committee and communicate with applicants. The loan officers can make decisions on small loans (max. EUR 2,000). A head of a lending departments is a member of the bank's credit committee and decides on loans (larger than EUR 2,000) together with other four members.

The documents observed in detail at one particular bank were:

- internal working instructions, such as a general directive of assignment (in force from 1.1.2002), a sample contract of employment, work rules for granting loans to enterprises and institutions (in force until 1.1.2002), lending procedure rules (in force from 1.1.2002), working instructions for the Credit Committee (in force from 1.1.2002), directives for portfolio management (draft),
- guidelines, such as credit policy (draft), credit risk assessment procedure (draft),
- management notes, such as the organisational structure of the Credit Department and Credit Department Restructuring Plan,
- portfolio analysis (first occurred in December 2001) including loan classification, watch list,
- credit files of ten granted loans – 4 short term and 6 medium term – these include credit application, credit memorandum, the minutes of the credit committee, credit information report, cash flow projections, spread sheet

format, cash flow statement, collateral, repayment schedule. These loans were granted to different small and large enterprises. They operate in trading – mostly technical machines and food – and in manufacturing – mostly export oriented products.

3.2.2 Instrumentation: Key Concepts and Questions

Concept mapping

Concept mapping is to some extent a kind of modification of a standardised open-ended interview. Both concept mapping and interviewing allow observation of how the people have organised the world and the meanings they attach to what goes on in the world. The difference is the interviewee or respondent is expressing his or her own understanding not in words, but by visualising their perceptions with maps. The advantages maps have over classical techniques are:

- another manner of presentation which differs from the selective and sequential manner and affords interviewees a better opportunity to illustrate their ideas;
- a faculty to diagnose structure.

Each banker is asked to produce maps on sub-domains or semantic cores "Risk and Risk Management", "Credit Risk Management and Credit Approval" and "Bank and Bank Regulation". The map on each sub-domain visualises the action-regulating knowledge of the banker in respect of the respective semantic core, thus his mental model. The composition of key concepts for semantic cores are illustrated below.

The number of node concepts for concept mapping differs in surveys from 10 to 50. There are likewise many varieties, from prescribed position of nodes and pre-labelled lines to free positioning and free-labelling, or mapping out freely with pencil and paper. The survey decided in favour of concept maps with 15 (map I), 48 (map II) and 25 (map III) nodes written on adhesive labels and the option of free placement of nodes and freely creation of propositions by labelling lines. This is justified by (i) a reasonable compromise between meaningful representation of the sub-domain and the danger of complexity – with regard to the number of nodes, and (ii) the fact that it is a research survey and not an audit test for students – free positioning and no pre-labelled lines. As already noted, the lists of concepts are founded by hypothetical models based on banking theory in a market-based economy and complemented with results of pre-tests with German bankers.

The first sub-domain "Risk and Risk Management" includes 15 concepts, thus different knowledge fields of the semantic core which are interrelated to each other (Figure 3.5):

- causality relations with concepts *Uncertainty*, *Return*;
- situational relations with concept *Risk;*
- goal with concept *Credit default;*
- operation and process with concepts *Bank supervision*, *Reserves;*
- benefits concepts *Information*, *Transparency*.

Additionally, further four concepts were added to give the interviewee the opportunity to make his or her own emphasis: *Chance*, *Avoidance*, *Bankruptcy* and *Probability*. These single concepts written on cards were handed to the interviewees, who were asked to build a map placing these concepts systematically and showing the interrelationship between them.

An important point here is to prepare the participants: introducing them to the method of concept mapping, doing exercises on relatively simple and easily comprehensible semantic cores, such as "Living things" or "Money". The following instructions given by the interviewer are guidelines. These can be oral first and than better displayed on a board or screen:

1. Please sort through the cards, and put to one side any that have a term you don't know or which you think is not related to any other term.
2. Put the remaining cards on the sheet of paper, and arrange them in a way that makes sense to you. Terms you see as related should be kept fairly close together, but leave space between even the closest cards.
3. When you are satisfied with your arrangement of the cards, stick them to the sheet.
4. Now, please draw lines between the terms you see to be related.
5. Write on each line the nature of the relation between the terms. It can help to put an arrowhead on the line to show how to read the relation.
6. If you put any cards to one side in the first step, go back to these and see if you now want to add any to the map. If you do add any, make sure you write the nature of the links between them and the other terms.

Figures 3.2 and 3.6 illustrate concepts for the second sub-domain "Credit Risk Management and Credit Approval". In order to allow an easy overview (illustration), this sub-domain has been split into two semantic cores, first "Credit Investigation" (33 concepts):

- causality relations with concept *Credit application;*
- situational relations with concept *Credit investigation;*
- goal concept *Credit risk;*
- operation concepts *Provision of data, Data processing, Data analysis*;
- conditions concepts *Reliability of data, Access to data;*
- means concepts *Market position, Personal conversation, On-site inspection, Quality of products;*
- partners concepts *Bank of Mongolia, Ratings, Acquaintance and friends, Loan Information Pool, History, Standard&Poor's;*
- results concepts *Financial situation, Quality of earnings, Leverage equity structure, Asset quality, Liquidity, Personal integrity, Credit facility.*

Alternative concepts, such as *Collateral, Guarantee, Reputation, Moody's, Parliament, Government, Relatives,* complement the list.

The second semantic core of this sub-domain is "Credit Risk Management" (15 concepts):

- causality concept *Credit risk* (already in the first semantic core);
- situational concept *Credit risk management;*
- goal concepts *Credit risk strategy, Bank's business policy, Safety, Profitability, Liquidity* (already in the first semantic core);
- operation concepts *Measuring, Screening, Diversifying, Monitoring*;
- conditions concepts *Bank supervision requirements, Bank internal instructions;*
- result concepts *Credit risk limitation.*

Additional concepts, such as *Credit policy, Credit committee, Portfolio,* were added as complements.

The sub-domain "Banking and Bank Supervision" consists of 25 concepts, a detailed listing of which is in the Annexes 3 and 4.

The maps built by bankers were than systemised and evaluated. The evaluation concludes (a) the presence of a particular concept in the map, (b) the position of the concept in the overall scheme, (c) whether a relationship is established to other concepts, and (d) if and how this relationship is described. After scoring the concepts and relationships, evaluation items are formulated (to follow in chapter 3.3 on data analysis and findings), which are a foundation for further content analysis.

Figure 3.5: Reference map for action-regulating knowledge on sub-domain "Risk and Risk Taking"
Source: own illustration

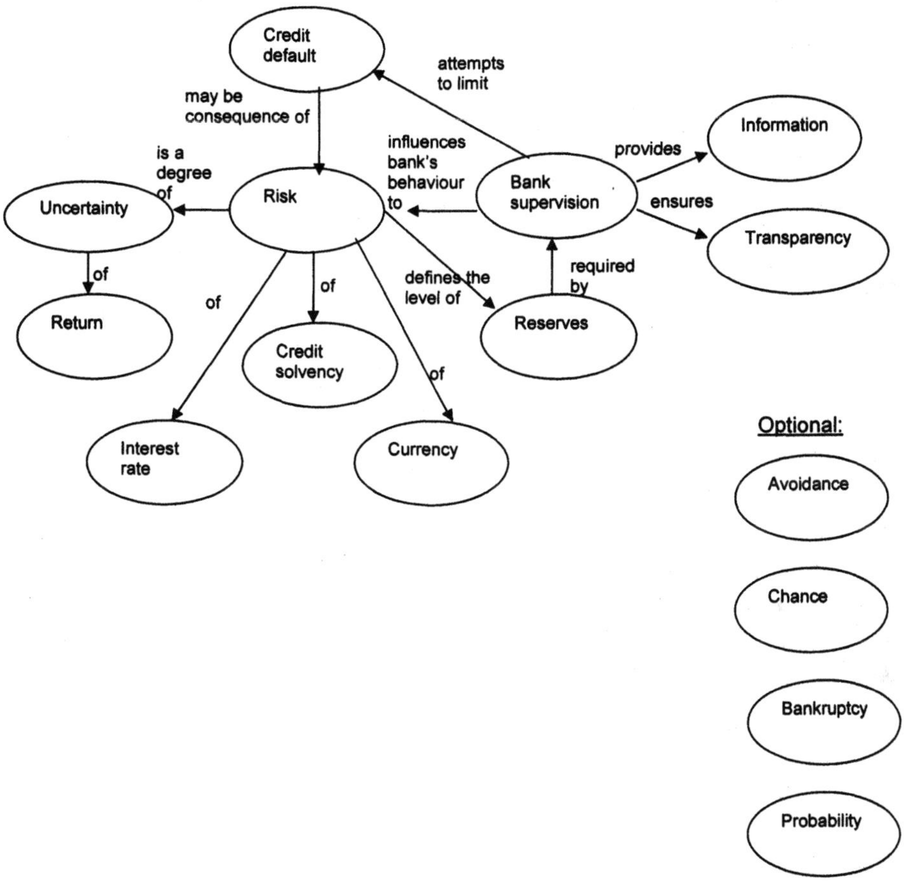

Figure 3.6: Reference map for action-regulating knowledge on sub-domain "Credit Risk Management"
Source: own illustration

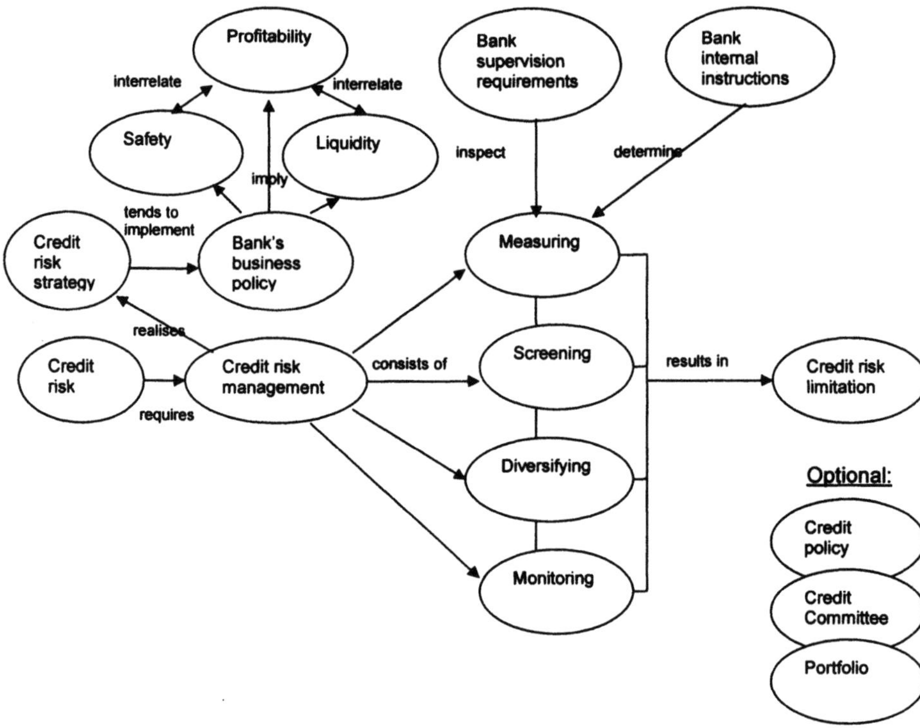

Individual interviews

As Patton (1987: 115) argues, "the fundamental principle of qualitative interviewing is to provide a framework, within which respondents can express their own understandings in their own terms".

In order to learn things which cannot be directly observed (feelings, thoughts, intentions; behaviours that took place at some previous time; situations which preclude the presence of an observer), a method of in-depth interviewing is used to enter the other person's perspective. This interviewing allows observation of how people have organised the world and the meanings they attach to what goes on in the world. An in-depth interview probes beneath the surface, soliciting detail and providing a holistic understanding of the interviewee's point of view. Interviews add an inner perspective to outward behaviours.

The three types of in-depth, open-ended interviews differ by the extent to which interview questions are determined and standardised before the interview is held: the informal conversational interview, the general interview guide approach, and the ***standardised open-ended interview***. The latter consists of a set of questions carefully worded and arranged for the purpose of taking each respondent through the same sequence and asking each respondent the same questions with essentially the same words.

The standardised interview may be particularly appropriate when several people are to conduct interviews and the researcher wishes to reduce the variation in responses. That ensures that the data obtained are systematic and thorough for each respondent. Limiting the variations in responses is also important due to the limited period of time. The data collected are still open-ended in the sense that the interviewee supplies his or her own words, thoughts, and insights in answering the questions. The main advantage of the standardised open-ended interview is that the systematic interview reduces the interviewer's judgement during the interview.

With the aim of adding an inner perspective to the outward behaviour of bankers, this study utilised standardised and open-ended questions. During an one and a half hours interview each, ten loan officers were asked 25 questions about their day-to-day work, their experiences (successes and failures), their opinion and feelings (co-operation within the bank).

The questions were conceptualised on the basis of the action-slot model. They were formulated in their content and in their sequence in a way appropriate to the knowledge fields of the action-slot model (Figure 3.1). Thus, for instance, the interviewees were asked about:

- causes of lending: "Which credit applications go through lending process?";
- signals: "How far are credit risk and trust cohered at your own option?";
- goals: "To which extent is your job concerned with credit risk?";
- process: "If there would be something you always have to keep in mind when granting a loan, what would it be?" and so forth.

Table 3.1 shows the knowledge fields and the actual interview questions. The questions are concerned with the present (which colleagues do you intensively co-operate with during credit analysis?), the past (how many of credit applications are returned without a credit investigation?) and involve one future-oriented question (what do you think, when will your bank and branches be able to grant loans with maturity of more than 2 years?). The exact sequence of the questions and the introductions to them are shown as an interview sheet in Annex 5.

On the basis of the interview notes, response units were formulated and the their strength was scored as a percentage. These response units are the foundation for further content analysis and conclusions (Table 3.10 to follow in chapter 3.3 on data analysis and findings).

Observing documents and records

Not only historians, but also scientists in other fields, deploy a method ***of historical studying***. Studying primary sources, documents created at the time in question, allows a development picture to be created of what happened. Examples of existing records – systematic accounts of regular occurrences – for any implementation are internal instructions and legal documents, progress charts and checklists, activity or field-trip rosters, correspondence, logs and diaries kept by personnel and management, circulation files and in-house memos, newspaper articles etc.

The important function of this method for analysing implementation is to answer the question: what are the materials, operations and administrative arrangements that constitute an activity, and if and how the combination of materials, operations, and administrative arrangements leads to the achievement of action's objectives (King et al.: 1987, 9)? As far as data collection and analysis are concerned – the process is not so much linear but rather holistic - they occur interactively as an observation. Other data suggest categories for the analysis and the analysis suggests additional

Table 3.1: Knowledge fields / semantic relations and questions of open-ended interview
Source: own work out

Knowledge fields / Semantic relations	Questions
Cause	Q3. Which credit applications go through credit investigation?
Signal / Activation	Q17. How far are credit risk and trust cohered at yours own option?
Goals	Q15. To which extent is your job concerned with credit risk?
	Q24. Suppose you are asked by an apprentice what is the best credit, what and how would you explain?
	Q14. Which basic principle is loan granting based on in your opinion?
Condition/ Process	Q18. If there would be something you always have to keep in mind, when granting a loan, what would it be?
	Q12. Suppose I would like to work as a loan officer. What skills should I have?
	Q20. What seems to be the most important factor for the ultimate decision on granting a loan?
	Q25. Which influence has the co-operation of international supervision institutions with the BOM on your activities?
	Q23. What do you think is the reason for the lack of long term loans?
	Q16. What relationship do you think exists between collateral and credit risk?
Measures/ Operations	Q5. How long does it take from the time of credit application receipt of a definitive decision?
	Q19. Which operation do you think is the most important for your job?
Means	Q6. Which documents and data, from where and from whom, do you use to conduct credit investigation?
	Q7. Which data do you usually have to procure in addition?
	Q8. How far are on-site inspections of significance? What is the objective of doing it?
	Q13. Which costs are incurred by credit investigation?
Partners	Q9. Which colleagues do you intensively co-operate with during credit analysis?
	Q10. Which colleagues do you work with after credit analysis but before a definitive decision is made on granting a loan?
	Q11. Which colleagues do you work closely with during the credit?
Results/ Benefits	Q21. How do you value the role and contribution of credit investigation for decision making on granting loans?
	Q22. How significant are the last legal reforms for granting loans?

data needs. Gradually the researcher produces a description of the events and an interpretation of them.

Records are kept independently of the researcher or evaluator, therefore the information found in records tends to be viewed as objective and credible. They also have the advantage of enabling data to be assessed without inconveniencing the staff. The main disadvantage is that records are very often incomplete. Due to the stress of day-to-day work or by other informal factors, people forget to sign in or to record an event or keep track of all the relevant information. Besides the fact that examining the existing records can be very time consuming, the researcher often has to overcome ethical or legal constraints and willingness problems.

The semantic relations of the action-slot model (Figure 3.1) – or knowledge fields - underlay the decision on categories to look for whilst examining the records. Critical categories are outlined in Table 3.2. The tangible remains of lending occurrences which could also be accessed and other documents listed in Sampling (3.2.1) were searched for the listed categories.

Table 3.2: Semantic relations / knowledge fields and critical categories of document observation

Source: own work out

Semantic relations/ Knowledge fields	Critical Categories
Cause	Definition of credit investigation within loan granting activity
Signal / Activation	Adherence of instructions
Goals	Definition of credit risk
Process / Conditions	Skills descriptions Procedures and instructions Compulsive activities Lines of authority for important decisions Further administrative arrangements, such as office discipline, abuse of power Any models of organisation that prescribe arrangements and procedures for effective management Group process models which underpin social action, loan handling, customers
	Changes occurred in these arrangements
Measures/ Operations	Offices and branches involved in lending Staff, including administrators, instructors, aides, secretaries and decision makers, including their number, the particular characteristics that made them eligible, and their level of competence, loan administration
Means	Resources, particularly resources purchased especially for credit investigation
	Materials used
	Level of expenditure
Partners	Staff, including administrators, instructors, aides, secretaries Procedures prescribed for the staff in their interaction with clients
Results/ Benefits	Credit portfolio, granted and withdrawn loans, earnings

The most challenging thing is the transfer data from the records examined. A lending procedure schedule was established for this purpose to visualise the collected data concerning who is doing what and when during lending. A short version of the schedule is contained in Table 3.3 (and a full version in Annex 6). Moreover, a data collection control roster (Annex 7) was set up with questions concerning the categories defined above. The notes from observation are formulated in form of observation items made in Table 3.10, the content of which is further analysed and formulated in findings (chapter 3.3).

3.2.3 Procedure

The steps taken to contact research participants, to obtain their co-operation and to administer the data collection instruments and their sequence are described in this sub-chapter. A schedule plan for data collection with successive phases is shown in Annex 8.

The preparatory logistics for the survey were not easy. Finding a partner interested in the research findings and willing to grant access to data was of key importance and the main difficulty in actually implementing the study. Several organisations were contacted, among these the Bank of Mongolia, the Ministry of Economy and Finance of Mongolia, five commercial banks and a German financial institution which co-operates with Mongolian banks in a development program to strengthen financial intermediation and services in Mongolia. Following an exchange of intents during phone calls and personal meetings, it was agreed that interviews could be held with bankers at three major banks, access to documents of program loans was granted at one particular bank. The next step was to obtain the acquiescence of Mongolian banks. Ensuring confidentiality on the part of the researcher and advising professors entailed entering a professional secrecy agreement and arranging the technical planning of the field excursion.

The field excursion started immediately thereafter and lasted a total of thirty five (22 plus 13) working days. The sequence of methods was chosen with the following points in mind:

- Some results from the document observation method can deliver information for better instrumentation of key concepts for the concept mapping method. Individual interviews enable missing data to be added after concept mapping.

- The less invasive (upon action-regulation) document observation method is implemented prior to the more invasive method of concept mapping (through thinking aloud).

Before starting the survey proper, the concepts chosen after the pre-tests in Germany needed to be pre-tested again. For this purpose, two bank supervision officers at the BOM, two bankers and a businessman were asked to build concept maps in relevant sub-domains. After evaluation, the concepts were slightly adjusted and the list of all concepts was ready to be printed out.

The first port of call was a two-week stay at one of the sampled banks. After being introduced to the staff and told of the administrative arrangements, the researcher was given intern status and a desk was provided in the office of credit department with ten other bank officers (HD, SLO, SCC, five LOs and two accountants). It was only possible to stay in the office during working hours from 9 a.m. till 6 p.m., except in three cases to 7 p.m. An overview of documents and records to be observed was also made on the same day in order to arrange a necessary modification to the timetable. The first six days involved intensive work with records (internal working instructions and policies, credit files of granted loans). This included obtaining documents, reading, checking up, comparing, transferring data, clarifying issues, feedback meetings and discussions, and assuring interim results. It should be pointed out that all staff were, on the whole, courteous and co-operative, except in one case of personal unwillingness (but solved by prescription of EXD) and a refusal as a matter of principle (no documents of withdrawn loans can be shown).

Inspecting the credit files more closely, the pre-arrangements for concept mapping were made by modifying the reference maps on the basis of interim results and making appointments with the head of credit department and senior loan officer. The data collection procedure with concept mappings was completed at the first bank within four days. Two groups of loan officers each drew concept maps during a three hours period in the bank's assembly room. The objective of the survey, the method of concept mapping and its role, were introduced to the loan officers in the first three quarters of the first hour. The loan officers were also given illustrated examples and practiced mapping techniques by building a map on "Money" (Figures 3.4). After reading carefully the instructions on steps given by interviewer once again, they were then given the remaining two and a quarter hours to each draw separate maps using the concept cards handed out. As the mapping took place during working hours (mandatory participation), a degree of hastiness was evident among the loan officers.

Two of them, seemingly pressurised by the volume of work planned for the rest of the day, delivered their maps in just over an hour. The remainder took around two hours.

The next stage, making appointments with bankers from the other two banks, turned out to be the most difficult one. The bankers preferred ad-hoc appointments, so that concept maps were generated in every location imaginable, from a conference room, office via doctor's waiting room to a restaurant and a pub. At times it took a whole day to construct one single map (including start-up, instructions, exercises etc). But once an appointment had been made and the interviewer and interviewee were sitting face to face, all those interviewed took sufficient time out to produce serious maps.
Having dealt with the maps, individual interviews were started whilst continuing the investigation of credit files, documents and clarifying talks with staff. The interview sheet was modified shortly beforehand due to interim results and several attempt made to arrange appointments. However, most of the loan officers wanted an ad hoc appointment for the interview and these took place in due course. Within a five day period, fifteen bankers were interviewed for up to two and a half hours each.

The interviews were started with an introduction, underlining their importance for the study. Four technical questions were then asked about the number of credit applications and the duration of the credit investigation process. These were followed by inquiries into the day-to-day work of bankers, accompanied by questions about their opinions, beliefs and knowledge. The interview was concluded with questions concerning their experiences and feelings. The interviewer additionally made notes on non-verbal observations made during the interview. It should be emphasised that all the bankers were interested in the interviews and took enough time out to answer the questions.

As the pre-tests had shown that recording an interview on tape detracted from the willingness of the bankers to open up and express themselves freely during the interview (some interviewees even explicitly rejected it), the interviewer decided in favour of taking detailed notes during the interview. Actual quotations were gathered as far as possible, for example, by reading the notes back to the interviewees and asking for their confirmation.

The follow-up activities to the field excursion consisted of checking the completeness of the collected data and obtaining any missing information during the last two days by meeting the bankers in their free time.

3.3 Lending Practice and Bank Regulation (Results)

The data collected by the triangulation of methods are now analysed and interpreted. Sub-chapter 3.3.1 analyses the data by ordering and organising it into categories and basic descriptive units – evaluation items, observation items, and response items. Sub-chapter 3.3.2 then attaches meaning to the analysis by explaining descriptive units and looking for relationships and linkages between the descriptive dimensions. Evaluation statements are thereby devised as initial insights.

3.3.1 Data Analysis

As previously explained about the qualitative design of the research, the data analysis procedure in the qualitative research is interactive and more fluid than quantitative approaches. Making sense of usually voluminous data in a naturalistic sense involves processing the data using techniques of inductive analysis. It is also necessary to go through a number of cycles of data analysis before arriving at the final findings. Figure 3.7 illustrates the data analysis procedure conducted here.

Analysing the data form concept mapping (main analysis)

The data from concept mapping is analysed in two stages: rough evaluation (qualitative) and detailed evaluation (qualitative-quantitative). The **rough evaluation** process provides an overall structure, leading to general conclusions and indications of where the main focus of the detailed evaluation should lie. The following questions paved the way for the rough evaluation analysis:

- Which concepts were sorted out?
- Are there any concepts situated in the centre with exceptionally many connections attached?
- Are the most important interrelations reproduced?
- Which conclusions can be drawn?

The results of the rough evaluation of the maps I ("Risk and Risk Taking") shown in Table 3.4 confirm the direction of study's analysis. *Chance* and *Probability* were the concepts most frequently sorted out. Although the *Risk* and *Bank Supervision* concepts were situated in the centre, the connections from and to them were misleading or not labelled. Thus the understanding of risk – its definition and classification – and risk behaviour of Mongolian bankers is deficient. Moreover, the majority of bankers do not see risk as a chance, but as a purely negative factor, which needs to be eliminated.

Table 3.3: Lending procedure (short version)

Source: own work out

Actions implemented by	SCC	LO	LR	LL	SLO	HD	CC	HC	EXD
1. Receiving the application, examining the satisfaction of the processing requirements	O								
2. Choosing a loan officer and forwarding the application for credit analysis	O, DM								
8. Inspecting the asset for pledging on site, taking photo or doing video tape-recording		O	O						
10. Evaluating the suggested collateral of the borrower			O	O					
11. Collecting appropriate data and information in order to analyse (screen) the credit		O							
13. Analysing the borrower and the credit risk		O							
14. Assessing the application documents (for conformity to legal requirements)				O					
16. Completing the analysis, making a suggestion (proposal) for granting the loan		DM							
19. Presenting the credit memorandum for further examination to the HC and SCC		O							
20. Examining the credit risk, the content of memorandum and credibility of loan assessment						O			
21. Making his or her own opinion (written and with a signature) before submitting to the CC members						O			
24. Studying the memorandum and writing his or her own opinion separately							O		
26. Deciding whether to discuss the applied credit within the CC								DM	
28. Examining the credit risk								O	
30. Chairing the meeting of the CC								O	
31. Reporting on the portfolio					O				
32. Monitoring the credit portfolio structure					O		O		
33. Deciding on the credit approval					(DM)	DM, T	DM, T	DM T	
37. Reporting the EXD about the decisions of the CC								O	
38. Monitoring the decisions of the CC									O
39. Veto for the decisions of the CC, if necessary									DM

Legend: **LO** Loan officer, **SCC** Secretary of the Credit Committee (called also as loan administration officer), **HC** Head of the Credit Committee (simultaneously first deputy director of the bank), **CC** Credit Committee (director and four members named by the executive director of the bank), **HD** Head of the Credit Department, **LR** Officer of the Loan Recovery Department, **SLO** Senior loan officer, **LL** Lawyer responsible for loan affairs, **EXD** Executive Director, **O** Operational action, **DM** Decision making action, **T** Team decision.

Figure 3.7: Data analysis procedure

Source: own work out

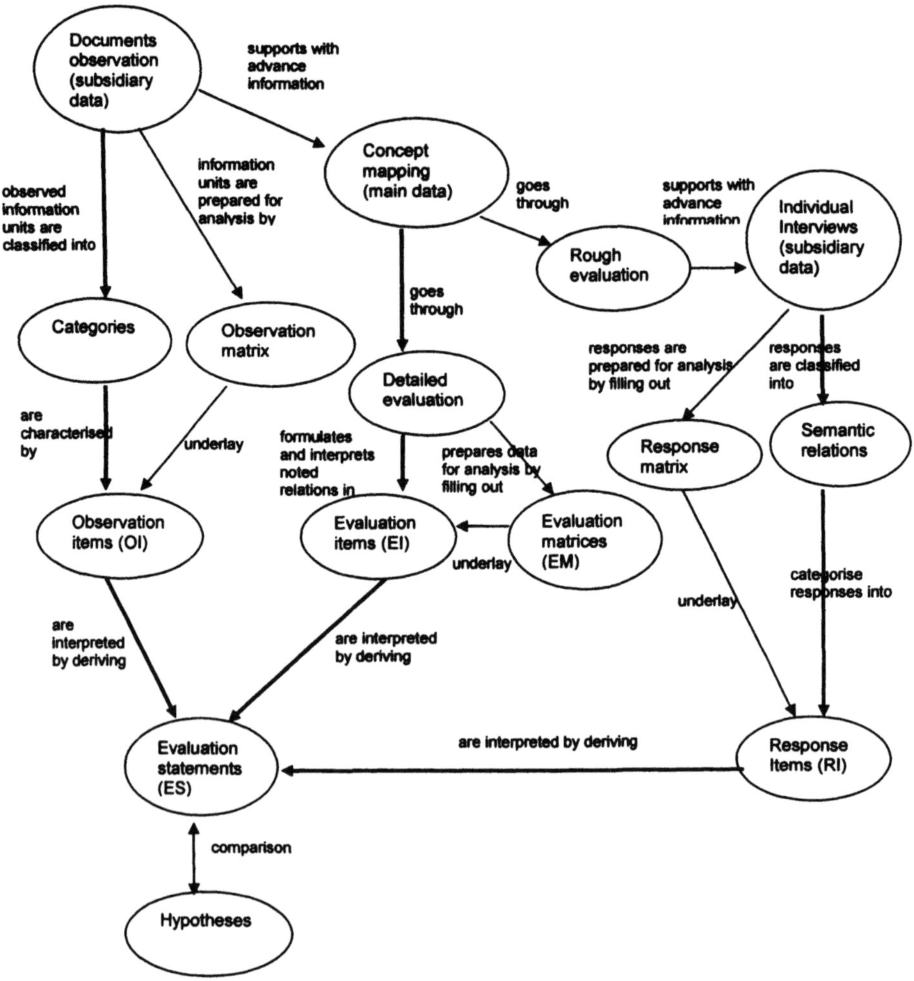

Table 3.4: Summing-up the rough evaluation results of map I "Risk and Risk Taking"
Source: own work out based on 15 maps, in brackets – number of maps concerned

	Map I **Risk and Risk Taking**
Concepts mostly sorted out	*Chance* (in 5 of 15), *Distance* (6), *Probability* (5)
Concepts centred, attached with many connections	*Bank supervision* (8), *Risk* (5)
Important interrelations produced	• In 7 maps, *Risk* is recognised as a main concept, but its definition and relation with other concepts is rather indistinct. • The relationship between *Risk* and *Reserves* is denoted (5) but not precisely defined. • The tasks of *Bank supervision* are to limit *Risk* in banking (4), to influence *Reserves* (3), to provide *Information* and to ensure *Transparency* (9), to guarantee *Credit solvency* (9), to allow *Chance* (3) and even to ensure *Return* (3). • Relations (9) linked from *Distance* to *Risk* (6), *Credit default* (2), *Bank supervision* (1). • No clearly defined relationship between *Chance* and *Risk* (14).
Conclusions	• The understanding of *Risk* (definition and classification) and its relation to *Reserve* and *Bank supervision* is deficient. • *Risk* is not seen as *Chance*, but as a purely negative factor which needs to be eliminated. • Banks are strongly reliant on *Bank supervision* for providing reliable data. • Bankers expect that *Bank supervision* would guarantee *Credit solvency*.

Figure 3.8: Examples of map I "Risk and Risk Taking"

Source: reproduction of the concept maps of participants 4 and 9.

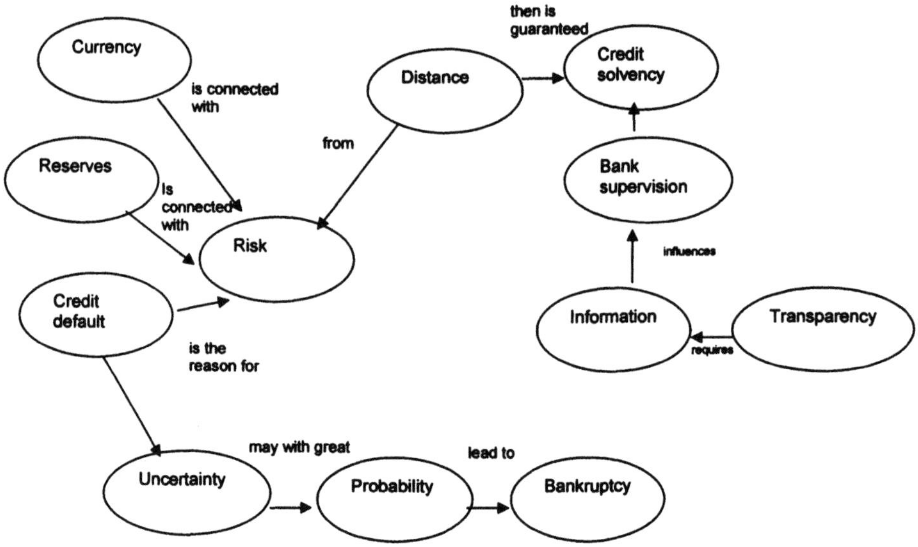

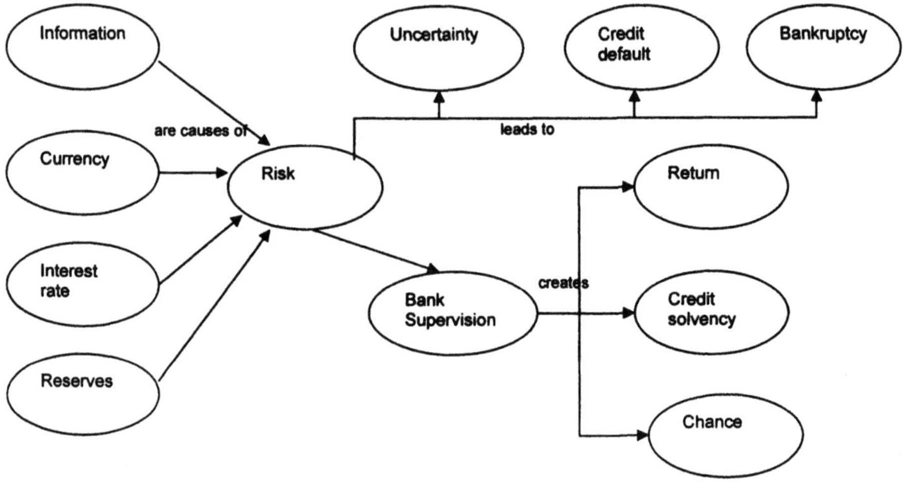

There is definitely an incomplete (if not erroneous) perception on the functions and targets of bank supervision in Mongolia – e.g. to guarantee credit solvency. Two examples of map I, drawn by participants 4 and 9, are reproduced in Figure 3.8.

The rough evaluation of maps II (Credit Risk Management and Credit Approval) would seem to indicate that Credit risk is a known and seemingly topical term, but bankers can do nothing about it as regards its content (Annex 9). The bankers point out structural components of the credit approval process with such concepts as Data analysis, Credit policy, Credit Committee, Credit investigation, Personal integrity and Financial situation. But the tasks of Credit risk management are not identified: it is neither defined nor its main components recognized. The bankers mostly built episodic, simple relations to this concept and it is not illustrated as a process.

In addition, importance is attached to personal relationships and state hierarchy during lending. If the concepts *Relatives* and *Clan* were not sorted out, they were linked to the concepts *Credit investigation*, *Personal integrity* and *Credit facility*. Moreover, *Acquaintance and friend* play an important role for the *Provision of data*. Concepts such as *Monitoring*, *Parliament* and *Government* are furthermore often centred and linked to concepts such as *Data analysis, Credit Committee* and *Management*. Finally, the maps demonstrate that banking in Mongolia is based on a house bank relationship (lines between concepts *Bank's business policy* and *Credit application* labelled with such words like current account etc.). Figure 3.9 illustrates a concept map drawn by one of the bankers.

In map III (Banking and Bank Supervision), key concepts such as *RAROC (risk-adjusted return on capital)* or *BIS (Bank for International Settlements), Basel Committee, Basel I* and *Basel II* were sorted out (Annex 10). Many connections were attached to concepts such as *Bank Activity, Bank Supervision* and *Bank Governance*, and most of these connections interlink with the *Guarantee* and *Warning* concepts. It can therefore be concluded that important issues of international bank supervision are not known by Mongolian bankers. Apart from accepting bank regulation as an significant institution, there is an incomplete, if not erroneous, perception of the functions and targets of bank supervision – as also shown in the results of map I ("Risk and Risk Taking").

Figure 3.9: Example of map II "Credit Risk Management and Credit Approval"
Source: reproduction of concept map of participant 10

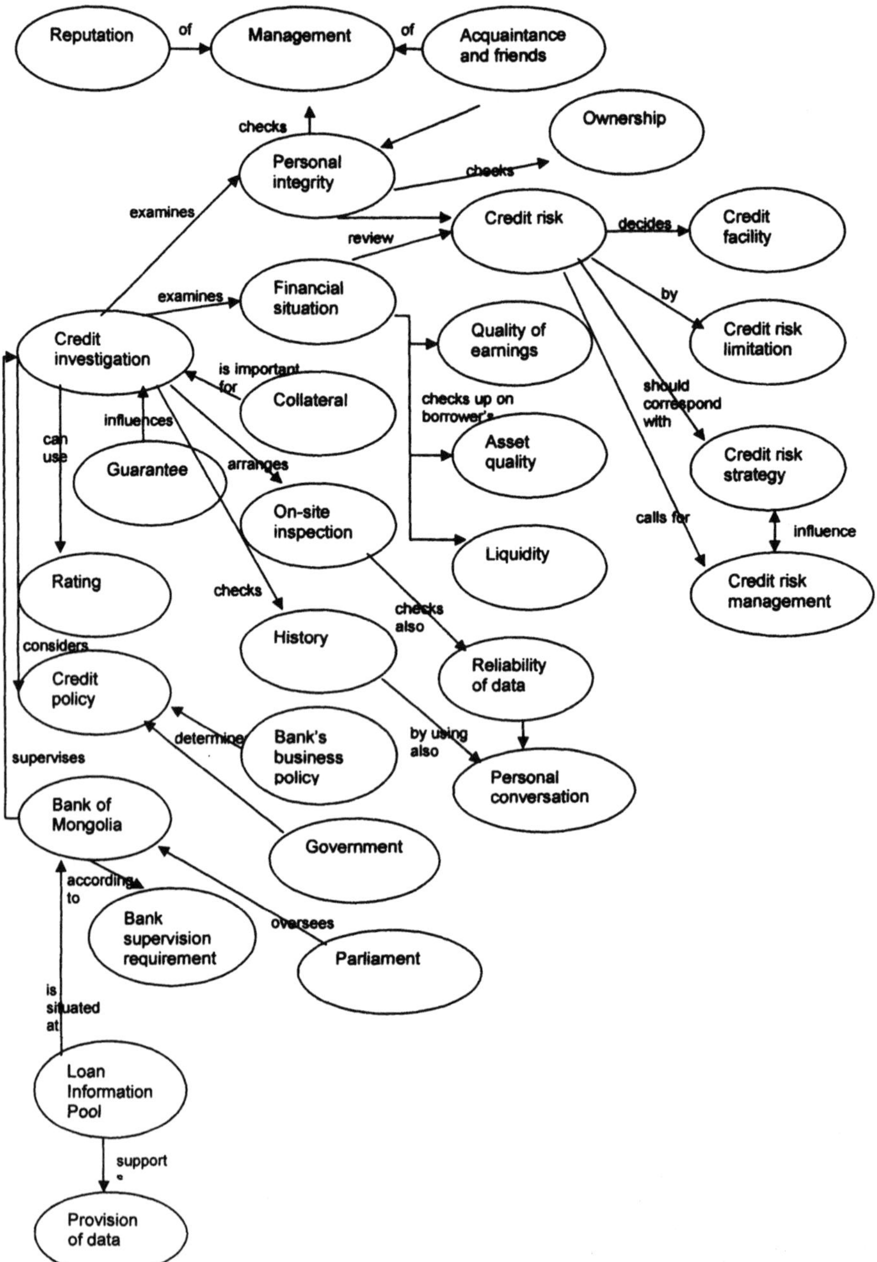

Guided by these general ideas, the **detailed evaluation** looks for meaningful insights. In order to prepare the data for analysis, an **evaluation matrix** (EM) for each concept map was produced by using the aforesaid codification[36] (Table 3.5) for revealed – or missing – relations between concepts (based on the action-slot model), thus for the propositions in the concept maps.

Table 3.5: Codification system for propositions in concept maps
Source: based on Peuckert et al. (1999: 124 et seq.)

Relationship (Proposition)	Example of Proposition	Objection of Relationship	Potentiality of Relationship
SR simple relation	*Risk* is somehow related to *Reserves.*	O(SR)	P(SR)
SC simple characteristic	*Risk* of *Interest rate, Risk* of *Currency.*	O(SC)	P(SC)
DR definitional relation	*Risk* is a degree of *Uncertainty* of *Return.*	O(DR)	P(DR)
D dependence	*Provision of data* depends on *access to data.*	O(D)	P(D)
C condition	*Measuring* and *Monitoring* of *Credit risk* have to conform to *Bank supervision requirements.*	O(R)	P(C)
R reason	*Uncertainty* causes *Risk.*	O(R)	P(R)
A activity / measure	*Financial situation* decides on *Credit facility.* *Bank supervision* attempt to limit *Credit default.*	O(A)	P(A)
MP mean or partner	*Data analysis* with support of *BOM.* *Data analysis* by means of *On-site inspection.*	O(MP)	P(MP)

An evaluation matrix for each concept map (of each participant) is filled out using the codification to prepare the data. 15 participants created 3 maps each (in 3 sub-domains), 45 evaluation matrices altogether were filled out. An evaluation matrix is shown below on the basis of map I ("Risk and Risk Taking") generated by participant 4 (P4) – Table 3.6. Table 3.7 gives an example of an evaluation matrix for map II from participant 10 (P10).

On the basis of 45 EMs, all types of proposition – two concepts connected with labelled or unlabelled line within a concept map – generated in the concept maps were specified. 30 different types of propositions[37] were classified in 15 concept maps I, 150 propositions in 15 concept maps II and 40 propositions in 15 concept maps III (altogether 220). Not only connections generated directly from one concept to another were considered here, but also connections across concepts, bearing in mind the content of propositions.

---

36 This codification is based on "Berliner-Codier-System" which was evolved by scientists of FU Berlin for research proposals with concept mapping.

37 This in fact refers to the number of proposition types and not the sum of all propositions in every concept map, i.e. propositions with similar meanings are counted as one type.

Table 3.6: Evaluation matrix for map I "Risk and Risk Taking"

Source: own work out based on map I by participant 4

Concepts	Ri	Re	Un	Pr	IR	CS	Cu	Re	BS	CD	Tr	Di	Ba	Ch	Inf	Sum	%
Risk																	
Return																	
Uncertainty				SR												1	
Probability													A			1	
Interest rate																	
Credit solvency																	
Currency	D[38]															1	
Reserves	D															1	
Bank supervision						SR										1	
Credit default	C		SR													2	
Transparency															SR	1	
Distance	SC					A										2	
Bankruptcy																	
Chance																	
Information									A							1	
Sum	4		1	1		2			1				1		1	11	
Percentage																	

Having prepared the data base, the next step was to make sense of it. For this purpose, propositions were selected according to the content depth and the frequency with which they occurred. This selection is useful because it allows propositions to be purposefully sought out – in a wealth of data – which are important for answering the research questions posed by the study. These particular propositions are named **evaluation items** (EIs). The EIs characterise the kind of relationship generated between concepts. In order to avoid content distortions during the selection process, a few propositions were modified into more general formulations. Of the 30 propositions from map I "Risk and Risk Taking", 15 were selected as evaluation items. Those are:

1. The relationship between *Risk* and *Uncertainty* relies on the fact that banking comprises uncertainties (of return).
2. The relationship between *Uncertainty* and *Return* is based on the circumstance that uncertainties in banking refer to the return situation of a bank.
3. The relationship between *Risk* and *Credit Default* addresses the potential consequence of risk taking.
4. The relationship between *Risk* and *Bankruptcy* is due to the possibility that uncertainties in banking could be reflected in bank insolvency.

[38] See the codification at Table 3.5.

5. The relationship between *Risk* and *Avoidance* (Distance) is based on the (presumed) perception of bankers to eliminate (cut out) risk by acting.
6. The relationship between *Risk* and *Interest rate* represents interest rate risk as a specific risk of banking.
7. The relationship between *Risk* and *Credit solvency* illustrates credit solvency risk as a specific risk of banking.
8. The relationship between *Risk* and *Currency* evaluates currency risk as a specific risk of banking.
9. The relationship between *Risk* and *Chance* emphasises the fact that risk taking contains both potent losses as well as the opportunity to make profits.
10. The relationship between *Risk* and *Reserves* rests on the facility of risk coverage by means of reserves.
11. The relationship between *Risk* and *Bank supervision* is based on the circumstance that bank supervision makes bankers aware of risk taking and thus influences their risk behaviour.
12. The relationship between *Bank supervision* and *Information* refers to the task of bank supervision to provide bank specific information, to evaluate and procure such.
13. The relationship between *Bank supervision* and *Transparency* reflects the bankers' perception that bank supervision should ensure transparency in the banking sector.
14. The relationship between *Bank supervision* and *Credit default* is based on the role of bank supervision to limit losses through deliberate risk taking and to thus lower the probability of failure in the banking sector.
15. The relationship between *Bank supervision* and *Credit solvency* rests on the (presumed) perception of bankers that bank supervision has the function of guaranteeing credit solvency.

Table 3.9 and Annex 11 show the 58 evaluation items selected (from 150 propositions) from map II and the 20 evaluation items selected (from 40 propositions) from map III.

Using the EIs and 15 EMs (15 participants) from map I, one overall or cumulated matrix for map I "Risk and Risk Taking" was aggregated, as shown in Table 3.8. As a consequence of selection, it should be borne in mind that not every proposition of each EM is present in the cumulated matrix. The respective cumulated matrices for map II "Credit Risk Management and Credit Approval" and map III "Banking and Bank Supervision" are shown in Table 3.9 and Annex 11.

Table 3.7: Evaluation matrix for map II "Credit Risk Management and Credit Approval"

Source: own work out based on map II by participant 10

Concepts	Credit investigation	Credit risk	Provision of data	Reliability of data	Personal integrity	Financial situation	Credit facility	Credit risk limitation	Credit risk strategy	Credit risk management	Guarantee	Collateral	Management	Reputation	Acquaintance and friends	Ownership	On-site inspection	Personal conversation	History	Quality of earnings	Asset quality	Liquidity	Rating	Credit policy	Bank's business policy	Bank of Mongolia	Government	Parliament	Loan Information Pool	Bank supervision requirements	Sum	%
Credit investigation					A	A											A		D				MP	MP							6	
Credit risk							A	SC	D	R																					4	
Provision of data																															-	
Reliability of data																		SR													1	
Personal integrity		C											D			D															3	
Financial situation		C																		D	D	D									4	
Credit facility																															-	
Credit risk limitation																															-	
Credit risk strategy																															-	
Credit risk management																															-	
Guarantee	A																														1	
Collateral	SR																														1	
Management																															-	
Reputation													SC																		2	
Acquaintance and friends					SR								SC																		2	
Ownership																															-	
On-site inspection				A																											1	
Personal																															-	

conversation																																
History																	MP														1	
Quality of earnings																															-	
Asset quality																															-	
Liquidity																															-	
Rating																															-	
Credit policy																															-	
Bank's business policy																								DR							1	
Bank of Mongolia	A																													D	2	
Government																								SR							-	
Parliament																										A					1	
Loan information Pool			A																							MP					2	
Bank supervision requirements																															-	
Sum	3	2	1	1	2	1	1	1	1	1	-	-	3	-	-	1	1	2	1	1	1	1	1	3	-	2	-	-	-	1	32	
Percent																																

The last column of the cumulated matrix shows the magnitude of EIs (93 = 15 + 58 + 20) as a percentage. On the basis of the magnitude of evaluation items in the cumulated matrices, the EIs are interpreted and **evaluation statements** (ESs) derived from them. Sub-chapter 3.3.2 on the findings of the survey provides details of the evaluation statements by summarising the (content) results from the analysis of the data collected by means of all three methods – the main method of concept mapping, and the subsidiary methods of document observation and individual interviewing.

Before giving a brief overview of the data analysis of documents and interviews, the steps taken to analyse the data in the concept maps are shortly summarised (see Figure 3.7):

1 A rough evaluation of the concept maps guided by four questions.
2 Detailed evaluation of the concept maps:
   - preparing the data: the evaluation matrices were filled out using the codification system,
   - preparing the data: 220 propositions (30 + 150 + 40) were classified,
   - making sense of the data: selection of 93 evaluation items (15 + 58 + 20) from among 220 propositions by examining the depth and frequency of propositions,
   - making sense of the data: aggregation of the cumulated matrix for each sub-domain (map I, map II, map III),
   - making sense of the data: calculation of the magnitude of evaluation items in cumulative matrices,
   - making sense of the data: interpretation of the evaluation items and formulation of the evaluation statements (to follow in sub-chapter 3.3.2).

Table 3.8: Cumulated matrix for map I "Risk and Risk Taking"

Source: own work out based on evaluation matrices of 15 maps

EIs	Content of EIs	P1	P2	P3	P4	P5	P6	P7	P8	P9	P10	P11	P12	P13	P14	P15	S	%
EI 1	The relationship between *Risk* and *Uncertainty* relies on the fact that banking comprises uncertainties (of return).	R	SR	-	-	SR	SR	-	-	A	SR	C	-	-	A	DR	9	60
EI 2	The relationship between *Uncertainty* and *Return* is based on the circumstance that uncertainties in banking refer to the return situation of a bank.	-	-	-	-	-	C	-	-	-	-	-	-	-	SR	SC	3	20
EI 3	The relationship between *Risk* and *Credit default* addresses the potential consequence of risk taking.	R	D	-	DR	SR	SR	-	C	A	SR	C	R	-	SR	-	11	73
EI 4	The relationship between *Risk* and *Bankruptcy* is due to the possibility that uncertainties in banking could be reflected in bank insolvency.	R	P(A)	A	-	SR	SR	-	SR	A	SR	C	SR	-	A	P(A)	12	80
EI 5	The relationship between *Risk* and *Avoidance* (Distance) is based on the (presumed) perception of bankers to eliminate (cut out) risk by acting. <u>(control item)</u>	SR	-	SC	SC	SR	-	-	SR	R	-	SR	-	SR	-	-	8	53
EI 6	The relationship between *Risk* and *Interest rate* represents interest rate risk as a specific risk of banking.	P(dr)	-	A	-	-	SR	-	-	R	-	-	SR	-	-	SC	6	40
EI 7	The relationship between *Risk* and *Credit solvency* illustrates credit solvency risk as a specific risk of banking.	SR	-	-	-	-	-	-	-	-	-	SR	-	-	SR	SC	4	27
EI 8	The relationship between *Risk* and *Currency* evaluates currency risk as a specific risk of banking.	SR	-	-	D	-	SR	-	-	R	SR	-	SR	-	-	SC	7	47
EI 9	The relationship between *Risk* and *Chance* emphasises the fact that risk taking contains both potent losses as well as opportunity to make profits.	-	A	-	-	-	-	-	-	-	-	-	-	A	-	DR	3	20
EI 10	The relationship between *Risk* and *Reserves* rests on the facility of risk coverage by means of reserves.	-	-	-	SR	-	SR	-	-	R	-	-	-	-	-	SR	4	27

EI 11	The relationship between *Risk* and *Bank supervision* is based on the circumstance that bank supervision makes bankers aware of risk taking and thus influences their risk behaviour.	-	-	-	-	SR	-	A	-	SC	-	-	SR	-	-	A	5	33
EI 12	The relationship between *Bank supervision* and *Information* refers to the task of bank supervision to provide bank specific information, to evaluate and procure such.	-	SR	DR	R	SR	C	DR	SR	-	SR	D	-	-	SR	-	10	67
EI 13	The relationship between *Bank supervision* and *Transparency* bears on bankers' perception that bank supervision should ensure transparency in the banking sector.	SR	SR	C	SR	SR	SR	DR	SR	-	SR	C	D	-	SR	-	12	80
EI 14	The relationship between *Bank supervision* and *Credit default* is based on the role of bank supervision to limit losses through deliberate risk taking and to thus lower the probability of failure in the banking sector.	-	-	SR	-	SR	-	A	R	-	-	-	SR	R	-	-	6	40
EI 15	The relationship between *Bank supervision* and *Credit solvency* rests on the (presumed) perception of bankers that bank supervision has the function of guaranteeing credit solvency. (control item)	SR	-	SR	SR	SR	SR	A	R	A	SR	-	C	R	A	-	12	80

Codification: The proposition (relation) results from the way of reading from left upwards:

SR	Simple relation	**O(SR)**	Objection of SR	**P(SR)**	Potentiality of SR
SC	Simple characteristic	**O(SC)**	Objection of SC	**P(SC)**	Potentiality of SC
DR	Definitional relation	**O(DR)**	Objection of DR	**P(DR)**	Potentiality of DR
D	Dependence	**O(D)**	Objection of D	**P(D)**	Potentiality of D
C	Condition	**O(C)**	Objection of C	**P(C)**	Potentiality of C
R	Cause, Reason	**O(R)**	Objection of R	**P(R)**	Potentiality of R
A	Activity	**O(A)**	Objection of A	**P(A)**	Potentiality of A
MP	Means and Partner	**O(MP)**	Objection of MP	**P(MP)**	Potentiality of MP

Table 3.9: Cumulated matrix for map II "Credit Risk Management and Credit Approval"

Source: own work out based on evaluation matrices of 15 maps

EIs	Content of EIs	P1	P2	P3	P4	P5	P6	P7	P8	P9	P10	P11	P12	P13	P14	P15	S	%
EI 16	The relationship between *Credit risk* and *Screening* relies on essential operation of credit risk management to identify credit risk.			SR		SR										DR	3	20%
EI 17	The relationship between *Credit risk* and *Measuring* relies on essential operation of credit risk management to measure risk.			SR		SR										DR	3	20%
EI 18	The relationship between *Credit risk* and *Diversifying* relies on the task of credit risk management to limit credit risk.											SR				DR	2	13%
EI 19	The relationship between *Credit risk* and *Monitoring* relies on the task of credit risk management to watch credit risk..		A			SR	SR										3	20%
EI 20	The relationship between *Credit risk* and *Collateral* bears on the relevance of collateral as an instrument of risk limitation.			SR								SR					2	13%
EI 21	The relationship between *Credit risk* and *Guarantee* bears on the relevance of guaranties as an instrument of risk limitation.			SR								SR					2	13%
EI 22	The relationship between *Credit risk* and *Credit Committee* bears on the fact that the subject matter of Credit Committee's decisions is the credit risk.	SR					SR	A	A	SR		SR		A		SR	8	53%
EI 23	The relation between *Credit risk* and *Credit policy* illustrates that risk taking is decided in the framework of credit policy of respective bank.					SC	C			SR	MP	SR				SR	6	40%
EI 24	The relationship between *Credit risk* and *Credit facility* relies on the importance of credit risk for the decision on credit facility.		SR		R		SR		A	SR	A	SR		A		SR	9	60%
EI 25	The relationship between *Credit facility* and *Credit Committee* is due to the fact that the Credit Committee makes decisions on any credit facility.		SR	SR	A	SR	SR	A	SR	SR		SR	SR	A	A	C	13	87%
EI 26	The relationship between *Credit facility* and *Credit policy* is based on the fact that decisions on credit facility are made within the framework of bank's credit policy.			SR			SR	SR		SR		SR			A	C	7	47%
EI 27	The relationship between *Credit facility* and *Credit investigation* emphases that the decision on credit facility premises a credit investigation.		A	C	SR	C	D		A	SR		SR	SR	C	A		11	73%
EI 28	The relationship between *Financial situation* and *Collateral* bears on the role of collateral for results of examination of financial situation.		SR	SR	C	SR	C		C	SR			SR	SR	C	D	11	73%
EI 29	The relationship between *Financial situation* and *Guarantee* bears on the role of guarantees for results of examination of financial situation.		SR		D	SR	D			SR		SR		D	D		8	53%

EI 30	The relationship between *Credit investigation* and *Rating* relies on the relevance of rating for results of credit investigation.				DR		MP				MP				MP		4	27%
EI 31	The relationship between *Rating* and *Moody's/ Standard&Poor's* relies on the acknowledgement about Moody's or Standard&Poor's as leading rating agencies.								SR	DR							2	13%
EI 32	The relationship between *Credit Committee* and *Credit policy* emphases that Credit Committee – in her decisions – has to abide by directives of bank's credit policy.			DR	A	SR	A		D			SR	SR		A	C	9	60%
EI 33	The relationship between *Credit investigation / Data analysis* and *History* emphases that the history of the borrower is of importance for analysis of credit investigation.		D	DR	A				SR		D	SR	SR		A	C	9	60%
EI 34	The relationship between *Data analysis* and *Market position* emphases that the market position of borrower is of importance for the analysis during credit investigation.		A	DR	SR		A		C	SR							6	40%
EI 35	The relationship between *Data analysis* and *Quality of products* emphases that during credit investigation quality of products or services of borrower are analysed.		A	DR	SR	SR	A			SR							6	40%
EI 36	The relationship between *Personal integrity* and *Management* is based on the role of management's quality and reputation of borrower for results of credit investigation and credit facility.				SR	SC					D						3	20%
EI 37	The relationship between *Financial situation* and *Quality of earnings* relies on the examination of profitability of borrower's activity.			A	SR	SR	A			SR	D		SR		D		8	53%
EI 38	The relationship between *Financial situation* and *Leverage equity structure* is based on the importance of capital structure of the borrower for the analysis during credit investigation.					SR				SR			SR				3	20%
EI 39	The relationship between *Financial analysis* and *Asset quality* relies on the importance of asset quality of borrowers for results of credit investigation.					SR				SR	D		SR				3	20%
EI 40	The relationship between *Financial situation* and *Liquidity* relies on the important role of liquidity facilities of the borrower for results of analysis during credit investigation.			D	D	SR	D			SR	D		SR		SR		8	53%
EI 41	The relationship between *Portfolio* and *Credit policy* emphasises that credit policy determines the composition of credit portfolio.	D		SR		SR	DR						SR			R	6	40%

EI 42	The relationship between *Relative/ Acquaintance & friends s* and ***Personal integrity*** relies on (presumed) perception that family ties can help to provide data for examination of personal integrity. (control item)		D	SR		D		SC		SR	MP		SC	D	MP	R	10	67%
EI 43	The relationship between *Relatives/ Acquaintance & friends* and ***Management*** relies on the importance of family ties for examination of management. (control item)		P(D)			SC		SC			SC			P(MP			5	33%
EI 44	The relationship between *Relatives/ Acquaintance & friends* and *Credit Committee* relies on (presumed) perception that Credit Committee often avails itself of services of familiar relations in order to provide data. (control item)			SC		SC		SC			SR			SR			5	33%
EI 45	The relationship between *Relatives / Acquaintance & friends* and ***Ownership*** relies on (presumed) perception that information about relatives and friends of owners (of borrowers) can deliver insight. (control item)			SR		SR	SR			SR		SR					5	33%
EI 46	The relationship between *Clan/Acquaintance/Friends* and *Credit Investigation* relies on (presumed) perception that credit investigation uses the service of relatives, friends etc. for providing information. (control item)	SR				SC							SC				3	20%
EI 47	The relationship between *Parliament* and ***Personal integrity*** relies on (presumed) perception of bankers that any relation to Parliament is a factor influencing examination of personal integrity during credit investigation. (control item)					SR	SR		SC								3	20%
EI 48	The relationship between *Parliament* and *Credit policy* relies on the (presumed) perception that the Parliament has an *influence on* bank's credit policy. (control item)	SR			SR			SR	SR	R		SR					6	40%
EI 49	The relationship between *Government* and ***Monitoring*** relies on supervision/influence of the government over banking.						SR										1	7%
EI 50	The relationship between *Government* and ***Personal integrity*** is based on (presumed) perception of bankers that any relation to Government is factor influencing credit investigation. (control item)						SR										1	7%
EI 51	The relationship between *Government* and *Credit policy* relies on the (presumed) perception that government has an influence on bank's credit policy. (control item)	SR			SR			SR		R	SR		SR				6	40%
EI 52	The relationship between *Government* and ***Management*** relies on the (presumed) perception that government can exert pressure on bank's management. (control item)	SR	C				SR		SR						SR		5	33%

EI 53	The relationship between ***Bank of Mongolia*** and ***Monitoring*** relies on the circumstance that the central bank supervises the banks.	DR		D	SR	A	A		R	A				A	A		9	60%
EI 54	The relation between ***Bank Supervision, BOM*** and ***Credit risk limitation*** relies on the task of bank supervision department of BOM bank to limit the risky behaviour of banks.																0	0%
EI 55	The relationship between ***Bank of Mongolia*** and ***Credit Committee*** is based on the (presumed) perception that the central bank can influence the actions of bank's Credit Committee. (control item)	SR			SR	SR	SR	SR		D				D	SR		8	53%
EI 56	The relationship between ***Bank of Mongolia*** and ***Credit policy*** relies on the (presumed) perception that the central bank can influence the bank's credit policy. (control item)	SR			SR	SR	SR	SR	A	SR		SR		SR	SR		10	67%
EI 57	The relationship between ***Safety, Credit facility*** and ***Manager*** relies on (presumed) perception that insider loans can ensure banks' security . (control item)				DR	MP	SC			MP					SR		5	33%
EI 58	The relationship between ***Manager, Credit facility*** and ***Profitability*** relies on (presumed) perception that insider loans bring profits. (control item)			MP	SC	SC	SR			SC					MP		6	40%
EI 59	The relationship between ***Safety, Credit facility*** and ***Ownership*** relies on (presumed) perception that insider loans (to owners) are practised. (control item)			P(D)	SC	SC	SC			P(D)							5	33%
EI 60	The relationship between ***Credit risk management*** and ***Bank supervision requirements*** bears on role of credit risk management as subject matter of bank supervision.																0	0%
EI 61	The relationship between ***Credit risk management*** and ***Credit risk strategy*** relies on the goal of credit risk management to realise credit risk strategy of bank.				A												1	7%
EI 62	The relationship between ***Credit risk strategy*** and ***Bank's business policy*** relies on the fact that credit risk strategy is elaborated to implement bank's business policy.				D												1	7%
EI 63	The relationship between ***Bank of Mongolia*** and ***Parliament*** emphasises the dependence of BoM on Parliament. (control item)		A	SC	D	D	D	C		A	A	SR		A	D		11	73%
EI 64	The relationship between ***Credit investigation / Credit risk*** and ***Financial situation / Personal integrity*** emphasises measures of credit investigation.		SC	SR	A	SR	SR	SR		MP	A, A	SR			MP		10	67%

EI 65	The relationship between *Credit investigation* and *On-site inspection* emphasises the importance of such inspection for credit investigation.		SC	MP	D	A	MP			MP		SR		MP	MP		9	60%
EI 66	The relationship between *Access to data / Provision of data* and *Loan Information Pool* bears on the fact that the LIP grant access to data.			SR		SR	A	SR		A	A				D		7	47%
EI 67	The relationship between *Bank of Mongolia* and *Credit facility* is based on (presumed) perception that the central bank can some how influence decisions of lending. (control item)				SC	SC	SC			D	A				A		6	40%
EI 68	The relationship between *Personal conversation* and *Reliability of Data / History* relies on the role of personal discussions and contacts for reliability of data. (control item)		SR	MP	DR	A	SR	SR			MP, SR				SC		8	53%
EI 69	The relationship between *Personal integrity* and *Ownership* relies on the impact of ownership's characteristics of borrower on credit investigation. (control item)						CR	SR			D				SC		4	27%
EI 70	The relationship between *Personal integrity / Financial situation* and *Credit risk* emphasises that examinations of personal integrity and financial situation lead to determination of credit risk.				SC, SC		SR, SR			A	C, C			A, A			5	33%
EI 71	The relationship between *Collateral / Guarantee* and *Reputation* relies on the influence of reputation on the quality of collateral and guarantee. (control item)		MP	D	SR	SR	P(D)			D				D	SR		8	53%
EI 72	The relationship between *On-site inspection* and *Reliability of data* emphasises that on-site inspections can influence the reliability of data.			SR				SR		SC	A			D	MP		6	40%
EI 73	The relationship between *Credit investigation* and *Collateral / Guarantee* emphasis the role of collateral and of guarantee for decisions on lending		D	D	SR		D	SR		D	A, SR			A	D		9	60%

Codification: The proposition (relation) results from the way of reading from left upwards:

SR	Simple relation	**O(SR)**	Objection of SR	**P(SR)**	Potentiality of SR
SC	Simple characteristic	**O(SC)**	Objection of SC	**P(SC)**	Potentiality of SC
DR	Definitional relation	**O(DR)**	Objection of DR	**P(DR)**	Potentiality of DR
D	Dependence	**O(D)**	Objection of D	**P(D)**	Potentiality of D
C	Condition	**O(C)**	Objection of C	**P(C)**	Potentiality of C
R	Cause, Reason	**O(R)**	Objection of R	**P(R)**	Potentiality of R
A	Activity	**O(A)**	Objection of A	**P(A)**	Potentiality of A
MP	Means and Partner	**O(MP)**	Objection of MP	**P(MP)**	Potentiality of MP

Analysing the data from documents and records

Analysing the data collected from records and documents meant unitising and categorising it. The information units were identified during a coding operation and categorised[39] in an on-going manner. The result is a kind of observation matrix, with 15 categories on the horizontal axis and data of days the observations were made on the vertical axis (Annex 12). Information units – notes, guidelines, procedures, content of credit files – were filled out in the intersections

After assigning the information units to categories, **observation items** (OIs) were devised to characterise each category's properties, as illustrated in Table 3.10. Some new categories were additionally formulated to capture information which could not been foreseen. Finally, the entire set of categories was reviewed, some of which were eventually discarded as being irrelevant. To determine when it was time to stop processing data, the four criteria proposed by Lincoln and Guba (1985: 207 et sqq.) were used: exhaustion of sources, saturation of categories, emergence of regularities and over extension. As a result, 31 observation items were devised which, for their part, individually or concertedly, should together with evaluation items complement (prove or disprove) the evaluation statements in sub-chapter 3.3.2 below.

The steps taken to analyse data from observation and records (see Figure 3.7) are summarised below:

- preparing the data: the observation matrix is filled out with information units, altogether 81 information units were noted during observation,
- making sense of the data: on the basis of observation matrix 31 observation items were devised to characterise each category's properties,
- making sense of the data: interpretation of observation items which, together with the evaluation items, should complement (prove or disprove) the evaluation statements in sub-chapter 3.3.2

[39] Categories were worked out based on semantic relations of action-slot model as shown in the Table 3.2.

Table 3.10: Categories and observation items of data analysis – documents and records

Source: own work out based on notes during document observation, a cut-out

Categories	Observation Items	Sources[40]
Existence of instructions and procedure guidelines	OI1. Procedure guidelines such as "Method of Credit Investigation", "Methods of Risk Assessment", and "Portfolio Management" are in the works.	Note1 (N1) from 25.01.
	OI7. First steps to completely standardise the loan granting process were taken in the middle of 2001. Implementation of guideline on "Loan Granting Procedure" – even fragmentary – began at 1.1.02.	LGP, WRof CC, N2 from 28.01
	OI21. The contradictions in the Mongolian and English versions of guideline on "Loan Granting Procedure" point at the potentiality to interpret the guideline.	LGP, item 4.6
CI definition	OI6. There is no explicit definition of credit investigation yet.	LGP, N7 from 25.01
Credit risk definition and assessment	OI30. There is no definition of credit risk and credit risk assessment process yet.	LGP
Line of authority	OI29. The authority to act is centred in hands of one person, executive director.	LGP
Level of competence	OI12. Level of competence, competence structures are in the process of being established. There still many obscurities: die competence of the secretary of Credit Committee is still vague.	N2 from 28.01.
	OI23. The prescribed task of secretary of Credit Committee to establish and manage a data base (pool) on granted and rejected loans is confined presently to manually administer three register books.	N3 from 4.04
	OI25. There are not any task description (competency) for central figures like loan officer, secretary of Credit Committee, director of Credit Department etc.	LGP
	OI2. The relationship between the secretary of Credit Committee and loan officers is rather hierarchical then team-structured.	N2 from 25.03.
Compulsive activities	OI24. Bureaucratic way of decision making ends with obligatory confirmation of the executive director (EXD) to every loan granting.	N4 from 5.04, LGP, Table „Actions"
	OI5. The structure of the guideline on "Loan Granting Procedure" is in so far interesting as it is concerned as first of all with examination of collateral requirements before going into financial analysis.	LGP, N6 from 25.01.
Models of organisation	OI11. Transparency in the sense of making steps traceable during decision making practice in lending could not be identified.	N from 28.01., CFs
	OI13. Working processes during lending, as far as it concerns the functional side (operating), are rather dynamic.	N3 f. 28.01.
	OI18. Bureaucracy within the bank, especially in respect to information flow and communication, is rigorous.	N1from 1.04.
	OI22. Due to shortage of time, secretary of Credit Committee can not hold down her job to "monitor the fulfilment of instructions on Credit Memorandum through loan officers".	N1 from 4.4

40 Sources are the information units identified during documents analysis, see hereto Annex 12.

Office discipline	OI19. The general working instructions of the bank could not be found in the credit department. After some "search operations", the officer of legal department fixed up with it.	N2 from 1.04., N2 from 2.04
Group process models	OI9. The decisions within the Credit Committee seem to be made on a principle of team work.	LGP, WRof CC, N2 from 28.01
	OI16. In her day-to-day work the secretary of Credit Committee conduct long, almost cautionary conversations with loan officers.	N4 from 29.01
Loan handling	OI4. The list with a classification of borrowers begins with the class of related persons (insider loans, such as loans to bank managers and loan officers).	LGP, N4 from 25.01.
	OI8. There is no classification of credit limits in respect to different business area or borrowers.	Portfoliomanag-R., N2 from 28.01
	OI20. Lending in terms of credo is not practised.	N2 from 3.04
Loan administration	OI10. Credit Files previous to first of January 2002 are organised very unsystematically.	CFs, N3 from 28.01, N1 from 2.01.
	OI14. The English version of Credit Files (Credit Files of those loans witch were supported within international projects) are much better systematised and clearly arranged.	N6 from 29.01
Resources	O31. In their day-to-day work, loan officers keep regular in touch with Loan Information Pool of BOM by telephone (there is no electronic network yet).	N8 from 29.01
Customers	OI27. Customer retention (loans are granted only to customers with house bank status) and strict collateral requirements strongly narrow the number and the circle of borrowers.	LGP
Granted and withdrawn loans	OI3. It was nearly impossible to have a look at the documents concerning rejected loans (no willingness, no justification).	N3 from 25.01
	OI15. Written formulations of members of Credit Committee concerning the reasons of their decisions are, in some Credit Files exactly the same.	CFs, N2 from 28.01
	OI17. During writing down the minutes of meetings of Credit Committee, the secretary of Credit Committee thinks really "loud" about what should she give as a reason for loan decisions.	N6 from 29.01
	OI28. As a matter of fact, some decisions on loans are contradictory to results of credit investigation and suggestions of loan officers (no explanations are given).	CFs
Credit portfolio	OI26. No putting on and weighing up of separate results to a joint finding in respect to portfolio management exists (in written form)	CFs, Notes from 4.01.

Analysing the data from individual interviews

The data collected during individual interviewing was to be prepared for analysis. For this purpose, the opinions most frequently expressed in open-ended individual interviews – **response items** (RIs) – were identified. Thus notes of narrative responses are categorised into response items by means of a response matrix. Guided by semantic relations/ knowledge fields which were used to formulate the interview questions (see Table 3.1), several search cycles within the interview notes were made. Moreover, it was necessary to organise the opinions into different response items: in some cases more in general, in others more narrow.

As shown in Table 3.11, the strength of the opinions expressed by each interviewee is rated with scores of five levels: very close (++), close (+), neutral (0), so-so (-) and contradictory (--). The last two columns calculate the number of very close and close opinions as a percentage. Using the magnitude of 21 response items, these were analysed by interpreting and devising together with EIs and OIs into evaluation statements. These are addressed in sub-chapter 3.3.2.

The steps taken to analyse the data from standardised, open-ended interviews with individuals (see Figure 3.7) are summarised below:

- preparing the data: 21 response items are identified by searching out the most frequently used wording and meaning,
- preparing the data: the response matrix is filled out and the strengths of response items given by each interviewee are noted,
- making sense of the data: interpretation of response items which, together with the evaluation items and the organisation items, should prove the evaluation statements in sub-chapter 3.3.2.

Table 3.11: Response matrix: response items and strength of responses

Source: own work out based on interview notes

Ris	Content of Response Items	P1	P2	P3	P4	P5	P6	P7	P8	P9	P10	P11	P12	P13	P14	P15	Sum	%
RI 1	Credit investigation process including ultimate decision on loan granting lasts maximum ten days.	+	++	++	++	++	++	+	+	++	++	++		++	+	++	14	93%
RI 2	Data of BOM (LIP) is important for bank's examinations during credit investigation.	+				++	++	++	+	+			+	++	+	+	10	67%
RI 3	Additionally to data in credit application, it is always needful to inform oneself about reliability of data – mostly by asking confident customers, past staff members and other acquaintances.	++	++				++	+			++		+	++	+	++	9	60%
RI 4	On-site inspections and personal discussions with owners are essentially important to check and supervise the collateral.	++		++	++		+		+	++	+	++	++	+	++	+	12	80%
RI 5	On-site inspections are very useful for loan officer to assure herself of facts.		++	++		+	++		+	++	++	+	++	+	++	+	12	80%
RI 6	The co-operation with other departments of the bank – payment settlement, customer service, international department etc., legal department – during loan granting is much intensive then it is the case after the actual loan granting.	++	+	+		+			+	++	+	++	+	+	++		12	80%
RI7	During credit investigation, loan officer always keeps in mind the question <u>how</u> can loan retirement be ensured.		+	++	++	+	++	+		+	+	+	+	++	+	+	13	87%
RI 8	Loan officer regards provision of detailed, reliable data as most important part of her job.	++				++		+	+	++	++	++		+	++	+	10	67%
RI 9	Loan officer regards credit investigation as most important part of her job.	+	+	++		+		+	+		+	+		+	+	+	11	73%
RI 10	Most important factors for decision on loan granting are the status of payment settlements of customer through the bank and her credit history at the bank.	++			++	++	++		++	++	++			++	++	++	10	67%
RI 11	Profitability of the business project is not as much important as the history of bank-customer relationship.	+			+	+	+		+	+	+	+	+	+	+		11	73%
RI 12	The most important factor for decision on loan granting is customer's reputation and history of customer's relationship.			++			++			++		++			++	++	6	40%
RI 13	The most important factor for decision on loan grating is characteristics of collateral.			++	++		+	+		+	+	+	+	++	+	+	11	73%
RI 14	Despite of importance of data provision, bank hardly spends funds for this purpose.	++	+	+	+			+		+			+	+	+	+	10	67%
RI 15	Banking in this country is not based on the principle of trust (in terms of credo) yet.	++	+			++	+		+	++			+		++	++	9	60%
RI 16	At present, it is imperative: "there is no credit without collateral".				++		++	+		+	+	+	+	+	+	+	10	67%

RI 17	Measures taken to standardise lending procedures are in so far useful if they do not bring bureaucracy.	++					+			++			+	++	+	+	7	47%
RI 18	The lack of long term loans is founded by availability of only short term deposits and absence of long term deposits in this country.	+	+		++		+		+	+			+	+	+	+	10	67%
RI 19	There is no instrument or mechanism which would allow to directly reflect and incorporate the experiences of loan officers into credit policy (credit lines, portfolio policy etc.).	+	+		+		+			+			+	+	+	+	9	60%
RI 20	The best credit is a credit without risk.		+		+		+	+		+	+		+		+		8	53%
RI 21	In the day-to-day work of bankers seem the role international supervision institution to be irrelevant.		+		+	+		+		+	+		+	+	+	+	10	67%

Levels of strength: ++ very close + close 0 neutral - so-so – contradictory

3.3.2 Findings

In order to interpret the data, descriptive units – EIs, OIs and RIs – were brought together to search for linkages among them. This involved identifying coherent and important items, looking for those which go together as being items of the same underlying idea or issue – an evaluation statement (Table 3.12). Special emphasis was placed on identifying those items underlying the hypotheses (formulated in 2.3.3). However, due to the nature of qualitative data, a conscious effort was made to look out for alternative explanations and contrary patterns. As a result, four groups of evaluations statements were devised for acknowledging the hypotheses (Table 3.12).

(1) Attitude to risk

ES 1.1 Understanding (definition and classification) of the concept risk is insufficient.

The banker's concept maps indicate that they do not comprehensively understand risk. Although 9 of 15 bankers are aware that banking comprises uncertainties (EI 1), only 3 were able to refer these uncertainties to the return situation of the bank (EI 2). Simple classifications of risk, such as interest rate risk or currency risk (EI 7, EI 8), were also not made.

The lack of any definitions of risk and risk assessment in the bank's procedure guidelines and instructions (OI 30) and the non-standardisation of credit investigation and portfolio management (OI 1) - which are still being processed – are further proof of the aforesaid insights.

Moreover, when asked to give reasons for the lack of long-term loans, two-thirds[41] of the bankers justified this by "availability of only short-term deposits and absence of long-term deposits in this country" (RI 18). It denotes the bankers' lack of procedural knowledge about the basic principles underlying the banking business – term transformation and risk taking.

ES 1.2 Though credit risk is a recognised term, which is seemingly up to date, in fact, bankers cannot use it in respect of content and praxis.

It is obvious that credit risk is going to find its way into bankers' knowledge models. Yet their concept maps show that bankers are far from implementing it in the context of their day-to-day work. About half the bankers see "credit risk as a matter of Credit Committee's decisions" (EI 22), and 9 of them illustrate the importance of credit risk

[41] The other third gave as reasons credit-worthiness of borrowers, high risk caused by volatile prices and uncertainties about economic policies.

for decisions on credit facilities (EI 24). And only one-third emphasise that credit investigation – i.e. examining the financial situation and personal integrity – allow credit risk to be determined (EI 70). Actions taken in respect of credit risk, such as screening, measuring, monitoring etc., were not recognised in the bankers' concept maps (EI 16, EI 17).

The missing definition of credit risk in internal instructions – as mentioned above – and the absence of credit limit classifications (OI 18) allied to purposeful recording (OI 10, OI 14) demonstrates that credit risk is not operationalised within lending processes.

ES 1.3 Loan granting (with credit investigation), but not credit risk management, is identified as a process.

The concept maps displayed the procedural knowledge of bankers concerning operations in the loan granting process, especially with respect to knowledge fields like goals, conditions, means and results of the credit investigation process. Many bankers (11 and 13) "emphasise that decision on credit facility premises a credit investigation" (EI 27). This decision is taken by the main body – the Credit Committee (EI 25). 9 bankers point out important role of collateral and guarantees for credit investigation (EI 73).

However, not more than the half revealed measures and means of credit investigation. There was little evidence of an examination of the financial situation – such as analysis of quality of earning (8), asset quality (3), leverage equity structure (3), liquidity of borrower (8) – as important action during credit investigation (EI 37-40). No propositions were made concerning an analysis of the market position, the quality of product etc. (EI 34, EI 35).

Only a few bankers (4) recognised the relevance of rating on the results of credit investigation and credit facilities (EI 30). Even fewer (2) recognised Moody's and Standard&Poor's as leading rating agencies. Thus procedural knowledge on credit risk management was not presented in the concept maps. Essential operations of credit risk management to identify and limit risk, such as screening, measuring, diversifying and monitoring, were proposed by just 2-3 bankers (EI 16-19), as already addressed.

Table 3.12: Findings of data analysis: evaluation statements derived from evaluation items, observation items and response items

Source: own work out

Evaluation items (EI) in			Observation items (OI)	Response items (RI)	Evaluation statements	Hypotheses
Map I	**Map II**	**Map III**				
EI 1, EI 3, EI 6, EI 7, EI 8, EI 2			OI 1, OI 30	RI 18	**ES 1.1** Understanding (definition and classification) of the concept risk is insufficient.	**H1.1** Despite the perception of risk as an important factor, it is not operationalised (risk management) in day-to-day business of banks. (ES 1.1, ES 1.2, ES 1.3, ES 1.4, ES 1.5, ES 1.6, ES 2.4) **H1.2** Risk taking and reserves are not recognised as being related to one another in terms of bank supervision. (ES 1.5, ES 2.4, ES 1.1, ES 1.2, ES 1.3, ES 2.1) **H1.3** The process of credit risk management is not perceived as a matter subject to bank supervision. (ES 1.5, ES 1.3, ES 2.1, ES 2.4)
	EI 22, EI 23, EI 24, EI 16, EI 18, EI 19, EI 31, EI 61, EI 70	EI 87	OI 30, OI 12, OI 23, OI 25, OI 8, OI 10, OI 14, OI 26	RI 6, RI 18	**ES 1.2** Though credit risk is known term which is seemingly up to date, in fact, bankers can not do anything with it in respect of content and praxis.	
	EI 16, EI 17, EI 18, EI 19, EI25, EI 27, EI 30, EI 31, EI 32, EI 34, EI 35, EI 38, EI 39, EI 40, EI 41, EI 60, EI 61, EI 62, EI 64, EI 73		OI 1, OI 7, OI 21, OI 30, OI 23, OI 25, OI 8, OI 26	RI 6, RI 8, RI 9, RI 19	**ES 1.3** Loan granting (with credit investigation), but not credit risk management, is identified as a process.	
EI 3, EI 4, EI 5, EI 9				RI 20, RI 16	**ES 1.4** Risk is not necessarily considered a chance: risk is assessed as a purely negative factor which ought to be eliminated.	
EI 10, EI 11	EI 60	EI 80, EI 81, EI 82, EI 86			**ES 1.5** Interrelation of risk taking with bank supervision and reserves is not realised.	
	EI 28, EI 73		OI 5, OI 20	RI 4, RI 7, RI 11, RI 12, RI 13, RI 16	**ES 1.6** Collateral is one of most important factors of decision on lending.	

EI 14, EI 10, EI 11	EI 54, EI 60	EI 80, EI 81, EI 82, EI 89, EI 90, EI 75, EI 76, EI 77, EI 78, EI 79, EI 88, EI 93			**ES 2.1** Understanding of bank supervision (fields of activity) is very general and its aims are not realised.	**H2** Bankers' perception concerning functions of bank supervision is to guarantee loan repayment and to provide information. (ES 2.1, ES 2.2, ES 2.3, ES 2.4, ES 1.5)
EI 12, EI 13		EI 89	OI 31	RI 2	**ES 2.2** Banks are reliant on bank supervision by being provided with reliable information.	
EI 15		EI 80, EI 81, EI 82, EI 89, EI 90			**ES 2.3** Bankers view bank supervision as an institution which ought to guarantee loan repayments.	
		EI 83, EI 84, EI 85		RI 21	**ES 2.4** The most important contents concerning international bank supervision (Basel Committee, Basel I, RAROC etc.) are unknown respectively disregarded.	
	EI 47, EI 48, EI 49, EI 51, EI 52, EI 55, EI 56, EI 63, EI 67	EI 91, EI 92			**ES 3.1** Bankers are aware of state influence on lending.	**H3** Decisions on lending are distinctly affected by official representatives (of the Parliament and Government). (ES 3.1, ES 2.2)
	EI 42, EI 43, EI 44, EI 45, EI 46, EI 57, EI 58, EI 59, EI 68		OI 4, OI 27	RI 3, RI 5, RI 11, RI 12	**ES 4.1** There is not an explicit, but an implicit influence of personal relationship in lending.	**H4** Decisions on lending are strongly influenced by personal relationships. (ES 4.1, ES 4.2)
	EI 69, EI 71			RI 4	**ES 4.2** Quality of collateral depends on personal characteristics of owners.	

Moreover, important propositions about the aim and conditions of credit risk management are not present in the bankers' concept maps. Only 1 banker shows "the role of credit risk management is realising bank's credit risk strategy" (EI 61), which "is elaborated to implement bank's business policy" (EI 62). And no banker gives "credit risk management as a subject matter of bank supervision" (EI 60).

The insight can be underlined by the responses of bankers to the most important part of their job: 10 bankers note the provision of the most detailed, reliable data (RI 8) and 11 – the credit investigation (RI 9).

ES 1.4 Risk is not necessarily considered a chance: risk is assessed as a purely negative factor, which ought to be eliminated.

Bankers perceive risk as a danger that needs to be avoided. 11 of 15 bankers emphasis credit default as a potential consequence of risk taking (EI 3) whilst 12 believe that uncertainties could be reflected in bank insolvency (EI 4). After all, 8 of them seem to mean that risk should be eliminated (EI 5). As EI 9 show, only 3 bankers perceive risk from both sides: potential for losses as well as an opportunity to make profit – chance.

RI 16 and RI 20 strongly exemplify this with the bankers' statement that "the best credit is a credit without risk" (8) and that at present, "there is no credit without collateral" (10).

ES 1.5 Interrelation of risk taking with bank supervision and reserves is not realised.

The concept maps reveal that there is a misconception among bankers not only about risk taking, but also about the aim and instruments of bank supervision. Only 5 bankers recognise the "circumstance that bank supervision makes bankers become aware of risk taking and thus influences their risk behaviour" (EI 11). The purpose of reserve requirements – among others – as a facility of risk coverage was expressed by 4 bankers (EI 10).

ES 1.6 Collateral is one of most important factors of decision on lending.

Previous remarks have implied that there are not any non-collateralised loans at present. Many bankers (11) even emphasise "the role of collateral for the results of examining a borrower's financial situation" (EI 28). And 9 bankers denote collateral's important role for decisions on lending (EI 73). It is interesting in this context that the guidelines for granting loans in the observed bank "is concerned as fist of all with examination of collateral characteristics before going into financial analysis" (OI 5).

In reply to the question of what the most important issue is that a loan officer keeps in mind during credit investigation, 13 of them emphasise the problem of "how loan redemption can be ensured" (RI 7). 11 bankers see the collateral characteristics as the most important factor for taking decisions on lending (RI 13). For this reason, they check collateral during on-site inspections (RI 4).

(2) Bankers' perception about bank supervision

ES 2.1 The understanding of bank supervision (fields of activity) is very general and the aims of bank supervision are not realised.

The bankers' understanding of risk and risk taking (based on EI 10, EI 11) also indicates that very few bankers (6) conceive the purpose of bank supervision as being "to limit losses through deliberate risk taking and thus to restrict the failure probability in the banking sector" (EI 14). None of the bankers' mental models visualise the aim of bank supervision requirements as being to limit the risky behaviour of banks (EI 54) by observing credit risk management of banks (EI 60).

ES 2.2 Banks are strongly reliant on reliable information of bank supervision.

The bankers partially realise the aim of bank supervision. The concept maps reveal that bankers (12, 10) expect bank supervision to ensure transparency in banking (EI 13) by providing bank-specific information and by evaluating and procuring such (EI 12). During individual interviews, bankers (10) emphasised the importance of the Loan Information Pool's data – placed at banks supervision department of BOM – for examinations made during credit investigation (RI 2). In fact regular telephone calls between the banks' loan officers and workers of LIP were observed during the day-to-day work in the credit department (OI 31).

ES 2.3 Bankers view bank supervision as an institution which ought to guarantee loan repayments.

The mental models of bankers (12) perceive the aim of bank supervision as ensuring credit solvency (EI 15).

ES 2.4 The most important contents of international bank supervision (Basel Committee, Basel I, RAROC) are unknown or disregarded.

Not only domestic bank supervision requirements, but also important concepts of international banks supervision are not recognised by all bankers (EI 80-82). Only one banker recognises the role of Basel Committee on bank supervision requirements and activities of BOM.

In response to an inquiry about the impact of international banking supervision institutions on bankers' day-to-day work, 10 bankers fail to see any direct connection and feel rather lost (RI 21).

(3) Social commitment: Commitment to the authoritative state

ES 3.1 Bankers are aware of state influence on lending.

The mental models of bankers in their concept maps show that there is significant intervention in banking by the state authorities. According to the Central Bank Act, the Bank of Mongolia is responsible for formulating state monetary policy and is authorised to implement this after having been adopted by Parliament. And many bankers (11) view the relationship between them as a dependency (EI 63). Moreover, bankers (10) believe that the BOM exerts influence on credit policy of banks (EI 56), 8 of them see an connection between the BOM and the actions of the main decision body of banks – the Credit Committee. However, they were not able to specify this in more detail (EI 55). The concept maps of 6 bankers perceive that the BOM influences decisions about credit facilities (EI 67).

Even though not the majority, some bankers are aware of the direct influence of state authorities. 6 bankers believed that Parliament and the Government interfere with the credit policies of banks (EI 48, EI 51). 5 also perceive that the "Government can exert pressure on banks' management" (EI 52). One of them uses the concept "monitoring" to demonstrate "supervision of government over banking" (EI 47). Additionally, 3 bankers see – even if not precisely stated – a linkage between parliament and examination of personal integrity (EI 47).

(4) Standards of ethics: Family ties and personal relations

ES 4.1 There is not an explicit, but an implicit influence of personal relations in lending.

Many propositions in the bankers' concept maps allude to personal relations – relatives, acquaintance and friends, but links between these concepts are either unlabelled or insufficiently marked. However, the importance of personal relations is visible, be it by way of data provision or guaranteeing credit solvency.

10 bankers perceive that family ties play an important role for data provision during credit investigation (EI 42). The mental models of 8 bankers see a role for personal discussions in verifying the reliability of data (EI 68). 5 bankers give personal relations as simple characteristics of borrower's ownership (EI 45), banks' Credit Committee (EI 44) etc. During individual interviews, 9 bankers stated that it is "necessary to inform oneself about the reliability of data – mostly by asking trusted customers, past staff members and other acquaintances" (RI 3).

Furthermore, the concept maps of one-third of the bankers perceive insider loans as ensuring the bank's security (EI 57, EI 59) and making profits (EI 58). This would seem to indicate that loans to unknown owners, management and workers are not particularly favoured. It should be mentioned that the loan classification list of the observed bank starts with "loans to related persons" (OI 4).

ES 4.2 The quality of collateral and guarantees depends on the personal characteristics of owners.

The bankers seem to rely upon inquiries about personal characteristics of owners whilst examining collateral and guarantees. The concept maps of 8 bankers mentioned the influence of reputation on their assessment of collateral's quality (EI 71) and 12 bankers stated explicitly that "on-site inspections and personal discussions with owners are essentially important to check collateral" (RI 4).

The impact of these findings will be discussed in Part 4 below.

Part 4 Institutions Building and Adjustment of Bank Regulation Norms in Mongolia

Having formulated findings on informal institutional constraints of lending in Mongolian banks in Part 3, Part 4 will now discuss them. Chapter 4.1 first reviews the significant findings and considers the impact of informal institutional constraints of lending on the enforcement of bank regulations on lending. Chapter 4.2 then attempts to devise implications of the study for the real world by looking at future challenges and putting forward suggestions for further reforms.

4.1 Discussion of Findings on Informal Constraints with Respect to Formal Institutions

4.1.1 Informal Constraints of Lending in Mongolia

Table 3.12 gave insights into existing informal institutions which channel the actions of Mongolian bankers in lending. By illustrating some issues of the bankers' mental models, the findings show weaknesses in the institutional framework of the Mongolian banking system.

The mental models of Mongolian bankers **lack a prudent attitude to risk.** The bankers' own perception of economic interrelations concerning risk and risk management identified opinions held by bankers on risk and other factors which influence the decision making process in lending. It reveals that Mongolian bankers perceive risk as an important factor, but risk is neither sufficiently understood nor operationalised in bankers' day-to-day work (hypothesis 1.1). Furthermore, bankers do not conceive risk in the context of bank regulation: they do not recognise risk taking and reserves as related in terms of bank regulation (hypothesis 1.2). And evaluation statements indicated that Mongolian bankers do not perceive credit risk management as a subject matter of bank supervision (hypothesis 1.3).

The bankers' mental models contain **an erroneous or one-sided perception about the way bank supervision functions**. The bankers see the targets of bank supervision as guaranteeing loan repayment and providing information (hypothesis 2). At present, they are strongly reliant on data provision through the bank regulation authority. The mental models do not reproduce the functioning of international bank regulation authority. Even members of senior management do not know much about the functions of the Basel Committee.

Mongolian bankers feel affected by officials when making their decisions on lending (hypothesis 3). The decision makers in enterprises and banks (at least those that are state-owned) are still aware of the status of the state and its hierarchy: **commitments to the authoritative state** are present in mental models of bankers. This kind of power of hierarchical authority is one of many examples of Mongolia's past. The state for its part bailed out enterprises, and this mechanism is now confronted with the realities of practicability in times of transition to market economy.

The bankers' own view of economic interrelations includes very **personalised exchange**. The bankers definitely make use of personal relations for data provision, but there is no strong evidence on the direct influence of family ties on lending decisions (hypothesis 4). As the quality of collateral and credit guarantees depends on their owner, the process of collateral and guarantee assessment is very exhausting and costly, if not infeasible. There is also no appropriate system of collateralisation in most Mongolian banks. Banks try to overcome this problem of infeasible collateral assessment by calling for a house bank relationship as a key condition for any loan application. Thus the profitability of the project to be financed is not a prior criterion as findings of all instruments show (adverse selection). Loans based on relationships were not found in records and documents, but content maps and interviews revealed that family and friendship ties play a role, less because they represent good collateral, but rather because they characterise credibility.

The observed informal institutions which constrain lending decisions of Mongolian banks – the insubstantial attitude to risk, the erroneous or one-sided perception of bankers on the functioning of bank supervision, the social commitment to an authoritative state and family ties and personal relations – thus account for the continuing "passivity" of Mongolian banks.

It can be concluded that the actions of Mongolian bankers are channelled by such informal institutions, which substantially differ from those assumed to be held in market economies. They have not yet adapted banking habits with a forward-looking nature, nor become an active participant in a market system. Bank behaviour in Mongolian economy is therefore different to that in market economies. This result is consistent with propositions of economists and politicians from the EITs and foreigners watching closely the transition process in general and keeping an eye on the banking sector reforms of these countries (e.g. IMF, World Bank, European Bank for Reconstruction and Development etc.): there is "a lack of skills and experiences concerning the running of a bank under the new system, and [...] institution building is a very important task" emphasised the Vice President at the European Bank for Reconstruction and former Governor of the National Bank of Poland Mrs. Hanna Cronkiewicz Waltz (CFS Even, 2002).

The main difficulties in this have been concretising informal institutions on the one hand, and providing scientific proof of this on the other. This study initially attempts to implicitly identify the informal institutions which constrain decisions made on lending at Mongolian banks. The compatibility of existing formal and informal institutions of lending in Mongolian banking is then discussed.

4.1.2 Incompatibility of Informal Institutions with Formal Institutions

If the informal institutions on lending already identified are compared with the formal institutions which also channel the actions of Mongolian bankers and constrain their behaviour, it can then be seen that the formal and informal rules of the "lending" game have not been altered simultaneously. As seen in Part 3, the bank regulation norms in Mongolia are based on the bank regulation norms of advanced market economies. They therefore assume that bankers have appropriate mental models of behaving and channel the actions of "active" banks. This is a prudent attitude to risk, a bankers' correct perception about the functioning of bank supervision and exchange processes, which are impersonalised, as well as social commitments which give incentives for productive activities.

Yet the frictions of transition from one system to another were not taken into account in evaluating the impact of reform policies in Mongolia. Thus in order to encompass the new system, institutional issues should be considered in switching from a centralisation to a decentralisation of financial banking services, such as lending. By addressing the institutional framework and its change, bank reform concentrated on modifying the formal rules of lending – laws, legal regulations, standardisation of bank regulation norms etc. Long into transition, the alteration of – or even establishment of new – informal rules was ignored by reform concepts. There is **incompatibility** between the existing regulation norms on lending and the informal institutional constraints of lending.

According to the Theory of Economic and Institutional Change (1.1.3), such incompatibility is evidence of discontinuity of change. Although new formal institutions are able to evoke changes in informal institutions (interaction of rules), the persistence of – deeply rooted – cultural traits in Mongolia makes informal institutions change at a different rate to that of formal institutions. There is thus a discontinuity of change, and **the enforcement of newly introduced formal rules** is endangered. Given compatibility, the theory presumes that institutions can be implemented at lowest cost. Yet in case of inconsistency between historically derived informal rules of the game deep-seated in bankers' mental models and newly established formal rules, bank regulation authorities would have to bear high additional costs to establish properly functioning control and sanction mechanisms.

Since the weak Mongolian economy has not been able to bear these expenses, formal bank regulation norms have only been partially met by banks, if at all. Moreover, the moral hazard problem characterised by the chance that banks may falsify data about their business operations helped banks to cut their own transaction costs. It has caused further difficulties in enforcing informal institutions of lending.

It appears that the lack of an extensive understanding of risk and risk management, the erroneous perception of bankers about the functioning of bank supervision and the influence of state authority and personal relationships lead to difficulties in enforcing existing bank regulation norms in Mongolia. The longer such a situation remains in place, the more difficult it will be to alter the direction of an institutional change and economic development – path dependence. Once this path is taken, bankers' learning processes, together with existing subjective modelling, will reinforce the course. This unproductive path[42] (since it is not market-oriented) would reinforce the existing disincentives and unproductive banks.

Thus Mongolia's economy is characterised by many unproductive banks, resulting in financial inadequacies. Banks can not properly accomplish the tasks assigned to them in a market economy: namely, to allocate capital, to ensure corporate governance and to transmit monetary impulses to the real sector. And as we have seen, this goes back to conditions at the microeconomic level. They are a consequence of the institutional legacy of the past and of incomplete reforms in transition.

If we view financial inadequacies, i.e. the passivity of credit allocation, as being at the core of Mongolia's economic problems, microeconomic reforms deserve greater attention. The next chapter puts forward some suggestions on how to address the problems in the banking and enterprise sectors of the Mongolian economy.

---

42 The compatibility of institutions is though not a sufficient, but necessary condition of economic efficiency and economic growth (1.1.3).

4.2 Implications and Future Challenges

4.2.1 Restructuring the Overall Institutions Over Time

Where incompatible institutions exist, North's Theory of Economic and Institutional Change suggests restructuring the overall constraints in both directions to produce a new institutional equilibrium.

For institutions of lending in Mongolia, this means that the existing informal institutions – e.g. the attitude to risk – should be changed faster than hitherto and the new "revolutionary" formal institutions – bank regulation norms - should be adapted to them. Moreover, this restructuring of overall constraints is a process that recurs over time. From time to time, bank regulation norms should adapt to a new constellation of informal rules: change is an incremental, ongoing process.

Thus the present mental models of bankers should be changed to those that integrate (accept) the arranged bank regulation norms. And mental models integrate new formal rules only if there is a simultaneous interaction of them with existing informal rules. Such a change to the mental models of Mongolian bankers would ensure an efficient enforcement of bank regulation norms. Under these circumstances, lending decisions should result in productive loan granting and thus in an effective allocation of even scarcer financial resources in Mongolia.

Meaningful institution reforms in Mongolia should address sources, agents and the direction of change – based on the Theory of Economic and Institutional Change (nature of institutional change in 1.1.3).

In Mongolia, changes in lending are a consequence of the daily choices made primarily by Mongolian bankers, but also entrepreneurs (borrowers), supervisors at the BOM (economists, bankers), members of Parliament and the Government (politicians). If these organisations, thus **agents of change in Mongolia**, perceive they could do better by restructuring exchange relations, institutional modification will occur. Addressing agents of change therefore involves implementing action which would improve bankers' abilities to detect profitable opportunities and realise them.

The same holds for the abilities of other agents, such as entrepreneurs, supervisors and politicians. If entrepreneurs recognised new opportunities to make from trade and were willing to exploit these, this would impel changes in the rules of the game in lending and exert pressure on bankers and banks. Seeking to improve their position, e.g. working conditions or work results, supervisors at the BOM could prompt bankers to organise themselves in order to gain the most best possible position in negotiations on the rules of the "lending" game.

However, an alteration of relative prices and preferences (new exchange situation) needs to occur – nature of institutional change in NIE - before the agents are activated or start to exploit profits from trading. Thus addressing the **sources of institutional change in Mongolian lending** could involve measures to import new knowledge on socio-economic coherence in general as well as new expert or technical knowledge on operations in money and capital markets. For example, new knowledge about the nature of financial products: loan is by nature risky, meaning hereby not only a possibility of loss but at the same time – a chance of gain. Moreover, measures supporting new techniques and instruments should alter relative prices, such as in credit investigation processes, interbank settlements or supervision activities. Finally, the alteration of resources of any kind, qualitative and quantitative, would shift relative prices and preferences. For example, the ongoing land reforms in Mongolia would definitely change the transaction costs of lending: the chance of owning a plot of land would change real estate prices and allow more active loan granting.

The **direction of change in Mongolia** is characterised by a path dependence which involved leaping the capitalist system and jumping into seventy years of communist rule. That makes it difficult for Mongolian bankers and borrowers to alter the direction abruptly to go down a completely different path. And after the shock of changing paths in 1991 when the development path of market-based lending was taken, the banking system in Mongolia had come "down-to-earth" around 1999. The learning process has now began after having overcome (at least partly) the strong reinforcement of historically derived subjective models of passive bankers.

For this reason, purposeful action should be taken to address this process by positively influencing the perceptions of individuals about the fairness of the rules of the "lending" game – ideology; by strengthening democratic infrastructures – political markets. The role of political markets and an understanding of the special features and anomalies of political markets in Mongolia then and today would be very supportive for economic reforms in general and banking in particular. The change in how individuals perceive fairness in the rules of "lending" game should be a step in the right direction. In the meantime, Mongolian banks are seen as producing nothing and ripping off their customers.

Thus the switch from passivity to activity in the banking system is a question that must be addressed by reforms which, as far as possible, simultaneously bring about change in formal and informal rules of lending – **institution building in lending,** e.g. by enhancing banking supervision norms. Some suggestions for institutional reforms in the Mongolian banking system are now made based on basic principles mentioned above.

4.2.2 Approaches to Institution Building in Lending in Mongolia

By addressing the sources, the agents and the direction of change in Mongolia, some concrete actions to change the informal institutions observed in this study are proposed. The vertical axis of Table 4.1 contains informal institutions which need changing – an insubstantial attitude to risk, erroneous perception of bankers about the functioning of bank supervision, the standard of ethics in personal relations, and commitment to the authoritative state. The elements of change are placed on the horizontal axis, these being new knowledge, innovation and resource alteration as sources of change; bankers as agents of change; ideology and democratic structures as the direction of change. These elements should be addressed by the suggested measures[43], which fill the intersection cells of the table.

Altering the insubstantial attitude to risk

In order to incrementally establish a prudent attitude towards risk, new knowledge and innovation should be created bringing about alteration of resources. Creating **new knowledge** refers to the general knowledge on the new socio-economic coherency on the one hand, and to new expert and technical knowledge on how loan markets operate and the nature of financial products on the other. This can be addressed in two ways:

> **A1:** Ensuring the professional knowledge/skills of bankers by an obligation – with qualitative bank supervision norm – to train loan officers abroad: for instance, in the form of internship at their correspondent banks abroad. Practical experience shows that it is not only possible but even supported by correspondent banks (in their business interest).

[43] The suggestions implicate change or adjustment of many laws and regulation norms such as civil law, economic laws, law on central bank, additional qualitative bank regulation norms as well as general economic policies, government policy towards banking infrastructure etc.

A2: Ensuring that loan officers learn by doing under an obligation – with qualitative bank supervision norm - to employ foreign experts on temporary contracts in some determined fields: e.g. risk and return, credit risk management, collateral assessment, portfolio management etc. This obligation can be graded by the economic ability of banks to afford it. However, every bank active in Mongolia is in such a position in the meantime.

New **innovative** techniques and instruments should target - in the first instance - the transformation of "uncertainty" into "risk" (see findings). That means:

A5: Operationalisation of risk in the day-to-day work of Mongolian bankers: making risk definable and measurable, calculable and limitable (risk management). In particular, deposit insurance initiatives should be encouraged, working groups of experts from banks, the BOM and politicians could jointly process risk diversification methods and hedge instruments against the volatility of the main products produced by the Mongolian economy. Thus both active measures of economic government policies and the co-operation of politicians, BOM and bankers are required. Moreover, a tremendous effort is needed to establish a sound deposit insurance sector in Mongolia. An obligation to inform depositors whether their deposits – with qualitative bank supervision norms - are insured or not could give an incentive to bankers to be more engaged in this matter.

A8: Introducing a system of collateralisation. The security of convenient property rights has to be ensured, the bundle of rights over collateralised property is of great importance: not only the right of use and to derive income, but also to exclude and exchange it. This requires an amendment to the constitution and existing economic laws.

Resources can be altered externally and internally, qualitative and quantitative:

A9: External alteration can be brought about by systematic support of foreign investments in banking (capital). As the domestic market of Mongolia is rather small, strategies which attract foreign investment in Mongolian banking in respect to regional gains could be imagined. The capital of Mongolia, Ulaanbaatar, is virtually the only economic centre of any size in Siberia, and is politically the most stable in Central Asia. Appropriate economic laws and policies are required.

A10: Internal alteration can be reached by changes in the quality of property rights. Up-to-date reforms in the law on land in sedentary areas will bring about movements in property structures. It will alter relative prices for some products and services, giving individuals incentives to change their behaviour, including the attitude of bankers to risk.

If this alteration of relative prices occurs (A1, A2, A5, A8, A9, A10), agents of change, thus financial organisations and their members – banks and bankers – could **be able to recognise the new opportunities** and jump at the chance. Hence:

A6: Obtaining and processing information should be made easier and more efficient. Bankers need comprehensive data to understand the complexity of a problem. The communication channels recently introduced by the Mongolian Government can be used to collect and report data on customers in the countryside – governmental policy towards banking infrastructure. These data can be transferred to Ulaanbaatar where the database is managed. Banks could be obligated – with qualitative bank regulation norms – to become a member of this data pool and pay their contributions.

A15: Improving the access of bankers to new knowledge by obligating banks to subscribe to a few main regional and international professional journals and newspapers – qualitative bank regulation norm.

Impersonalising the exchange relationship

Apart from the previously proposed suggestions in respect to **new knowledge A1** (obligation to train loan officers abroad) and **A2** (obligation to employ foreign experts), personalised relationships (based on historical standards of ethics) can also be changed to impersonalised relations by:

A4: Standardisation of key activities in lending within banks and within the banking system as a whole – qualitative bank regulation norms including unitised accounting and reporting standards. That would create new knowledge and information, bringing transparency into the system.

Innovative techniques should shift the emphasis of economic thinking of individuals into the analyses of contracting and contractual relationship by:

A12: Introducing qualified contractual instruments and mechanisms. Thinking in contracts is one of main targets to be achieved if Mongolia's economic system is to become a market-based one. Economists and lawyers (as well as politicians) are required to work together to establish the culture of contracts. Collective (joint) training of bankers and borrowers could be useful in this context.

Table 4.1: Suggestions on further institutional reforms of banking in Mongolia

Source: own work out

Informal constraints (informal institutions) to be changed	**Addressing source of change** (alteration of relative prices)		**Addressing agent of change**		**Addressing direction of change**	
	New knowledge: General knowledge on socio-economic coherence as well as expert knowledge and technical knowledge on operations at money markets	**Innovation:** New techniques and instruments	**Resources alteration:** Resources alteration of any kind, quantitative as well as qualitative	Bankers recognising new possibilities of gains from trade and pressing to change the rules	Influence of the games of rules of political markets: democratic infrastructures (path-dependence)	Ideology: Perception about fairness of the rules of the game; ability to realise and reorganise
Insubstantial attitude to risk	**A1**: Ensuring the professional skills of banker by an obligation to train loan officers abroad – qualitative bank regulation norm. **A2**: Ensuring learning by doing of loan officers by an obligation to employ foreign experts under limited contract in determined fields – qualitative regulation norm.	**A5**: Operationalisation of risk by an extra encouraging deposit insurance initiatives, by initiating diversification methods, by provisions of hedge against price volatility in main products – government's economic policies. **A8**: Introducing system of collaterisation by ensuring the security of convenient property rights – economic laws.	**A9**: External alteration of resources by support of foreign investments in banking (capital as well as know how) – appropriate economic laws and policies. **A10**: Internal alteration of resources by changing respectively reforming the law on land in sedentary areas.	**A6**: Improving provision and processing of information by making the government's communication channels available to banks – government's policy towards banking infrastructure. **A15**: Improving access to new knowledge by obligating banks to subscribe main regional and international professional journals and newspapers.		

Erroneous perception of bankers about functioning of bank supervision	**A1, A2, A15** **A13**: Close co-operation of BOM with banks to enlighten the nature of financial products and its special influence on macroeconomic performance of Mongolia – BOM's engagement.	**A5, A8**		**A6** **A14**: Making the bank regulation authority independent either by disconnecting bank supervision department of BOM or by task sharing within several authorities – changes in law on central bank.		**A7**
Standard of personal relations	**A1, A2** **A4**: Standardisation of key activities in lending within banks – qualitative bank regulation norms.	**A12**: Shifting the emphasis in economic thinking into analysis of contracting by introducing qualified contractual instruments and mechanism – government policies.	**A 11**	**A6**	**A12**	**A7**: Changing the individual perception about the fairness and justice of the rules of the game by disputing intensively in the public and clarifying the elements of socio-economic system chosen for Mongolia – government policy as well BOM's engagement. **A12**
Commitment to authoritative state				**A1, A2** **A3**: Improving the ability of bankers to organise themselves by e.g. a strong and influential professional lobbing and NGOs – laws on representation of interests.	**A3** **A11**: Based on the strong traditional adaptability and the positive previous experience, medium and long term learning should strengthen democratic structures.	**A1, A2**

Under the new opportunities of A1, A2, A4, A12, the agents should **be able to identify new opportunities**. Apart from **A6** (obtaining and processing information to be made easier and more efficient by using the governmental communication channels), the bargaining power of bankers to apply pressure should improve by learning a banking habit of forward-looking evaluation in market economies.

Ideology consisting the **perceptions of individuals about fairness in the rules of the "lending" game** is a significant criteria for institutional change towards productive lending. Thus:

> **A7:** Changing the perception of individuals about the fairness and justice of the rules by extensive public debate and by clarifying the elements of the socio-economic system that has been chosen for Mongolia. On the one hand, this involves the macro- and microeconomic role of banks, and on the other, focusing public disputes (with depositors, borrowers, lenders etc.) on an objective evaluation of past banking crises, which strongly weakened confidence in the new banking system. This requires the active engagement of the Government and the BOM. Due to the traditional culture and mentality of Mongols, economists and politicians who enjoy public confidence may have a quite viable impact on public opinion.

Altering the mental models of individuals regarding the role of the state

Social commitments, such as that to the authority of state, have been one of obstacles of transition. Changing these is still painful due to the traditional, strong reliance on the state, which is a "corporate" identification, if not with a kind of "almighty" power. Now, in the new system of democratic and market order, the role of the state shifts from that of bailing out to providing services. Mongols are currently redefining the role and functions of the institution "state" within the new order. In this context, the suggestions for improving the professional sphere within the mental models of bankers **A1** (ensuring the professional skills of bankers by an obligation to train loan officers abroad) and **A2** (loan officers working with foreign experts under contract in some determined fields) should be complemented with along with alterations to other spheres in the mental models of agents, especially bankers:

> **A3:** Improving the ability of bankers to organise themselves, e.g. by strong and influential professional lobbing and NGOs. The existing Association of Mongolian Bankers is still weak due to the lack of awareness of the need for such an organisation among financial institutions. A push might be given by the activity of competitive groups (at political markets) like borrowers or politicians seeking to make the most gain, as well as by laws regulating representation of interests.

The rules of the game in political markets are in the process of being established and have not yet stabilised. However, looking back on the experiences of political processes during transition in Mongolia, the traditional ability of Mongols to adapt and adjust can be recognised. A relatively stable political situation has been created and past experience has been moulded to form democratic structures. Thus:

> **A11:** Based on the strong traditional adaptability and the positive previous experience with democratic structures, the path of political change and the role of state can be influenced with medium- and long-term learning at best.

Altering bankers' perception about the functioning of bank supervision

The current mental model of Mongolian bankers sees the purpose of bank supervision as guaranteeing credit solvency. This must be altered so that bank supervision is perceived as aiming to limit systemic risk within the banking system (by protecting depositors and improving confidence in banks). The perception of bank supervision is, insofar, related to the attitude that Mongolian bankers have towards risk, so that suggestions **A1**, **A2**, **A5**, **A8**, **and A6** would also have an impact on altering how bankers perceive the functions of bank supervision. Additionally:

> **A13:** The BOM should co-operate closely with banks to raise understanding of the nature of financial products and their special influence on the macroeconomic performance of Mongolia – active engagement of BOM. Moreover, an instrument to cumulate experiences made by bankers (banking crises etc.) might support learning and brain-storming within banking.
>
> **A14:** Making the bank regulation authority independent will give incentives to both bankers and supervisors. That can be done either by decoupling the bank supervision department from de jure independent (from parliament) but de facto contingent BOM, or by spreading responsibilities among several authorities. And it would require changes in civil law as well as to the Central Bank Act.

Some suggestions, especially those which contain qualitative bank regulation norms, have a very regulative character. However, they are temporary measures necessary to establish the mental model of an “active” banker, and should become redundant in the course of time, once market mechanisms function on their own.

Part 5 Conclusions

Despite some economic progress, the present realities in Mongolia do not match the initial hopes placed in the outcome of reform. Although the reforms followed the suggested approach of liberalisation and privatisation, the response at the microeconomic level remained unsatisfactory. The reforms did not create properly functioning markets as had been expected. The transformation program placed greater emphasis on macroeconomic policy whilst microeconomic issues were not thoroughly tackled.

The lack of reform at the microeconomic level has therefore made it harder to implement strict macroeconomic policies. The reason for this is that the programmes implemented and the models they are founded on mostly failed to take into account the behaviour of economic agents in transitional Mongolia. The behaviour of enterprises, bankers etc. differs from that in market economies and the response is in fact different to reform measures. Looking at the microeconomic conditions and considering the existing specific characteristics of the behaviour of economic agents should bring more insights for further economic policies towards stabilisation and growth, – systemic change.

Due to its important role as a financial intermediary within the economy, the banking system is a supporting element of a systemic change. The behaviour of individuals – bankers, borrowers, state authorities etc. – within the banking system significantly influence the allocation of financial resources. Applying the arguments of NIE to analyse lending in banks with respect to bankers' behaviour helps to explain some crucial issues of financial intermediation and imperfections within the banking system in Mongolia.

The purpose of the present study was to identify the informal institutions which channel the actions of Mongolian bankers. A cognitive approach was chosen to frame the survey on mental models of bankers. According to the principles of NIE, especially the Theory of Economic and Institutional Change by North, and of cognitive psychology, (informal) institutions channelling decisions of bankers are the external (to the mind) mechanism, which individuals use to order and structure their environment, whereas cognitive/mental models are internal representations.

The present study therefore assumed that diagnosing the mental models that Mongolian bankers have with regard to lending could indirectly bring insights into these informal institutions, direct observation and measurement of which is one of the outstanding challenges for economists and psychologists at the present. Based on existing models for observation of cognitive/mental models, which assume that mental models are shaped by knowledge – both conscious and unconscious, a research approach was evolved to diagnose the action-regulating knowledge of Mongolian bankers during lending.

Whereas the interrelation of institutions, mental models and knowledge is founded by the conception of knowledge organisation in memory, the conception and approaches of knowledge content help to indirectly observe informal institutions by diagnosing the content of this knowledge in memory.

A triangulation of methods – concept mapping, inspecting documents and interviews with individuals – was used to collect and analyse data to diagnose the action-regulating knowledge of Mongolian bankers. During the main method, that of concept mapping, bankers produced concept maps representing the main aspects of their current knowledge in the "lending" content domain. This "network" of concepts illustrated how bankers see the relation between things, ideas and people by showing their own interpretation of "risk and risk taking", "credit risk management and credit approval" and "banking and bank supervision".

The results indicate that the actions of Mongolian bankers are channelled by informal institutions which differ substantially from those assumed to be held in market economies. Mongolian bankers have not yet adapted a banking habit of a forward-looking nature:

- The mental models of Mongolian bankers lack a prudent attitude to risk. It was shown that Mongolian bankers perceive risk as an important factor, but risk is neither sufficiently understood nor operationalised in bankers' day-to-day work (hypothesis 1.1). Additionally, they neither recognise risk taking and reserves as related in terms of bank regulation (hypothesis 1.2), nor do they perceive credit risk management as a subject matter of bank supervision (hypothesis 1.3).
- The bankers' mental models contain erroneous or one-sided perception about the functioning of bank supervision. Mongolian bankers comprehend the targets of bank supervision as being guaranteeing loan repayment and providing information (hypothesis 2). They perceive supervision not as a regulating, but rather as bailing out mechanism.
- Mongolian bankers feel influenced by officials in making decisions on lending (hypothesis 3). The decision makers in banks are still aware of the status of the state and its hierarchy: commitments to the authoritative state are present in the mental models of bankers.

- Bankers definitely make use of personal relations for data provision, but there is no strong evidence for a direct influence of family ties on lending decisions (hypothesis 4). Although relationship lending has not been explicitly proved, it was revealed that ties of family and friendship play a significant role, less so because they represent good collateral, but rather that they carry credibility.

The continuing "passive" behaviour of Mongolian banks is thus accounted for by the informal institutions identified which constrain the lending decisions of Mongolian banks – an insubstantial attitude to risk, the erroneous or one-sided perception of bankers about the functioning of bank supervision, the commitment to authoritative state, and the standards of ethics in personal relations.

Formal and informal rules in lending have not been altered simultaneously – there is an incompatibility between the existing regulation norms on lending and informal constraints of lending. As the bank regulation norms in Mongolia are based on the norms of advanced market economies, these assume that bankers have appropriate mental models to channel the actions of "active" banks.

By addressing the institutional framework and its change, banking reforms concentrated on modifying the formal rules of lending – laws, legal regulations, standardisation of bank regulation norms etc. Long into transition, the alteration of – or even establishment of new – informal rules was ignored in reform concepts. Thus, due to this discontinuity of change, the enforcement of newly introduced formal rules is endangered.

In order to address this deficiency, the overall institutions should be changed incrementally over time. This means that the existing informal institutions – e.g. attitude to risk – should be changed faster then hitherto, and the new "revolutionary" formal institutions – bank regulation norms – should be adapted to them. The existing mental models of bankers need to be changed to integrate the arranged bank regulation norms. Such a change in the mental models of Mongolian bankers would ensure enforcement of bank regulation. Under such circumstances, lending decisions should result in productive loan granting and – with sensible macroeconomic policies – in effective allocation of even scarcer financial resources in Mongolia.

The switch from passivity to activity in the banking system therefore must be addressed by reforms which lead to as simultaneous as possible change of formal and informal rules of lending – institution building in lending – e.g. by enhancing banking supervision norms. Some suggested approaches are:

- Instalment of appropriate – qualitative – bank regulation norms to provide new knowledge and innovation, such as an obligation to train loan officers abroad (e.g. in the form of internship at their correspondent banks abroad) or to employ foreign experts under temporary contracts in some determined fields. Additionally, obliging banks to subscribe to a few main regional and international professional journals and newspapers or to standardise the main elements of operations during lending – portfolio management procedure, credit risk management procedure etc. – are another examples of qualitative norms.
- Measures to modify individual perceptions about the fairness and justice of the rules of the "lending" game. This should involve extensive public debate and clarification of the elements of the socio-economic system chosen for Mongolia. The nature of financial products and their special influence on macroeconomic performance should be explained. Public disputes should focus both on the intrinsic features of the lending business and on an objective evaluation of past banking crises, which strongly weakened the confidence in the new banking system (to counter the image of banks as producing nothing real and ripping off their customers).
- Measures to grant access to data: the Government could possibly make its recently introduced communication channel available to the banking system for a fee.
- Legal amendments to make the bank regulation authority independent and ensure the quality of property rights.
- The aforesaid measures require the co-operation of politicians, BOM and bankers: working groups of experts from banks, the BOM and politicians could jointly process such matters as risk diversification methods and hedge instruments against the volatility of main products in the Mongolian economy, or evolve instruments to cumulate the experience of bankers (from banking crises etc.) to support learning within banking.

Although some of these suggestions are rather regulatory, they are temporary measures necessary to establish the mental models of "active" bankers and should become redundant in the course of time.

Summing up, by identifying informal institutional constraints on lending and showing the discrepancy between rapidly adapted formal rules and slowly changing informal rules, the present study described the conditions at the microeconomic level in the banking system in Mongolia which has led to low macroeconomic progress. The entire economic system is characterised by this constellation of economic policies in many EITs and has to be taken into account in order to ensure long-term economic development.

Moreover, applying an institutional approach to the analysis not only of the economic system but also of the political and social systems in EITs would yield much insight. The lack of appropriate (for the chosen socio-economic system) mental models of individuals is also observable at the political and social markets – behaviour of politicians during election campaigns in Mongolia like road making in their constituencies, bestowing food and clothes for voters, or promising these activities in case of election victory. The individuals' mental models do not differentiate between the duties of legislative and judicative powers.

The questions addressed by transition go far beyond the transition process itself. Institutional perspectives and the cognitive approach could also support research on the microeconomic foundations of the economic environment and macroeconomic reforms in advanced market economies. The difficulties in implementing the recent social and health reforms in Germany – underlain by inconsistent formal and informal institutions – or the incompatibility of rules within the drafted European Constitution (consisting institutions of a federal state as well as of a confederation) show the impact of institutions on change.

For further research, many worthwhile questions can be posed. A question of whether a pure market-based economy is the optimal one for countries such as Mongolia with very low population density and what might be a more appropriate one, is the subject to a separate study. Research on how to quantify institutions and to improve evaluation techniques for survey of informal institutions, would contribute to incorporation of institutional sets as variable into economic analysis.

Annex 1: Reserve requirements for Mongolian banks

Source: Regulation for Calculating and Controlling Reserve Requirements, 10th of April 2001, Regulation No. 181

Deposit liabilities of a bank for determining the minimum level of required reserves shall be comprehended as outstanding balance of domestic and foreign currency denominated accounts of business entities, citizens, Government demand deposits and time savings that are on the bank's balance sheet. Bank's cash in-vault, cash foreign currencies and cheques, domestic and foreign currency denominated demand deposits at the current account with the BOM will be considered as an available reserve of that particular bank. The percentage rate of required reserves, penalties for failure and remuneration of fulfilled part shall be determined by Governor's Resolution of the BOM. Domestic and foreign currency denominated demand deposits of the current account with the BOM accounts shall be calculated on the calendar date basis. The position of non-business day should be accepted by the position of the previous working day.

In order to control bank's liquidity on daily basis, the required reserves will be determined as a minimum level of daily average position of bank's demand deposits of the current account with the BOM. The MPRD shall monitor a maintenance of required reserves for each bank. The MPRD shall carry out the following measures in the case of certain bank's failure to meet reserve requirements: Penalties should be set for the failed bank and a maximum level of such penalty shall not exceed the BOM's highest lending rate to banks by more than 5 percentage point. Penalties will be directly deducted from the failed bank's current account with the BOM. Remuneration paid for the fulfilled reserves (domestic and foreign currency) and penalty imposed on unfulfilled parts should be calculated once a month for both first and last 15 days of that particular month and will be approved by the Governor's Resolution. Banks shall be informed as shown in Appendix 6. The Accounting and Automatization Department of BOM shall inform the failed bank every time, when direct deduction from its deposit account has taken place as penalty.

In the case, when a particular bank has failed to comply the reserve requirement for more than 3 consecutive months, the MPRD shall make a proposal and submit to the Board of Directors a set enforcing measures. The Bank Supervision Department, Internal Audit Department, Monetary Policy and Research Department and the BOM Branches in aimags shall control on credibility, timeness of data provided by banks and their branches. The MPRD should inform the Governor of BOM on the compliance of reserve requirements and bank liquidity position.

Annex 2: Prudential ratios for Mongolian banks

Source: Prudential Ratios Regulation, 3rd of October 2001, No. 459, Ulaanbaatar

The purpose of this regulation is to establish prudential ratios for evaluation of compliance of banks with Article 15 of the Banking Law, and control their fulfilment, and undertake enforcement measures stated in Article 31 of the Banking Law. Banks should evaluate risks inherent to the banking business by the following prudential ratios: capital adequacy ratio, liquidity ratio, credit concentration ratio, and forex risk ratio. They should calculate prudential ratios using their financial statements, and determine factors, which influenced major changes of these ratios, thereby properly manage relevant risks.

Capital adequacy of banks should be evaluated on the basis of the following ratios: the total risk-assessed capital adequacy ratio, (RACAR), the Tier I risk-assessed capital adequacy ratio, (RATCAR), and the Tier I capital adequacy ratio(CAR). If the general level of risks of the bank is higher than the system average then the Governor of the Bank of Mongolia can impose minimum requirements for that bank greater than those mentioned in 2.2,2.3 and 2.4 provision of this regulation.

Prompt corrective actions should be taken for undercapitalised banks. On the basis of compliance with capital adequacy ratios, the banks shall be classified as follows : well capitalised (RACAR of 10 percent or greater, RATCAR of 5 percent or greater and CAR of 5 percent or greater), undercapitalised (RACAR within 6-10 percent, RATCAR or CAR that any of this two ratio is within 3- 5 percent), significantly undercapitalised (total risk-based capital ratio that is within 3-6 percent, either Tier 1 risk-based capital ratio or leverage ratio that any of this two ratio is within 1- 3 percent), critically undercapitalised (RACAR within 1-3 or RATCAR or CAR within 1- 3 percent), uncapitalised bank (RACAR lower than 0).

Concerning the liquidity ratio, liquid assets is the sum of vault and other cash, deposits with the Bank of Mongolia, deposits with other banks, the Bank of Mongolia bills, the Government securities less by clearing payment delays. The Government bills, which terms haven't been specified by the contract, including bank restructuring bonds, deposits with the banks placed under conservatorship or receivership, and deposits pledged as warranty for the certain payment guarantee and)or letter of credit shall not be treated as liquid assets. Total liabilities is the sum balances of all types of deposits, including deposits of private enterprises, households, the Government, and other banks, inter-bank borrowing, funds attracted from the NBFIs, investment funds, and other liabilities less by clearing payment delay. Liquidity ratio is the comparison of liquid assets to total liabilities, which is calculated in Togrog, forex, and in their total sum. The bank should keep the liquidity ratio level over 18 percent.

Important issue in respect to lending concern the credit concentration risks. The credit concentrations limits are established in order to prevent the deterioration of the bank's financial condition due to losses incurred by the large exposures to a single borrower or group of related borrowers. The compliance of banks with single borrower and related borrowers exposure shall be evaluated on the basis of the report prepared in accordance with the appendix 3 of this regulation. Total amount of loan to single borrower or related borrower should not exceed 20 percent of the bank's capital. The bank shall determine the credit concentration limit level regarding geographic location, sectors of economy, guarantees and collateral on its own and those limits should be enforced.

Forex risk ratio evaluates impact of forex revaluation loss to the bank's financial standing. Forex prudential ratio is calculated as a ratio of on-balance and off-balance items between assets and liabilities denominated in forex over- the paid up capital. (See attachment 9) Prudential ratio is calculated for overall and each forex open positions. Forex risk report shall cover forex derivatives, guarantees, letter of credit, income and expenditure, and options, which will become due in period of 3 months, from the date of compiling period. Difference between forex assets and liabilities should not exceed 40 percent of paid up capital. Bank may calculate the prudential ratio of foreign exchange risk by VAR method. (See attachment 10) To use this methodology a special permission is required from the Supervision Department. The bank with this permission will be eligible not to follow limitations stated 6.6 and 6.8 of this regulation and the loss amount calculated by VAR method should not exceed 10% of paid up capital.

Credit risk management or structure of internal audit.

1) The bank has unit for risk management, where calculates daily risks by using mathematical and software systems for probability of loss that bank might occur from market risk, and this is provided report to management.
2) The manager of risk management unit has a right to trade assets, liabilities under the management, use the risk measuring scores derived from special software and programmes for setting up trading limit level.
3) Bank has approved internal regulations, special recommendations and resolutions of staff's right and responsibility on risk management.
4) Bank's internal audit unit has embedded the following items in its regulations and documentation.

Software and assumptions used to calculate a risk should meet the following standards:

- capability of calculating the VAR on a daily basis,
- error probability has to be 99 % and normally distributed,
- calculate the result of VAR for 10 working days,
- in calculating exchange rate volatility to use random research methodology, and at least 250 independent observation or 5 years results to be covered. (For the banks using weighted average and other methodologies, the weighted average periods time gap should be not less than 6 months),
- to update related information base at least once in every 3 months .

Annex 3: Concepts of sub-domain " Banking and Bank Supervision" (map III)

Source: own work out

25 concepts:

- causality concepts *Bank activity*, *Lending;*
- situational concepts *Bank supervision*, *Bank of Mongolia;*
- goal concepts *Risk taking*, *Financial stability;*
- operation concepts *Licensing*, *Bank supervision requirements*, *Capital requirements*, *Reserve requirements*, *CAR (capital adequacy ratio)* ;
- partners concepts *Basel Committee*, *Basel I*, *Basel II*, *BIS;*
- means concepts *Reports, On-site inspection;*
- results concepts *Risk management, Credit risk management, RAROC.*

Alternative concepts are *Government*, *Insolvency*, *Guarantee*, *Bank governance, Warning.*

Annex 4: Reference map for action-regulating knowledge on sub-domain "Banking and Bank Supervision"

Source: own illustration

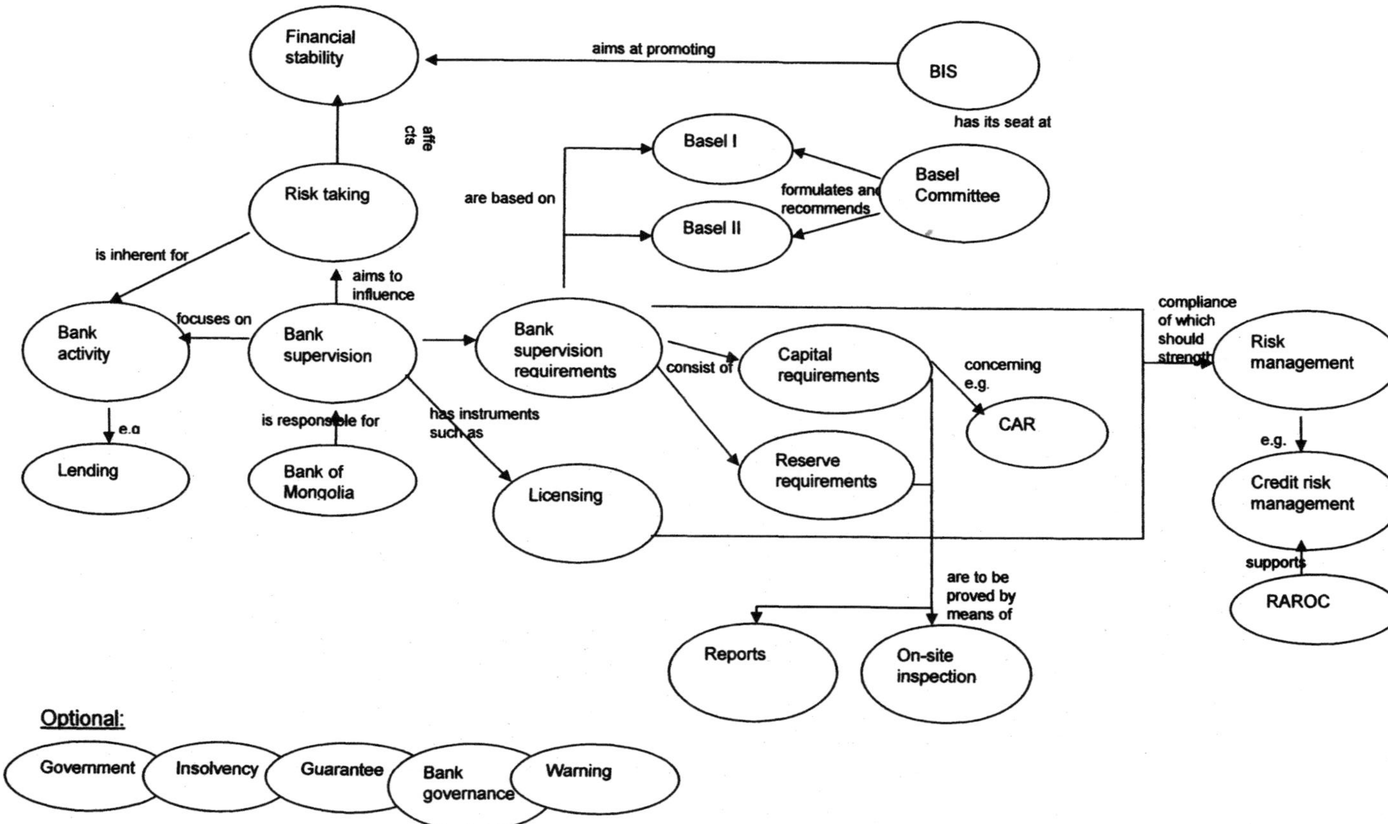

Annex 5: Individual Interview Sheet

Source: own work out

A. First, I would like to ask you some technical questions about credit applications:

1. **How many** credit applications do you receive **per month**?
2. Which of them are usually **returned** (without a credit investigation)?
3. Which of them **go through** credit investigation?
4. How many credit files do you have **right now**?

B. Now, please tell me about your day-to-day work at the bank by answering the following questions:

5. **How long does** it take from the time of credit application receipt to the ultimate decision?
6. **Which documents** and data, from **where** and from **whom** do you use to conduct credit investigation?
7. Which data do you usually have to **procure in addition**?
8. How far are on-site inspections of **significance**? What is the objective of doing it?
9. **Which colleagues** do you intensively co-operate with **during credit analysis**?
10. Which colleagues do you work with **after** credit analysis but before a definite decision is made on granting a loan?
11. Which colleagues do you work closely with **during the credit**?

C. It would be very helpful to learn more about your opinion of credit investigation. I would like to ask you to talk about it answering these questions:

12. Suppose, I would like to work as a loan officer. What **skills** should I have?
13. Which **costs** are incurred by credit investigation?
14. On which **basic principle** is loan granting based on in your opinion?
15. To what extent is **your job** concerned **with credit risk**?
16. What **relationship** do you think exists between collateral and credit risk?
17. How far are credit risk and trust **cohered** in your own option?

D. And finally, in order to learn about your experience and feelings I would like you to answer the following six questions:

18. If there would be something you **always have to keep in mind** when granting a loan, what would it be?
19. Which **operation** do you think is **the most important** for your job?
20. What seems to be the **most important factor for the ultimate decision** about loan granting?
21. How do you value the **role and contribution** of credit investigation for decision making on granting loans?
22. How significant are the last legal **reforms** concerning the loan granting?
23. What do you think is the **reason** for the **lack of long term** loans?
24. Suppose you are asked by an apprentice what is **the best credit**, what and how would you explain?
25. Which influence has the co-operation of **international supervision institutions** with the BOM on your activities?

Annex 6: Lending procedure (complete version)

Source: own work out

Actions implemented by	LO	LOB	LR	LL	HD	SCC	SLO	CC	HC	EXD	NOTE
0. Consulting and advising on credit	O	O									
00. Advising on loan application						O					
1. Receiving the application, examining the completion and satisfaction of the processing requirements		O				O					
2. Choosing a loan officer and forwarding the application for credit analysis						O, **DM**					
3. Registering the application in the Application Book		O				O					
4. Opening a Credit File	O										
5. Checking whether the documents have any incompleteness	O	O									
6. If so, asking to eliminate the drawback	O	O									Within 5 days
7. If not met the deadline, returning the application	O	O									
8. Inspecting the asset for pledging on site, taking photo or doing video tape-recording	O	O	O								
9. Explaining the guarantor about his duties	O	O									
10. Evaluating the suggested collateral of the borrower			O	O							
11. Collecting appropriate data and information in order to analyse (screen) the credit	O	O									
12. Examining the data and information	O	O									
13. Analysing the borrower and the credit risk	O	O									
14. Assessing the application documents (for conformity to legal requirements)				O							
15. Evaluating the borrower				O							
16. Completing the analyses, deciding whether to discuss further or not	**DM**	**DM**									Within 10 days
17. In negative case, writing motivations and returning the application to the borrower	O	O									Appendix 14
18. In positive case, preparing a memorandum on loan application assessment	O	O									Appendix 15
19. Presenting the memorandum t for further examination to the DCD and SCC	O	O									
20. Examining the credit risk, the content of memorandum and credibility of loan assessment					O						
21. Making his own opinion with a signature before submitting to the CC members					O						
22. Revising filling requirements with a checklist						O					
23. Copping the memorandum and submitting to the members of the CC	O	O									App. 16
24. Studying the memorandum and writing own opinion separately								O			Every member
25. Introducing to the DCC as a point of agenda for CC meeting						O					
26. Deciding whether to discuss the applied credit within the CC									**DM**		
27. Examining the properness of the credit analyses, of the memorandum									O		

28. Examining the credit risk									O		
29. Writing own opinion about the applied loan									O		
30. Chairing the meeting of the CC									O		
31. Monitoring the credit portfolio							O	O			
32. Reporting on the portfolio							O				
33. Deciding on the credit approval					DM, T		DM, T	DM, T	DM, T		SLO only within the subcommittee (up to 20 Mio)
34. Preparing the CC decision and giving it for HCs signature						O					Within one day
35. Handing over the copies of CC decision to LO for inserting it to Credit File						O					
36. Writing minutes of the CCs meeting						O					Within 5 days
37. Reporting the EXD about the decisions of the CC									O		
38. Monitoring the decisions of the CC										O	
39. Veto for the decisions of the CC, if necessary										DM	
Suggesting (requesting) a particular borrower (which has not passed the normal procedure, but potential in the sense of established business with minimum risk, sufficient source of income, quality collateral)					D				DM		
Suggesting new loan limit lines to the Assets and Liability Committee									O		
Implementation of the credit management								O			
Monitoring the loan repayment	O	O									
Monitoring the collateral	O	O	O								

Codification

LO Loan officer,
SLO Senior loan officer,
LOB Loan officer of the branch,
SCC Secretary of the Credit Committee (called also as loan administration officer),
HC Head of Credit Committee,
CC Credit Committee (director and four members named by the executive director of the bank),
HD Head of Credit Department,
LR Officer of the Loan Recovery Department ,
LL Lawyer responsible for loan affairs,
EXD Executive Director,
O Operational action,
DM Decision making action,
T Team decision.

Annex 7: Control roster for data collection during documents and records observation

Source: relied on Patton (1987)

Critical Characteristics and Questions	If and where data available	Notes
Which offices, or sites?		
Which staff? (including administrator, instructors, aides, secretaries)		
Which resources? (particularly resources purchased especially for CI)		
Which decision makers? (their number and particular characteristics that made them eligible, their level of competence)		
What materials used?		
Were they used as indicated?		
What procedures were prescribed for the CI staff in their interactions with clients?		
Were this procedures followed?		
In what activities were participants supposed to participate? (management, assistants, loan officers, clients)		
Did they?		
What administrative arrangements did the CI include?		
What lines of authority were to be used for making important decisions?		
What changes occurred in these arrangements?		
What kind of instructions? (modifications, office discipline, abuse of power)		
Is there any skills description for a loan officer?		

Annex 8: Schedule plan for data collection

Source: own work out

Action/ Operation	Where?	With whom?	How?
1. PRIOR LOGISTICAL CONSIDERATIONS: ARRANGING A SURVEY			
1.1. Pre-contact, reconcilement with project co-ordinators	Dresden, Frankfurt	Project co-ordinator	Exchange of intents in two meetings in Frankfurt, e-mails and calls
1.2. Approach and agreement with Bank	Dresden – UB	EXD, HD	Exchange of intents in calls, e-mails and faxes
1.3. Accord and supplement of professors	Dresden – UB	Two professors advising study	Approval of research objectives and ensuring confidentiality with professional secrecy agreement via fax
1.4. Technical planning and time table	Dresden –UB	Professors, HD	Confirmation of time table via fax
2. GOING INTO FIELD EXCURSION: GETTING STARTED			
2.1. Arrival on-site	Dresden –UB	-	Flight Berlin-Ulaanbaatar
2.2. Introduction and getting started	UB, BHO	HD, SPO, Los	Meeting, introduction round, working hours 9 a.m. till 6 p.m. (latest 6.30), work table
2.3. Agreeing on professional secrecy	Admin. Office	Officer	Signing an agreement on professional secrecy to get an access to minutes of CC meeting
3. DATA COLLECTION: DOCUMENTS AND RECORDS			
3.1. Overview of internal work instructions	BHO: CD	HD	Handing in of instructions: lending procedure rules, working instructions for CC
3.2. Checking up, plan modifications	At home	-	After getting an overview, the time table is modified and adapted
3.3. Feed back meeting	CD	HD	Asking him for old instructions, getting a work rules for granting loans to enterprises and institutions (in force until 1.1.2002); information on a new credit policy (draft in process). Asking about decision making structure and lines of authority: information on last developments in this field
3.4. Working with instructions	CD	-	Reading and transferring data from records?
3.5. Speedy sight on first credit files	CD	SPO, LOs	Getting an overview about structure, completeness, actuality. Asking to provide an insight into withdrawn loans: negative
3.6. Check up of instruction data	At home	-	Determining missing documents of instructions, formulating unclear points to ask
3.7. Feed back meeting	CD	HD	Exchange of information about incompleteness of credit files. He gives me his own notes on reformation issues of CD. Asking to provide an insight into minutes of CC's meetings: positive, but SCC protests, need to ask EXD.

3.8. Working with instructions	CD	Los	Reading and transferring data from records?
3.9. Meeting with EXD	EXD's office	EXD	Asking to allow to sight into minutes of CC's meetings: positive for some 4-5 cases.
3.10. Working with notes of HD	CD	-	Reading and transferring the data
3.11. Short conversation with project co-ordinator from Frankfurt	CD	Project co-ordinator	Exchange of information and suggestions: compare the past, present for future
3.12. Working with credit files	CD	-	Reading and transferring the data
3.13. Summary of records on instructions	At home	-	Building the credit investigation procedure table, checking data collection control roster
3.14. Working with credit files	CD	-	Reading and transferring the data
3.15. Interim records analysis	At home	-	Checking up data for de jure situation, summarising first findings of interim analysis
3.16. Interim records analysis	CD	-	Preparing the comparison on situations: de jure and de facto
3.17. Interim findings, planning days 6,7	At home	-	interim results
3.18. Interim findings, planning days 8-12	At home	-	formulating facts, questions to clarify
3.19. Working with credit files	CD	-	Credit memorandums,
3.20. Feed back discussions	Lunch	Bank officer	Discussion transparency and bureaucracy in the bank
3.21. Working with instructions	CD	Bank officer	Asking for a general directive assignment but getting a sample for a contract of employment: misunderstanding or ignorance?
3.22. Feed back meeting	CD	HD	Asking among other things for a sample of general directive assignment: no copy at the CD, but to find in the administration office
3.23. Feed back meeting	CD	SPO	Discussions about credit investigation procedure and the role of CC, its activities
3.24. Feed-back meeting	CD	SLO	Asking questions concerning responsibilities in administration affairs of the department
3.25. Working with credit files	CD	-	Reading and transferring data
3.26. Evaluating credit files	At home	-	Systematisation and prudence
3.27. Working with research proposal	CD	-	Working with my research design and procedure in order to make an overview of things done and to be done
3.28. Feed back talk	CD	LO	On the spur of the moment came about a talk with her, just after finish of concept mapping: banking system, financial intermediation in Mongolia, loan granting in the bank
3.29. Interim evaluation of data collection	At home	-	Interim evaluation of data collection, determining missing data, formulating questions
3.30. Feed back meeting	CD	SLO	Asking questions concerning portfolio management (procedures, responsibilities, experiences, opinion)
3.31. Feed back meeting	CD	SCC	Asking about her responsibilities, new requirements and possibilities of implementation, capacities and experience.
3.32. Feed back discussion	Bank's casino	HD	Overview of the stay, impressions and difficulties, additional questions

3.33. Attending internal seminar (tutorial)	Bank's seminar room	HD, Los	Seminar of credit investigation procedure, especially financial analysis in respect to the reliability and validity of data. One loan officer presents his own strategy, discussions.
3.34. Feed back discussion	A pub in the city	LO	Asking additional questions; discussions about the incentive structure in the bank, loan granting activities, experiences, granting priorities and about the seminars of the development project of Germany.
3.35. Systematisation of collected data	At home	-	Checking up, systematising collected data
4. DATA COLLECTION: CONCEPT MAPPING			
4.1. Modifying the reference map	At home	-	On the basis of interim findings, the reference map is amended with some new concepts
4.2. Making appointments for realisation of concept mapping	CD	HD, SLO	Asking to allow the concept mappings with loan officers: after instruction of HD the SLO builds two groups of five
4.3. Building concept Mapping, group 1	CD	5 Los	After introducing my self and the objectives of the study, an introduction to the concept mapping methods and instruction for mapping is given that followed by a sample and exercise. Administering cards and asking to build mappings (2,5 hours all together)
4.4. Building concept mapping, group 2	CD	5 Los	The same as 4.3.
4.5. Check up	At home	-	Checking the completeness of mappings
5. DATA COLLECTION: IN-DEPTH, INDIVIDUAL INTERVIEWS			
5.1. Modifying and re-fining the questions	At home	-	On the basis of interim findings some questions are added and some are modified
5.2. Making appointments for interviews	CD	LOs	After informing the HD an individual appointments are sought to make, but most want an ad hoc appointment
5.3. Individual interviewing	CD	10 LOs	Interviewing for one and a half hours each, 22 questions
5.4. Check up	At home	-	Checking the completeness , preparing additional questions
6. CLOSURE			
6.1. Leaving site	UB- Dresden	-	Flight Ulaanbaatar – Berlin
6.2. Systematisation of collected data	Dresden	-	Restructuring, reorganising the data (by using recording modes) for further analysis

Annex 9: Summing-up the rough evaluation results of map II "Credit Risk Management and Credit Approval"

Source: own work out based on 15 maps, in brackets – number of maps concerned

	Map II **Credit Risk Management and Credit Approval**
Concepts mostly sorted out	3 groups of concepts : • *Relatives* (in 11 of 15), *Clan* (12), • *Moody's* (10), *Standard&Poor's* (15), • *Measuring*(9), *Screening* (9),
Concepts centred, attached with many connections	The emphasis done in mappings is rather homogenous except following combination of concepts centred: • *Monitoring, Parliament,* and *Government* (2) • *Credit policy* and *Data analysis* (3) • *Credit committee* and *Data analysis* (2)
Important Interrelations produced	• Bankers point out structural components of the process credit approval: *Data analysis, Credit policy, Credit Committee, Credit investigation.* • Credit risk management is not defined and a few relations were noted to it: mostly episodic, simple relations. • If the concepts *Relatives* and *Clan* were not sorted out, they were linked (directly or indirectly) to concepts *Credit investigation, Personal integrity, Credit facility. Acquaintance and friend* play an important role for *Provision of data.* • Concepts like *Monitoring, Parliament, Government* are often centred and attached with concept such as *Data analysis, Credit Committee, Management.*
Conclusions	• *Credit risk* is a known and seemingly topical term, but as regards its content bankers can't do anything with it. The *Credit risk management* is not identified as a process. • Bankers are aware of the status of the state and its influence during lending. • There is an implicit indication of an importance of personal relationships in lending. • Banking in Mongolia is based on a house bank relationship.

Annex 10: Summing-up the rough evaluation results of map III "Banking and Bank Supervision"

Source: own work out based on 15 maps, in brackets – number of maps concerned

	Map III **Banking and Bank Supervision**
Concepts mostly sorted out	*BIS* (15), *Basel Committee*(14), *Basel I* (14), *Basel II* (14), *RAROC*(15),
Concepts centred, attached with many connections	*Bank activity* (13), *Bank supervision* (14), *Bank governance* (9)
Important interrelations produced	• The tasks of *Bank supervision* are to influence *Risk taking* in banking (5) by overseeing the implementation of *Capital requirements* (13) and of *Reserve requirements* (6), to provide *Warning* (10) and to *Guarantee* (9). • No clearly defined relationship between *Bank supervision* and *Risk management/ Credit risk management* (1). • Bankers often point out the interrelation between *Bank supervision* and *Government* (8).
Conclusions	• Apart from accepting bank regulation as an significant institution, there is an incomplete, if not erroneous, perception of the functions and targets of *Bank supervision*. • Important issues of international *Bank supervision* are not known by Mongolian bankers. • Bankers are aware of the role or the influence of the *Government* in *Bank supervision*.

Annex 11: Cumulated matrix for map III "Banking and Bank Supervision"

Source: own work out based on evaluation matrices of 15 maps

EIs	Content of EIs	P1	P2	P3	P4	P5	P6	P7	P8	P9	P10	P11	P12	P13	P14	P15	S	%
EI 74	The relationship between *Bank supervision* and *Bank governance* relies on the perception that supervisory activities influence the way bank governance is shaped .	-	-	C	C	DR	SR	-	SR	D	R	SR	-	-	D	-	9	60
EI 75	The relationship between *Bank governance* and *Risk taking* is based on the circumstance that the form of bank governance shape the pattern of risk behaviour.	-	DR	A	DR	SR	SC	-	SC	R	-	SR	-	R	C	SR	11	73
EI 76	The relationship between *Bank supervision* and *Reports* shows the way of proving the compliance of bank supervision requirements.	MP	C	MP	MP	-	MP	C	MP	C	MP	-	MP	MP	MP	SR	13	87
EI 77	The relationship between *Bank supervision* and *On-site inspection* shows the ways of proving the compliance of bank supervision requirements.	-	-	MP	MP	-	D	-	-	MP	A	-	-	-	MP	-	6	40
EI 78	The relationship between *Bank supervision requirements / Capital requirements* and *CAR* refers to precise norms and ratios of bank supervision instruments.	SR	-	DR	DR	SR	DR	DR	-	DR	DR	SR	SC	SC	DR	SC	13	87
EI 79	The relationship between *Bank supervision* and *Bank supervision requirements / Licensing* shows the important instruments of bank supervision.	SR	SC	DR	MP	SC	SR	A	A	A	SR	SR	SR	A	SC	SC	15	100
EI 80	The relationship between *Risk taking* and *Bank supervision* is due to the aim of bank supervision to influence the bank's risk behaviour.	-	-	-	-	SR	-	D	-	R	-	R	-	-	R	-	5	33
EI 81	The relationship between *Bank supervision* and *Financial stability* is based on the pursuit of bank supervision to promote financial stability.	-	-	SR	-	SR	-	-	-	R	-	-	-	-	SR	R	5	33
EI 82	The relationship between *Bank supervision* and *Reserve requirement* illustrates the instrument of bank supervision to cover bank's risk by means of reserves.	-	-	C	SC	-	SR	-	-	C	SR	-	-	-	SR	-	6	40
EI 83	The relationship between *Bank supervision / Bank supervision requirements* and *Basel I, Basel II* relies on the fact that supervision requirements are based on international standards and guidelines for best supervisory practice (Basel I, II).	-	-	-	-	-	-	-	-	-	-	-	-	-	SC	-	1	7
EI 84	The relationship between *Basel Committee / BIS* and *Financial stability* bears on the fact that the Basel Committee has its seat at the BIS which on her part makes an effort to promote financial stability.	-	-	-	-	-	-	-	-	-	-	-	-	-	-	-	0	0

EI 85	The relationship between ***Basel Committee*** and ***Basel I / Basel II*** is based on the task of the Basel Committee to formulate and recommend broad supervisory standards and guidelines in order to ensure prudent supervision.	-	-	-	-	-	-	-	-	-	-	-	-	-	SR	-	1	7
EI 86	The relationship between ***Risk taking*** and ***Bank activity*** refers to the fact that risk is an inherent feature of banking.	SR	SR	-	SC	SR	SR	-	-	SC	-	-	-	SR	SR	-	8	53
EI 87	The relationship between ***Risk taking / Credit risk management*** and ***RAROC*** refers on one of widely used methodologies to quantify the level of risks in each business unit in order to manage these risks.	-	-	-	-	-	-	-	-	-	-	-	-	-	-	-	0	0
EI 88	The relationship between ***Bank supervision*** and ***Insolvency*** rests on perception of bankers that bank supervision should save banks from insolvency. <u>(control item)</u>	-	-	A	D	SR	SR	-	SC	A	D	-	D	-	A	-	9	60
EI 89	The relationship between ***Bank supervision*** and ***Warning*** bears on the task of bank supervision to forewarn banks and bankers in their risky activities. <u>(control item)</u>	-	SR	SR	A	SR	SR	-	SR	A	A	-	A	-	A	-	10	67
EI 90	The relationship between ***Bank supervision*** and ***Guarantee*** and ***Insolvency*** is based on (presumed) perception of bankers that bank supervision warrants prevention of insolvency. <u>(control item)</u>	-	-	A	SC	SR	SR	-	SR	A	D	-	A	-	SR	-	9	60
EI 91	The relationship between ***Bank supervision*** and ***Government*** is based on the (presumed) perception that Government has an influence on bank supervision activities. <u>(control item)</u>	-	-	SR	D	SC	SR	D	A	A	-	SR	-	-	-	-	8	53
EI 92	The relationship between ***Bank governance*** and ***Government*** relies on the (presumed) perception that Government can interfere banking activities. <u>(control item)</u>	-	-	-	SR	-	SR	SC	SC	SC	-	SC	-	-	-	-	6	40
EI 93	The relationship between ***Bank supervision / Bank supervision requirements*** and ***Risk management*** is based on the impact of bank supervision activities to strengthen risk management of banks.	-	-	-	-	-	-	-	-	-	-	-	-	-	-	-	0	0

Codification: The proposition (relation) results from the way of reading from left upwards:

SR	Simple relation	**O(SR)**	Objection of SR	**P(SR)**	Potentiality of SR
SC	Simple characteristic	**O(SC)**	Objection of SC	**P(SC)**	Potentiality of SC
DR	Definitional relation	**O(DR)**	Objection of DR	**P(DR)**	Potentiality of DR
D	Dependence	**O(D)**	Objection of D	**P(D)**	Potentiality of D
C	Condition	**O(C)**	Objection of C	**P(C)**	Potentiality of C
R	Cause, Reason	**O(R)**	Objection of R	**P(R)**	Potentiality of R
A	Activity	**O(A)**	Objection of A	**P(A)**	Potentiality of A
MP	Means and Partner	**O(MP)**	Objection of MP	**P(MP)**	Potentiality of MP

Annex 12: Model of observation matrix: categories and information units (notes and sources).

Source: own work out

Date	Instructions and Procedure Guidelines	Credit Investigation Definition	Credit Risk Definition and Assessment	Line of Authority	Level of Competence	Compulsive Activities	Models of Organisation	Office Discipline	Group process models	Loan Handling	Loan Administration	Resources	Customers	Granted and withdrawn loans	Credit portfolio
25.01.02	N1: ...; LGP, §4.6: ...														
28.01.02	N2: ...				N2										
...															
...															
...															

Codification of information units:

N1, N2 ...	Numbered notes of the day
LGP	Loan Granting Procedure
WR	Work rules of CC
CC	Credit Committee
CF1, CF2	Numbered credit files

References

Aitchison, J. (1987): Words in the Mind: An Introduction to the Mental Lexicon, Oxford: Blackwell.

Alchian, A., **Demsetz,** H. (1972): Production, Information Costs, and Economic Organisation, American Economic Review, 62.

Allais, M. (1953): Fondements d'une Théorie Positive des Choix Comportant un Risque et Critique des Postulats et Axiomes de L'Ecole Américaine, in : Économétrie, Colloques Internationaux due Centre de la Recherche Scientifique, Volume XL, 257-332, Paris. (Translated into English in M. Allais and O. Hagen (eds.): Expected Utility Hypotheses and the Allais Paradox, D. Reidel Publishing Company, Dortrecht, Holland, 1979.)

Anderson, J. (1976): Language, Memory, and Thought, Hillsdale, NJ: Erlbaum.

Anderson, J. (1983): The Architecture of Cognition. Cambridge, MA: Harvard University Press.

Arestis, P., **Demetriades**, P. (1997): Financial Development and Economic Growth: Assessing the Evidence, Economic Journal, vol. 197, 783-799.

Ariunkhishig, G. (2003): Banks and Non Bank Financial Institutions Data, Research Bulletin, Bank of Mongolia, 5, Ulaanbaatar.

Arthur, B. (1989): Competing Technologies, Increasing Returns, and Lock-In by Historical Events, Economic Journal, March 1989, 99 (394), 116-131.

Ausubel, D. (1968): Educational Psychology: A Cognitive View, New York.

Bank of Mongolia (1996): Annual Report 1996, Ulaanbaatar.

Bank of Mongolia (2000): Annual Report 2000, Ulaanbaatar.

Bank of Mongolia (2001): Report 2001, manuscript, Ulaanbaatar.

Banking Law of Mongolia (1996): Banking Law of Mongolia, in: The Great Khural of Mongolia (Parliament), Laws of Mongolia, unofficial English translation, Ulaanbaatar.

Begg, D., **Portes**, R. (1993): Enterprise Debt and Economic Transformation: Financial Restructuring in Central and Eastern Europe, in: Mayer, C., Vives, X. (eds.), Capital Markets and Financial Intermediation, Cambridge, 230-361.

Bigman, D. **Leite**, S. (1993): Enterprise Arrears in Russia: Causes and Policy Options, IMF Working Paper, No. 61, August.

Black, S. (2002): Obstacles to Faster Growth in the Mongolian Transition, Journal of Asian Economics 13, 357-369.

Boote, P., **Tarvaa**, B., **Tsend**, A., **Tsendjav**, E., and **Unenburen**, N. (1997): Mongolia's Transition to a Democratic Market System, in: Woo, W., Parker, S, and Sachs, J., Economies in Transition: Comparing Asia and Eastern Europe, London: the MIT Press, 103-129.

Braun, H. (1997): Historische Wurzeln spezifischer Transformations- und Entwicklungsprobleme der Mongolischen Republik, in: Pohl, H., Gömmel, R. (eds.), Sozial- und Wirtschaftsgeschichte, Stuttgart, 512-543.

Braun, H., **Sedjav**, Ts. (1999): Das Geld- und Bankwesen der Mongolei eine historische Wurzel der Transformationsprobleme dieses Staates, manuscript, Regensburg.

Buch, C. (1993): An Institutional Approach to Banking Reform in Eastern Europe, Kiel Working Papers, No. 560, February, Kiel Institute of World Economics.

Campbell, D. (1995): Incentives: Motivation and the Economics of Information, Cambridge: Cambridge University Press.

CFS Even, (2002): Financial Market Development in Central Europe: The Banking Sector and Capital Markets, lecture given by Hanna Gronkiewicz Waltz.

Chimeddagva, D., **Jargalsaikhan**, J., and **Walters**, B. (2000): Macroeconomic Policy and Performance, in: Nixson, F. et al. (eds), The Mongoliian Economy: a Manual of Applied Economics for a Country in Transition, 41-70.

Coase, R. (1937): The Nature of the Firm, Economica, 4, 386-405.

Coase, R. (1991): The Institutional Structure of Production, The American Economic Review, vol. 8, issue 4, 713-719.

Cohen, L., **Lawrence**, M. (1994): Research Methods in Education, 4th Edition, London: Routledge.

Constitution of Mongolia (1992): The Constitution of Mongolia, in: The Great Khural of Mongolia (Parliament), Laws of Mongolia, unofficial English translation, Ulaanbaatar.

Davaajargal, L., **Ariuntungalag**, T., **Enkhuyag**, B. (2001): Bank Profitability in Mongolia, Research Bulletin, Bank of Mongolia, 1, Ulaanbaatar.

David, P. (1995): Clio and the Economics of QWERTY, in American Economic Review, May (Paper and Proceedings), 75 (2), 332-337.

Deese, J. (1965): The Structure of Associations in Language and Thought, Baltimore.

Demetriades, P., **Hussein**, K. (1996): Does Financial Development Cause Economic Growth? Times-Series Evidence from 16 Countries, Journal of Development Economics, Vol. 51, 357-411.

Diamond, D.W. (1984): Financial Intermediation and Delegated Monitoring, Review of economic Studies, 51, 393-414.

Dochy, F. (1994): Assessment of Domain-Specific and Domain-Transcending Prior Knowledge: Entry Assessment and The Use of Profile Analysis, in: Birenbaum, M., Dochy, F. (eds.), Alternatives in Assessment of Achievement, Learning Process and Prior Knowledge, Boston, 93-129.

Eberleh, E., **Neugebauer**, K., **Sträter**, O. (1989): Modelle des Wissens und Methoden der Wissensakquisition: eine Übersicht; erweiterte Fassung eines Vortrages am Forschungsinstitut für Anthropotechnik (FAT) der Forschungsgemeinschaft für Angewandte Naturwissenschaften (FGAN), Wachtberg-Werthhoven, Aachen.

Edwards, W. (1954): Behavioral Decision Theory, Annual Review of Psychology, 12, 473-498.

Eger, T., **Nutzinger**, H.G. (1999): Ordnungstheorie, Institutionenökonomik und Evolutorische Ökonomik, in: Cassel, D. (ed.), Perspektiven der Systemforschung, Berlin: Duncker und Humblot, 23-29.

Elmes, D. (1999): Research Methods in Psychology, Pacific Grove: Brooks Publications.

Enkhhuyag, B. (2002): Lessons From Past Ten Years (1991-2001) of Transition in the Banking System of Mongolia and Future Objectives, Research Bulletin, Bank of Mongolia, 4, Ulaanbaatar.

Enkhuyag, B., **Ariunkhishig**, G. (2002): Lenders' Survey, Research Bulletin, Bank of Mongolia, 4, Ulaanbaatar.

Erlei , M., **Leschke**, M., **Sauerland**, D. (1999): Neue Institutionsökonomik, Stuttgart: Schäffer-Poeschel.

Ernst, M., **Alexeev**, M., **Marer**, P. (1996): Transforming the Core – Restructuring Industrial Enterprises in Russia and Central Europe, Boulder.

Fama, E, **Jensen**, M. (1983): Agency Problems and Residual Claims, Journal of Law and Economics 26, 327-349.

Fama, E. (1980): Banking and the Theory of Finance, Journal of Monetary Economics, 10, 10-19.

Fama, E. (1985): What 's different About Banks?, Journal of Monetary Economics, 15, 29-36.

Fischler, F., **Mandl**, H. (2000): Wissen Sichtbar Machen: Wissensmanagement mit Mapping-Technicken, Göttingen.

Fraser, K., **Edwards**, J. (1985): The Effects in Training in Concept Mapping on Student Achievement in Traditional Tests, Research in Science Education, 15, 158-165.

Freinkman, L. (1995): Financial-industrial Groups in Russia: Emergence of Large Diversified Private Companies, Communist Economies & Economic Transformation, Vol. 7, No. 1, March 1995, 51-66.

Fürstenberg von, G. (1990): Acting Under Uncertainty: Multidisciplinary Conceptions, Boston: Kluwer.

Geweke, J. (1992): Decision Making Under Risk and Uncertainty: New Models and Empirical Findings, Boston: Kluwer.

Glaser, R., **Bassok**, M. (1989): Learning Theory and The Study of Instruction, Annual Review of Psychology, 40, 631-666.

Goldberg, V. (1976): Regulation and Administered Contracts, The Bell Journal of Economics, 7, 426-448.

Grunert, K. (1982): Informationsverarbeitungsprozesse bei der Kaufentscheidung: Ein Gedächtnispsychologischer Ansatz, Frankfurt: Lange.

Grunert, K. (1990): Kognitive Strukturen in der Konsumforschung, Heidelberg: Physica.

Grunert, K. (1993): Essen und Emotionen: die Selbstregulierung von Emotionen durch das Essverhalten, Weinheim: Psychologie-Verl.-Union.

Grunert, K. (1994): Cognition and Economic Psychology, in: Brandstätter, H., Güth, W. (eds.), Essays on Economic Psychology, Berlin: Springer, 91-108.

Hacker, W. (1992): Expertenkönnen: Erkennen und Vermitteln, Göttingen: Verlag für angewandte Psychologie.

Hacker, W. (1996): Diagnose von Expertenwissen: Von Abzapf- (broaching) zu Aufbau- (reconstruction) Konzepten, Sitzungsberichte der Sächsischen Akademie der Wissenschaften zu Leipzig, Band 134, Heft 6, Berlin, Akademie Verlag.

Hacker, W. (1999): Informationsökonomie aus Psychologischer Sicht: Wissensmanagement, Frühes Prototyping bei der Produktentwicklung, Technische Universität Dresden, Institut für Allgemeine Psychologie, Forschungsberichte, Band 70, August.

Hacker, W. (2003): Action Regulation Theory – A Practical Tool for the Design of Modern Work Processes? Technische Universität Dresden, Institut für Psychologie I, Arbeitsgruppe "Wissen – Denken - Handeln", Projektberichte, Heft 23, Mai.

Hacker, W., **Grossmann**, N., **Teske**, S. (1991): Knowledge Elicitation: A Comparison of Models and of Methods, in: Bullinger, H.-J. (ed.), Human Aspects in Computing: Design and Use of Interactive Systems and Information Management, Elsevier Science Publishers B.V.

Hacker, W., **Jilge**, S. (1993): Vergleich verschiedener Methoden zur Ermittlung von Handlungswissen, Zeitschrift für Arbeits- und Organisationspsychologie, 37 (N.F. 11) 2, 64-72.

Hackman, (1969): Nature of the Task as a Determiner of Job Behaviour, Personal Psychology, 22, 435-444.

Handlbauer, G. (2000): Decision-Making and Institutionalised Cognition, in: Streit, M., Mummert, U., Kiwit, D. (eds.), Cognition, Rationality and Institutions, Springer, 161-180.

Harriss, J., **Hunter**, J. and **Lewis**, C. M. (eds.) (1995): The New Institutional Economics and Third World Development, London & New York: Routledge.

Hartmann-Wendels, T., **Pfingsten**, A., **Weber**, M. (1998): Bankbetriebslehre, Springer.

Hayek, F. A. (1952): The Sensory Order – An Inquiry into the Foundations of Theoretical Psychology, Chicago: University of Chicago Press.

Herr; H. (2003): Makroökonomische Rahmenbedienungen der Unternehmensfinanzierung in der Mongolei, unpublished paper.

Hoen, H. (1997): Is Economic Theory Able to Underpin the Transition to a Market Economy in Eastern Europe?, Journal of International and Comparative Economics, Vol. 5, 153-175.

Ickes, B. (1994): Stabilisation and Privatisation in Russia: An Attempt at Perspective, Paper prepared for the symposium on privatisation in Russia, United States Airforce Academy, February.

Ickes, B., **Ryterman**, R. (1992): The Inter-Enterprise Arrears Crisis in Russia, Post-Soviet Affairs, Vol. 8, No. 4, 331-361.

Ickes, B., **Ryterman**, R. (1993): Roadblock to Economic Reform: Inter-Enterprise Debt and the Transition to Markets, Post-Soviet Affairs, Vol. 9, No. 3, 231-252.

Ickes, B., **Ryterman**, R. (1994): Financial Underdevelopment and Macroeconomic Stabilisation in Russia, in: Caprio, G., Folkerts-Landau, D., Lane, T. (eds.), Building Sound Finance in Emerging Market Economies, Washington DC, 60-83.

International Monetary Fund (1994): Country Report Mongolia, Washington.

Itgel, M., **Ariuntungalag**, T., **Enkhhuyag**, B. (2001): Summary of the One Time Questionnaire on Allocation of Savings, Research Bulletin, Bank of Mongolia, 2, Ulaanbaatar.

James, C. (1987): Some Evidence on the Uniqueness of Bank Loans, Journal of Financial Economics, 19, 217-235.

Jensen, M., **Meckling**, W. (1976): Theory of the Firm: Managerial Behaviour, Agency Costs and Ownership Structure, Journal of Financial Economics 3, 305-360.

Johnson, S. , **Kroll**, H., **Horton**, M. (1993): New Banks in the Former Soviet Union: How Do They Operate?, in: Aslund, A., Layard. R. (eds.), Changing the Economic System in Russia, London, 183-209.

Kahneman, D. (2003): A Psychological Perspective on Economics, AEA Papers and Proceedings: Views of Economics form Neighbouring Social Sicences, Vol. 93, No. 2, 162-168.

Kahneman, D., **Tversky**, A. (1979): Prospect Theory: An Analysis of Decision Under Risk", Econometrica 47, 263-291.

Kahneman, D., **Tversky,** A. (eds.) (2000): Choices, Values and Frames, Cambridge: Cambridge University Press.

Karmann, A. (1992): Prinzipal-Agent-Modelle und Risikoallokation, Wirtschafts-wissenschaftliches Studium, Heft 11, 557-562.

King, J., **Morris**, L., **Fitz-Gibbon**, C. (1987): How to Assess Program Implementation, Newbury Park, California: Sage Publications.

King, R., **Levine**, R. (1993): Finance and Growth: Schumpeter Might Be Right, Policy Research Working Series, World Bank, Washington DC,

Kletzer, K., **Roldos**, J. (1996): The Role of Credit Markets in a Transition Economy with Incomplete Public Information, IMF Working Paper, No. 18.

Kohonen, T., **Oja**, E., **Lehtiö**, P. (1981): Storage and Processing of Information in Distributed Associative Memory Systems, in: Hinton, G., Anderson, J. (eds.), Parallel Models of Associative Memory, Hillsdale, NJ: Erlbaum, 105-143.

Lachman, L.M. (1984): Marktprozeß und Erwartungen: Studien zur Theorie der Markwirtschaft, München: Philosophia Verlag.

Lakatos, I. (1974): Falsifikation und die Methodologie wissenschaftlicher Forschungsprogramme, in: Lakatos, I., Musgrave, A. (eds.), Kritik und Erkenntnisfortschritt, Braunschweig, 89-189.

Law on Central Bank (1996): Law on Central Bank of Mongolia, in: The Great Khural of Mongolia (Parliament), Laws of Mongolia, unofficial English translation, Ulaanbaatar.

Law on Deposit Taking, Payment Services and Lending Activities (1995): Law on Deposit Taking, Payment Services and Lending Activities in Mongolia, in: The Great Khural of Mongolia (Parliament), Laws of Mongolia, unofficial English translation, Ulaanbaatar.

Law on Non-bank Financial Activities (2003): Law on Non-bank Financial Activities of Mongolia, in: The Great Khural of Mongolia (Parliament), Laws of Mongolia, unofficial English translation, Ulaanbaatar.

Lunt, P. (1989): The Perceived Causal Structure of Unemployment, in: Grunert, K., Ölander, F. (eds.), Understanding Economic Behaviour, Dordrecht: Kluwer, 107-120.

Lunt, P., **Livingstone**, S. (1991): Everyday Explanations for debt: A Network Approach, British Journal of Social Psychology, 30, 309-323.

Malone, J., **Dekkers**, J. (1984): The Concept Map as an Aid to Instruction in Science and Mathematics, School Science and Mathematics, 84(3), 220-231.

Mandl, H., **Spada**, H. (eds.) (1988): Wissenspsychologie, München: Psychologie-Verl.-Union.

Markham, K., **Mintzes**, J. (1994): The Concept Map as a Research and Evaluation Tool: Further Evidence of Validity, Journal of Research Science Teaching, Vol. 31, No. 1, 91-101.

McClelland, J., **Rumelhart**, D. (1985): Distributed Memory and the Representation of General and Specific information, Journal of Experimental Psychology: General, 114, 159-188.

Mearns, R. (1995): Environment Entitlements: An Outline Framework for Analysis, and a Mongolian Case Study, Working Paper, February, Institute for Development Studies.

Ministry of Finance and Economy (2003): The Economic and Social Development of Mongolia in 2002.

Minsky, M. (1975): A Framework for Representing Knowledge, in: Winston, P. (ed.), The Psychology of Computer Vision, New York: McGraw Hill, 211-277.

Mishkin, F., **Eakins**, S. (1998): Financial Markets and Institutions, Addison-Weasly.

Murzaev, E. (1954): Die Mongolische Volksrepublik: physisch-geographische Beschreibung. Cotha: Geographisch-kartographische Anstalt.

Naishul, V. (1992): Institutional Development in the USSR, Cato Journal, Vol. 11, No. 3., Cato Institute, 489-496.

Neisser, U. (1976): Cognition and Reality. Principles and Implications of Cognitive Psychology, San Francisco: Freemen.

Neuberger, D. (1994): Kreditvergabe durch Banken: Mikroökonomische Theorie und Gesamtwirtschaftliche Implikationen, Tübingen: Mohr.

Norman, D., **Rumelhart**, D. (1975): Explorations in Cognition, San Francisco: Freeman.

North, D. (1990): Institutions, Institutional Change and Economic Performance, Cambridge: Cambridge University Press.

North, D. (1991): Institutions, Journal of Economic Perspectives, Vol. 5, No. 1, 97-112.

North, D. (1992): Institutions, Ideology and Economic Performance, Cato Journal, Vol. 11, No.3, Cato Institute, 477-488.

North, D. (1994): Economic Performance Through Time, The American Economic Review, Vol. 84., Issue 3, 359-368.

North, D. (1997): The Contribution of the New Institutional Economics to an Understanding of the Transition Problem, WIDER Annual Lectures 1, World Institute for Development Economic Research, Helsinki.

North, D., **Denzau**, A. (1994): Shared Mental Models: Ideologies and Institutions, Kyklos International Review for Social Sciences, Vol. 47.

Novak, J. (1972): Audio-tutorial Techniques for Individualised Science Instruction in the Elementary School, in: Triezenberg, H. (ed.), Individualised Science: Like it is , Washington DC, 14-30.

Novak, J. (1990): Concept Mapping: A Useful Tool For Science Education, Journal of Research in Science Teaching, Vol. 27, No. 10, 937-949.

Novak, J. (1997): A Theory of Education, Ithaca, N.Y.

Novak, J. (1998): Learning, Creating, and Using Knowledge: Concept Maps as Facilitative Tools in Schools and Corporations, London: Lawrence Erlbaum.

Novak, J., **Gowin**, D. (1984): Learning How to Learn, New York: Cambridge University Press.

Novak, J., **Musonda**, D. (1991): A Twelve-Year Longitudinal Study of Science Concept Learning, American Educational Research Journal, 28 (1), 117-153.

OECD (1998): Country Note of Mongolia, in: Centre for Co-operation with economies in Transition, Fourth Conference on Financial Sector Development in the Central Asian Countries, Azerbaijan and Mongolia, draft, Paris.

Onoodor (2001): Bank Supervision in the Last 10 Years, in: the Mongolian Daily Newspaper "Today", the 4th of June, 4.

Patton, M. (1987): How to Use Qualitative Data, Newbury Park, California: Sage Publications.

Pankratus, W. (1990): Building an Organised Knowledge Base: Concept Mapping and Achievement in Secondary School Physics, Journal of Research in Science Teaching, 27 (4), 315-333.

Perotti, E. (1994): A Taxonomy of Post-Socialist Financial Systems: Decentralised Enforcement and the Creation of Inside Money, Economics of Transition, Vol. 2, No.1, 71-81.

Perotti, E. (1994): A Taxonomy of Post-Socialist Financial Systems: Decentralised Enforcement and the Creation of Inside Money, Economics of Transition, Vol. 2, No. 1, 71-81.

Peter, J., **Olson**, J. (1990): Consumer Behaviour, 2nd ed., Homewood, IL: Irwin.

Peuckert, J., **Rothenhagen**, A., **Sylvester**, U. (1999): Concept Mapping – Lernen Wir unsere Schüler kennen! Teil 2: Diagnose von Wissensentwicklungen mittels Concept Mapping: ein Bericht aus der Praxis, Physik in der Schule 37, 1999(2), 122-128.

Portes, R. (1994): Transformation Traps, Economic Journal, Vol. 104, Sept, 1178-1189.

Quillian, M. (1968): Semantic Memory, in: Minsky, M. (ed.), Semantic Information Processing, Cambridge, Mass.: MIT Press, 216-270.

Ray, W. (2000): Methods Towards a Science of Behaviour and Experience, London: Wadsworth.

Richter, R. , **Furubotn**, E. (1999): Neue Institutionenökonomik, Tübingen: Mohr Siebeck.

Richter, R. (1990): Banking Regulation as Seen by the New Institutional Economics, in: Furubotn, Richter, The Economics and Law of Banking Regulation, Centre for the Study of the New Institutional Economics, Occasional Papers, No. 2, 135-160.

Rowell, R. (1978): Concept Mapping: Evaluation of Children's Science Concepts Following Audio-Tutorial Instruction, Unpublished Doctoral Dissertation, Cornell University.

Royer, J., **Cirsero** C., **Carlo**, M. (1993): Techniques and Procedures for Assessing Cognitive Skills, Review of Educational Research, 63, 201-224.

Ruiz-Primo, M., **Shavelson**, R. (1996): Problems and Issues in the Use of Concept Maps in Science Assessment, Journal of Research in Science Teaching, Vol. 33, No.6, 569-600.

Rumelhart, D., **Ortony**, A. (1997): The Representation of Knowledge in Memory, in: Anderson, R., Spiro, R., Montague, W. (eds.), Schooling And The Acquisition of Knowledge, Hillsdale, NJ: Lawrence Erlbaum, 99-135.

Rutherfold, M. (1994): Institutions in Economics: the Old and the New Institutionalism, Cambridge: Cambridge University Press.

Sanders, A. (1978): Mongolia Lays Down the Law, in: The Far Eastern Economic Review, May 26th, 87.

Schank, R., **Abelson**, R. (1997): Scripts, Plans, Goals, and Understanding, Hillsdale, NJ: Lawrence Erlbaum.

Schlicht, E. (1985): Isolation and Aggregation in Economics, Berlin: Springer.

Schmidt, S. (1995): Mongolia in Transition: The Impact of Privatisation on Rural Life, Bielefelder Studien zur Entwicklungssoziologie, Bank 62, Saarbrücken.

Schotter, A. (1986): The Evolution of Rules, in: Langlois, R. (ed.), Economics as Process: Essays in the New Institutional Economics, Cambridge: Cambridge University Press, 117-133.

Simon, H. (1955): A Behavioural Model of Rational Choice, Quarterly Journal of Economics, 69, 99-118.

Simon, H. (1956): Rational Choice and the Structure of the Environment, Psychological Review 63, 129-138.

Simon, H. (1957): Models of Man: Social and Rational, New York: Wiley.

Simon, H. (1979): Rational Decision Making in Business Organisations, The American Economic Review, Vol. 69, Issue 4, 493-513.

Simon, H. (1986): Rationality in Psychology and Economics, in: Hogarth, R,, and Reder, M. (eds.), Rational Choice: Contrast between Economics and Psychology, Chicago: University of Chicago Press, 1986, 25-40.

Sommer, B., **Sommer** R. (1997): A Practical Guide to Behavioural Research: Tools and Techniques, New York: Oxford University Press.

Stein, H. (1995): Institutional Theories and Structural Adjustment in Africa, in Harriss, J., Hunter, J. and Lewis, C. M. (eds.), The New Institutional Economics and Third World Development, 109-132.

Stringer, E. (1999): Action research: A Handbook for Practioners, Thousand Oaks, California: Sage Publications.

Sujan, M., **Bettman**, J. (1989): The Effects of Brand Positioning Strategies on Consumer' Brand and Category Perceptions: Some Insights From Schema Research, Journal of Marketing Research, 16, 454-467.

Thomas, M. (1999): Neoinstitutionalismus, Economic Sociology und der Transformationsfall, Heft am Frankfurter Institut für Transformationsstudien, Frankfurt /Oder.

Tversky, A., **Kahneman**, D. (1992): Advances in Prospect Theory: Cumulative Representation Under Uncertainty, Journal of Risk and Uncertainty, 5, 297-323.

Veblen, T. (1919): The Place of Science in Modern Civilisation and Other Essays, New York: Huebsch.

Weick, K. (1995): Sense Making in Organisations, Thousand Oaks, California: Sage Publications.

Weick, K., **Burgon**, M. (1986): Organisations as Cognitive Maps: Charting ways to Success and Failure, in: Sims, H., Gioia, D. (eds.), The Thinking Organisations, San Francisco: Jossey-Bass, 102-135.

White, R., **Gunstone**, R. (1992): Probing Understanding, New York: Falmer.

Williamson, M., **Wearing**, A. (1991): Cause and Effect Relations in Cognitive Models of the Economy, paper presented at the IAREP/SASE conference, Stockholm, June 16-19.

Williamson, O. (1967): The Economics of Defence Contracting; Incentives and Performance, in: McKean, R. (ed.), Issues in Defence Economics, New York, 217-271.

Williamson, O. (1975): Markets and Hierarchies: Analysis and Antitrust Implications: A Study in the Economics of Internal Organisation, New York: Free Press.

Winitzky, N., **Kauchak**, D., **Kelly**, M. (1994): Measuring Teachers' Structural Knowledge, Teaching and Teacher Education, 10 (2), 125-139.

World Bank (1997): Mongolia: Country Economic Memorandum: Policies for Faster Growth, Report Number 16749-MOG, World Bank, Washington DC.

Zedevijn, G. (1998): Das Mongolische Bankensystem: Die Erben Dschingis Khans und ihre Banken, Bank Magazin 3/98, 72-75.

MIX
Papier aus verantwortungsvollen Quellen
Paper from responsible sources
FSC® C105338

If you have any concerns about our products,
you can contact us on
ProductSafety@springernature.com

In case Publisher is established outside the EU,
the EU authorized representative is:
Springer Nature Customer Service Center GmbH
Europaplatz 3, 69115 Heidelberg, Germany

Printed by Libri Plureos GmbH
in Hamburg, Germany